# THE BEST-LAID SCHEMES

# THE BEST-LAID SCHEMES
A Tale of Social Research and Bureaucracy

Seymour J. Deitchman

The MIT Press
Cambridge, Massachusetts, and London, England

This book was typed on IBM Selectric by Nancy Talbott,
printed on R&E Book,
and bound in Roxite B53501
by Halliday Lithograph Corporation
in the United States of America.

Library of Congress Cataloging in Publication Data

Deitchman, Seymour J
      The best-laid schemes.

      Bibliography:  p.
      Includes index.
      1.  Vietnamese Conflict, 1961-1975--United States.
I.  Title.
DS558.D44     959.704'3373          75-31736
ISBN 0-262-04049-2

# CONTENTS

To Rains

"But Mousie, thou art no thy lane
In proving foresight may be vain;
The best-laid schemes o' mice and men
    Gang aft agley,
An' lea'e us nought but grief an' pain,
    For promised joy!"

Robert Burns, 1785

My purpose in this book is to tell the story of a great experiment in social research, in which I participated and whose events were important and instructive for American social science in the mid-1960s and later.

I have attempted to limit what I have written to that which I experienced or observed, and to limit personal aspects of the narrative to those which are useful to portray the context and the atmosphere of the events. It has been necessary, nevertheless, to describe some of what others, with whom I may have had little contact, experienced and expressed. Such descriptions cannot but be tempered by my own views. Thus I am afraid the reader will find those views pervading everything, even though I have made a conscious attempt to minimize my intrusion. I regret any resulting distortion of "truth" that other participants may find, but at the same time I will defend opinions and conclusions expressly identified (and some that are implicit).

In the interest of saving time and effort I have taken some liberties with the usual practices of scholarship in annotating references and supporting material. Such annotation is given wherever I believed it important to support statements of fact that may not be generally known or that may be controversial, but there are two important exceptions. Official records, correspondence, or documents that are described and discussed can be presumed to exist, but I have not listed them as explicit references if they have not

been published or otherwise made generally available.
Newspaper articles identified in the text by source,
author, and date did not seem to me to warrant the em-
bellishment of formal citation. (Permissions to quote
from other copyrighted material will be found in the
Credits following this Preface, or, where it has been
requested by the copyright holders, as footnotes to the
text. Full bibliographic citation of generally available sources will be found in the References at the end
of this volume.)

Some of the events described in this narrative are
"recorded" only in the memories of the individuals involved, including my own, and in such cases the responsibility for errors of fact or differences of perception is purely my own.

The reader will find that in many cases I have gone
to some lengths of circumlocution to avoid naming
scientists, civilian or military officials, and even
countries, in connection with particular aspects of
the events or particular research projects. As the
book will show, the material has in it, often at unexpected turns of subject and time, the capacity to
stimulate controversy and cause embarrassment. This
applies especially to many members of the academic community, who are still feeling the effects of the parts
of these adventures that touched on them, and who have
in some cases been subject to attack and vilification
because of the parts they played. It has definitely
not been my purpose to write an exposé, and I have

tried to avoid mentioning names wherever I judged that spectres from the past would be unwelcome and would add little of importance to the narrative.

My heartfelt thanks are in order to many individuals. They include those who supported the efforts that, if events had taken a different turn, might have affected more history than simply that of social research; those whose comments and assistance were invaluable both during the events the book describes and in helping to shape the manuscript; and those without whose help on workaday matters I could not have finished it.

Among the first are Drs. Harold Brown, John McLucas, Charles M. Herzfeld, and Eberhardt Rechtin, all of whom perceived potential value in the efforts that I undertook to stimulate and guide, and gave me the freedom and the strong support within the Defense Department bureaucracy to make and sustain the attempt, despite the problems that were created and diversions from other perhaps more pressing business. The late Dr. S. Rains Wallace, Drs. Jesse Orlansky and Eugene Webb were sources of knowledge and understanding about the intricacies of the world of social science, without whose help and advice I would indeed have been lost in a strange forest. Their knowledge of the events made their comments on the manuscript especially helpful and valuable. Mrs. Edna Majors deserves a special note of thanks for having borne the tedium of typing and retyping, for what must have seemed endless time.

It would have been impossible to track down references
lost in the pressure of events without the able assistance of Mrs. Evelyn Fass and Mrs. Thomasina Jones.
My wife observed the passing events from a ringside
seat, and shared with me the strain of long hours and
stressful conflicts.  Finally, to all those others,
scientists, managers, and "target populations," who
helped, who participated, and who bore suffering they
did not see, I must express my gratitude and, where
appropriate, my sympathy.

It should be obvious to all readers that although
I have worked for the government, and currently work
for an organization that serves the government, I am
speaking for neither of them in any part of this book.
The book is about government programs.  But the descriptions and interpretations of those programs, of
the events surrounding them, and of the policies that
supported or affected them are mine, alone.  It must
be remembered, also, that the programs and policies I
have thus described existed at another time and in
circumstances different from those that apply today.
It is de rigueur in modern bureaucratese to admonish
that nothing in this book should be taken as implying
that the programs and policies that are described still
exist in the Defense Department or any other agency,
or that anything like them will be espoused in the
future.

CREDITS

Permission to reprint excerpts from the following is
hereby gratefully acknowledged:  Pages 25-26 from
Charles W. Bray, "Toward a Technology of Human Behavior
for Defense Use," American Psychologist, Vol. 17, 1962.
Page 87  from Gene M. Lyons, The Uneasy Partnership:
Social Science and the Federal Government in the Twen-
tieth Century,  © 1969 by the Russell Sage Foundation.
Page 88  from Chester L. Cooper, The Lost Crusade:
America in Vietnam, Dodd, Mead & Company, 1970.
Page 244  from Robert H. Thouless, How To Think
Straight, Simon & Schuster, 1947.  Permission courtesy
of Ms. Clare Bristow,  Hodder and Stoughton Ltd,
London.  Pages  257-258, 264  from Kalman H. Silvert,
"American Academic Ethics and Social Research Abroad,"
American Universities Field Staff, Reports Service,
West Coast/South America Series, Vol. XII, No. 3(KHS-
1-65), July 1965.  © 1965 by the American Universities
Field Staff, Inc.  Pages  261-263  from Irving Louis
Horowitz, "The Life and Death of Project Camelot,"
Transaction, Vol. 3, No. 1.  Published by permission
of Transaction, Inc. © 1965 by Transaction, Inc.
Pages  268-270  from Michael T. Klare, "Counterinsur-
gency's Proving Ground," The Nation, April 26, 1971.
© Michael T. Klare.  Pages  270-272  from Ralph L.
Beals, Politics of Social Research:  An Inquiry into
the Ethics and Responsibilities of Social Scientists,
Aldine Publishing Company, 1969.  Page 275 from
Arnold Thackray, "Reflections on the Decline of Science
in America and Some of Its Causes," Science, Vol. 173,

pp. 27-31, July 2, 1971. © 1971 by the American Association for the Advancement of Science. Page 449
from Donald T. Campbell, "Reforms as Experiments,"
American Psychologist, Vol. 24, 1969. Pages 449-450 from
Daniel P. Moynihan, "Eliteland," Psychology Today,
September 1970. © 1970 by Ziff-Davis Publishing Company. All rights reserved. Page 453 from D.
Shapley, "Education Research: HEW Auditing Two SRI
Contracts," Science, Vol. 177, p. 973, September 15,
1973. © 1973 by the American Association for the Advancement of Science.

For permission to quote from their letters, I am
grateful to Joseph E. Barmack (pp. 279-280) and
Ithiel de Sola Pool (pp. 280-282).

ABBREVIATIONS AND ACRONYMS

| | |
|---|---|
| AFOSR | Air Force Office of Scientific Research |
| AID | Agency for International Development |
| ANZUS | Australia, New Zealand, U.S. Treaty |
| ARO | Army Research Office |
| ARPA | Advanced Research Projects Agency |
| CI | Counterinsurgency |
| CIA | Central Intelligence Agency |
| CINCSO | Commander-in-Chief, Southern Command |
| CINCPAC | Commander-in-Chief, Pacific |
| CINFAC | Counterinsurgency Information and Analysis Center |
| DCSOPS | Army Deputy Chief of Staff for Operations, and his "office" |
| DDR&E | Director of Defense Research and Engineering |
| DOD (DoD) | Department of Defense |
| DSB | Defense Science Board |
| FAR | Foreign Area Research Coordinating Group |
| FCRC | Federal Contract Research Center |
| GAO | General Accounting Office |
| GVN | Government of Vietnam (refers to South Vietnam) |
| HumRRO | Human Resources Research Organization |
| IDA | Institute for Defense Analyses |
| INR | State Department Bureau of Intelligence and Research |
| ISA | International Security Affairs (refers also to the Assistant Secretary of Defense for International Security Affairs, and his "office") |
| JUSPAO | Joint U.S. Public Affairs Office |

| | |
|---|---|
| MAAG | Military Assistance Advisory Group |
| MACV | Military Assistance Command, Vietnam |
| MIT | Massachusetts Institute of Technology |
| NAS | National Academy of Sciences |
| NATO | North Atlantic Treaty Organization |
| NLF | National Liberation Front (South Vietnam) |
| NRC | National Research Council |
| ODDR&E | Office of the Director of Defense Research and Engineering (i.e., the director's staff) |
| ONR | Office of Naval Research |
| OSD | Office of the Secretary of Defense |
| RAC | Research Analysis Corporation |
| RAND | The RAND Corporation |
| R&D | Research and Development |
| SAC | Strategic Air Command |
| SECDEF | Secretary of Defense |
| SORO | Special Operations Research Office |
| SRI | Stanford Research Institute |
| USAPRO | U.S. Army Personnel Research Office |
| USIA | United States Information Agency |
| VC | Viet Cong |

THE BEST-LAID SCHEMES

# I GREAT EXPECTATIONS

# 1  ANTECEDENTS

In the early 1960s, while the United States was becoming involved in a long and difficult war in a
strange and far-off corner of the world, the Defense
Department undertook what turned out to be a painful
research experiment intimately connected with and
driven largely by that war.  That experiment, which
is the subject of this book, was to have profound implications, still not fully recognized, for social research in the service of the federal government.

The research and the war grew together from America's increasing involvement, after the Second World
War, in the affairs of the former European colonial
empires.  Conditioned by our deep cultural and historical interrelationships with the nations of Western
Europe, and reinforced by the ebb of their power in
Asia and Africa, we believed it essential to our own
safety and theirs to block the advance of a new and
hostile ideology which seemed to be on the verge of
sweeping the world with the same force as the earlier
advance of Islam.  We were involved in the Berlin
blockade, the Korean War, the "loss" of China and
Cuba, and lengthy conflicts in Greece and several
countries of Southeast Asia.  The increasingly stri-
dent Soviet and Chinese promises to support "wars of
national liberation" were taken to be a euphemism for
a new and (for us) dangerous approach to "conquest" of
regions where we deemed our influence, and therefore

our ultimate survival, to be at stake. While there
were obviously many nonmilitary facets--political,
economic, cultural, informational--to the defenses we
had constructed over the years, the military aspects
of the worldwide "cold war" conflict also loomed large
to successive American governments. By the late 1950s
a large, worldwide American military presence had become an integral part of our policy and of our attempts
to contain expansion of the major communist powers--
powers that were not then viewed as a group holding
diverse and subtly different creeds. But by the early
1960s it was becoming clear that despite this military
presence, and despite our aid programs, we were not
succeeding as we hoped we would in trying to transmit
military capability for local self-defense to the developing countries over whom we had thrown our protective mantle.

Enter, now, into the ambience of the early Kennedy
era. There had grown, in America, an uneasiness about
our image and our position in the world. Nixon had
been mobbed in South America; Eisenhower had been prevented by mob action from visiting Japan; the embarrassment of the U-2 affair was still palpable. The
essence of Kennedy's election campaign was that he
would "get America moving again." When he took office
he brought with him intellectuals and intellectualism
from the Northeastern Universities--especially Harvard
and MIT. Some of the Defense thinkers of the RAND
Corporation--Charles Hitch, Alain Enthoven, Henry

Rowen--entered the Defense Department. Theories of
strategy, economic development in the new world, the
formation and use of military power, and foreign policy that had been incubating during the Eisenhower
presidency blossomed, and those who held them were
placed in positions from which they could apply them.
The atmosphere was one of change, of ferment, of self-
confidence--of "knowing" what had to be done and of
unquestioning "can do." It would all lead to a better
world. It was the time of Camelot.

President Kennedy took office to face a crisis
over Berlin, the beginning of active guerrilla warfare
in Vietnam, a Laos whose shaky neutrality had been
upset in favor of a Western-oriented government which
communist-supported forces were in the process of
attacking and defeating, and a government in Cuba
openly hostile to the United States and declaring both
its orientation toward the Soviet Union and its intention to carry _Fidelismo_ to the rest of Latin America.
All this was duly noted from the start. In his inaug-
ural address Kennedy said:

Let every nation know, whether it wishes us well or
ill, that we shall pay any price, bear any burden,
meet any hardship, support any friend, oppose any
foe to assure the survival and the success of liberty
... In the long history of the world, only a few generations have been granted the role of defending
freedom in its hour of maximum danger. I do not
shrink from this responsibility--I welcome it.

This was to become the call to resistance against the
"wars of national liberation" for which Khrushchev, in
January 1961, promised "resolute" Soviet support.[1]
Kennedy met with Khrushchev in Vienna, and left the
meeting feeling that he was up against a tough oppo-
nent, one who would not "give" easily, in Europe or
elsewhere.[2] He found at the Bay of Pigs that guerrilla
warfare is not an easy instrument to use; and there
were the experiences of China, Indochina, Greece,
Malaya, the Philippines, Algeria, and Laos to show
that when it was used by a tough, well-organized and
resourceful enemy it was not easy to counter. Taking
seriously the threat to American power and influence
implicit in Khrushchev's words, and in the later elaborations on the theme by Khrushchev and the Chinese
Communists,[3] he set about building our military and
government instruments to meet an obvious and serious
challenge. That challenge may appear shadowy and
full of braggadocio from the vantage point of the
bitter experiences of all parties in the later sixties.
But who can deny that it was uttered seriously, and
was meant to succeed, if it could, ten years earlier?

To meet it, Kennedy built the Army from 11 to 16
active divisions, with corresponding increases in the
strategic and tactical naval and air forces. He added
to airlift and sealift to improve our ability to de-
ploy overseas--the prospect and the propriety of intervention to meet the threat were foreseen and accepted. The U.S. Army Special Forces became a favorite

of the President, and were expanded and oriented toward the problem of training foreign troops in counterguerrilla warfare.[4] The President stressed the need for the military to learn about what seemed to be a new kind of warfare. He said in an address at West Point in June, 1962:[5]

It is a form of warfare uniquely adapted to what has been strangely called "wars of liberation," to undermine the efforts of new and poor countries to maintain the freedom that they have finally achieved. It.... preys on economic unrest and ethnic cultures... These are the kinds of challenges that will be before us in the next decade if freedom is to be saved, a whole new kind of strategy, a whole different kind of force, and therefore a new and wholly different kind of military training... The mission of our armed forces...is to master these skills and techniques and to be able to help those who have the will to help themselves...

The justification for this interest was at once simple and lofty. A year earlier Walt Rostow, then in the State Department, had said[6] "...it will permit American society to continue to develop along the old humane lines which go back to our birth as a nation-- and which reach deeper into history than that--back to the Mediterranean roots of Western life. We are struggling to maintain an environment on the world scene which will permit our open society to survive and to flourish." There was a pervading sense of the importance and of the urgency of undertaking the task of assistance overseas. In his statement in the spring of 1962, supporting the fiscal 1963 Defense budget, Robert McNamara said:[7]

> There has come into prominence, in the last year or
> two, a kind of revolt which Mr. Khrushchev calls wars
> of national liberation or popular revolts, but which
> we know as insurrection, subversion and covert armed
> aggression. I refer here to the kind of war which we
> have seen in Laos and which is now going on in South
> Vietnam... Actually, it is not a new Communist tech-
> nique. We have seen it in many other parts of the
> world since the end of World War II... We have a long
> way to go in devising and implementing effective
> countermeasures against these Communist techniques.
> But this is a challenge we must meet if we are to de-
> feat the Communists in this third kind of war. It is
> quite possible that in the decade of the 1960s, the
> decisive struggle will take place in this arena.

At the same time, he recognized that "to meet successfully this type of threat will take much more than
military means alone. It will require a comprehensive
effort involving political, economic, and ideological
measures as well as military."[8]

President Kennedy started to organize and inter-
connect the Defense Department and the other parts of
the government to undertake the task. The State Department was assigned diplomatic and political roles,
and the responsibility for coordinating the efforts of
the other key agencies of government. The Agency for
International Development would continue its task of
economic assistance, but also was given the responsibility for tailoring this assistance, where necessary,
to help the recipient nations build their strengths
against subversion and insurgent forces. This included

responsibility for helping to build police and other
paramilitary internal security forces. The United
States Information Agency, through its overseas offices, was supposed to carry out not only its tradi-
tionally assigned duties of information gathering and
dissemination, and studying the U.S. image overseas,
but it was also to render assistance to the countries
under insurgent attack by helping them learn to undertake and counter psychological warfare.[9] (The Peace
Corps was also organized at this time with a purely
people-to-people role that was the obverse of the coin
of security-related assistance.) It is clear from
later news stories and books about American involvement in Southeast Asia that the CIA was given an operational role in supporting combat and irregular
forces that went beyond its intelligence mission
alone.[10]

All of these agencies and the Defense Department
were instructed about the parts they were to play in
a coordinated program, with the President's assignments to each telling them what they were supposed to
do and how, and in what areas they were to work with
each other. The Defense Department's role was made
broader than simply undertaking military operations;
it was to work with the other agencies at the "inter-
faces" between civil and military operations--
psychological operations, searching for guerrillas
and protecting local populations against them, and
forms of small-scale and local economic assistance

that could be clustered under the rubric of "military civic action."

To help coordinate all these activities from the top, the President established what came to be called the Special Group (CI).[11] This included the second-ranking men in the State and Defense Departments; the Chairman of the Joint Chiefs of Staff; the Directors of the CIA, AID, and USIA; and a representative from the office of McGeorge Bundy, the President's Special Assistant for National Security Affairs. The Attorney General, the President's brother, was a member of the group. He could obviously help keep the President closely informed about its activities, and carry the President's direct authority and interest into the group and its deliberations.

In the spring of 1962, the Laotian government army moved against the Pathet Lao but was routed at Nam Tha, by what had been said to be an inferior force which then seemed to be on the verge of crossing into Thailand. The President moved American troops into Thailand near its northern border.[12] Then in difficult and sensitive negotiations at Geneva a treaty was patched together that brought Souvanna Phouma back to power in a troika of incompatibles, temporarily stabilizing a very shaky situation. There had been one obvious fact: the Laotian army, which we had helped equip and train, had folded and couldn't withstand an attack.

There were other signs of similar problems. Even

earlier the Draper Report had stated that our military
training programs in the developing nations weren't
achieving their objectives.[13]  In the critical area of
military logistics--simply maintaining equipment and
keeping the armed forces supplied--our training efforts
were not succeeding.  These armies were therefore not
very effective, and instead of operating in the field
they clustered around a few base areas near the
national capitals and regional centers of population
and power.  The Draper Report stated that their effectiveness for conventional wars left much to be desired.
It was worse still for counterguerrilla warfare, where
these armies needed extreme flexibility, good intelligence, and the ability to disperse into small groups
against bands of a tough and resourceful enemy who
used a secret, cellular, hierarchical organization
that was very hard to penetrate.  Additionally, in
many countries the armed forces served a political
purpose in being the muscle that kept existing regimes
in power.  This, too, kept them near the population
centers where they could be watched and used as instruments of politics.

Moreover, the developing countries faced severe economic problems, and their societies were characterized
by a lack of national cohesion, as well as a political
elite usually separated and different, by wealth, education, and a degree of Westernization, from the population they governed.  Thus it appeared that for most
of our allies outside NATO and ANZUS the political

climate and military capability were not well suited
to fighting a tightly organized conspiratorial group
able to play on local disaffections and to take advantage of the political as well as geographical remote-
ness of most of the people from the influence of the
central government.  There were, during this period,
about 30 internal wars or conflicts, at various stages
of maturity, in various parts of the world.[14]  Such
problems were coming to the fore in Southeast Asia,
in both Laos and Vietnam.  They were not everywhere
recognized very early, but they became obvious and insistent with the events that ultimately led to the
overthrow of Diem and the consequent series of military coups and countercoups in South Vietnam.

Drawing on some of the results of the research I
will later talk about, we can now appreciate some of
the underlying reasons for the increasing difficulties
American policy and its implementation were facing in
these areas.  We didn't really understand the countries
we had undertaken to help.  We learned ultimately that
the guerrillas in South Vietnam did their work in the
villages, gaining the confidence of the population or
using terror to separate them from the government and
to wipe out the government's sparse cadre of trained
administrators.  But, if we came to recognize early
that it was a war for the sympathy and support of the
people--largely a rural people--in which we were trying
to play the important role of guiding and assisting
the central government, we then found that we did not

really understand the relationships between that
government and its people, or among the various factions who might be involved, both in the government
and without.  Their history and their political and
cultural motivations were mysterious to most Americans
involved; it was not clear what divided all these
groups from each other, much less how they might be
drawn together.  All this was proof, if any was needed,
that the processes of social development, revolution,
and internal warfare in a country with which we had
undertaken a sort of marriage contract were not very
clearly understood by those who were most deeply involved in the events.  The philosophical underpinnings
of the political and economic theories on which we
based our actions were complex and more specific to
our culture than to that of the Vietnamese--or, for
that matter, the culture of other countries with which
we had become involved.  Experts differed on the nature
of the problems, on who the key players were and what
motivated them, and on what should be done or how.
And in any case few of the experts were consulted,
nor was their advice often followed, as policies were
made at the highest levels and orders given to carry
them out.  At the same time the Vietnamese Communists,
and Marxist revolutionary groups in other countries,
had a firmly based social theory--founded on Marx,
Lenin, Mao, Giap, Che--which, whether it might be
right or wrong about processes of social evolution and
revolution, nevertheless lent cohesiveness and the

discipline of dogma. So the other side held this important advantage while we moved pragmatically from
one step to the next, without fully understanding the
players on both sides, or the implications of our
moves, their moves, or the interactions between them.

Much of the burden fell on American advisors overseas, at all levels. When all was said and done,
policy was made in Washington, incorporating the advice of our ambassadors and sundry other high officials.
It then had to be implemented in the field. While
ambassadors and theatre commanders and mission chiefs--
the chiefs of the Military Assistance Advisory Groups,
the AID missions overseas, the U.S. Information Service, and others--worked with the top levels of the
local government, they were assisted by staffs which,
in the military case, could number in the hundreds and
in Vietnam even before the entry of American combat
troops came to be numbered in the thousands. These
staffs had the "nuts and bolts" job of making the
policy work by interacting with lower-level officials
and officers in the foreign armed forces. While this
job may have held a certain glamour, it eventually
emerged as difficult and frustrating. There were a
few Americans who had long local experience and were
intimately acquainted with the local cultures and
people, but the advisory staffs and the staffs responsible for administering American programs were
composed, in the main, of short-timers who had had a
minimum of training to prepare them for the nontechni-

cal parts of their tasks. It was difficult for most
of them to understand a people and a culture having the
ingrained patterns of thousands of years of evolution,
totally different from their own. In general, staff
personnel did not speak the local language. The orientations of the Americans and those they came to assist
toward getting a job done were poles apart.

In Indochina, for example, the South Vietnamese
officer corps were likely to have been politically
appointed and to be politically motivated. They were
not aggressive and job-success-oriented, but rather,
survival-oriented. Many were foreign trained--French
or American--and were themselves culturally not in
rapport with their enlisted troops. Some had been
fighters with or against the Viet Minh, and the instruction they received from their American advisors
was often not compatible with their understanding of
the ways necessary to organize and fight in Vietnam.
The Army Special Forces, in the job given to them, had
to deal with primitive tribesmen, the Montagnard of
the Vietnamese Highlands, and in the process they became involved in the long-standing animosity between
the Montagnard and the Vietnamese. The latter looked
on the mountain tribesmen as little better than ani-
mals, while the tribesmen viewed the lowland, agricul-
turally-oriented Vietnamese as enemies who were trying
to steal their land and stifle their freedom. In one
case, when an anthropologist asked a Montagnard village
chief what he would do with the weapons he had asked

for--ostensibly to fight the Viet Cong--the chief
answered very frankly, "If we have guns we can drive
all those Vietnamese out of here."

In other areas of the world the United States was
making policies about its relations with, and giving
aid to, countries in transition from colonial to
modern status. These were fragmented societies just
coming into the twentieth century. Age-old differences
and antagonisms existed among many groups. These ultimately became known to the few Americans assigned in
those countries who became deeply involved with the
inhabitants for long periods of time, but they were
not usually known to those in Washington making policy
or to those serving a conventional "three-year tour"
in the country. Politically, these countries were
not generally oriented to or familiar with democratic
government as we know it and could be sympathetic with
as a people, and yet our aid had to be justified at
least partly on the basis of building defenses for
Western democracy. On the economic level, these
countries were struggling, with small, capitol-
oriented educated elites and masses of relatively
primitive peasant populations, to make the transition
from suppliers of raw materials to the West to states
undertaking modern commercial and industrial activities.

All of this led to the kinds of social stresses that
must, in any case, create conflict, violence, and revolutionary forces. It was not surprising that the mili-

tary often couldn't learn to maintain and use modern
equipment and its required forms of organization,
since they had no basis of technology and industry on
which to build. These conditions existed everywhere
in varying degrees, but they were not always obvious
to American policymakers at high levels or advisors
and trainers at low levels. Yet judgments based on
far-from-adequate knowledge had always to be made in
an environment of communication across cultures where
even simple acts or words in the wrong pattern could
destroy a man's usefulness for the remainder of his
"tour," be he ambassador or simple soldier.

This, then, is how the situation had evolved as
American foreign policy led to widening American involvement in the world's affairs. Historically, Western nations in colonial times had a lode of data deriving from and relevant for the master-slave relationship between governors and governed. Such data were
often not germane, and the learning problem was much
more severe, in the more egalitarian relationship we
had undertaken with the Vietnamese. We had insufficient knowledge to do the job as well as we wanted
to, and while this may be typical of the international
efforts of all nations, growing awareness led to a
strong feeling at the highest levels of American
government that we would have to do better. By 1964,
the kind of opinion held by some who had key roles in
participation with or observation of the American advisory effort in Vietnam, that only about 15 percent

of the American advisors could establish effective relationships with their counterparts, was beginning to
be heard, and questions about how this performance
could be improved were beginning to be asked.

From our current view, all the above could look like
parts of an argument saying we shouldn't have become
involved.  But however we might view it now in rueful
retrospect over Vietnam, the point at the time was
not whether the job should be done, or even whether it
could be done, but rather how to do it better.

## 2 SOCIAL SCIENCE TO THE RESCUE

In its action-oriented view the government had much re-
inforcement from an important part of the social
science community.  Among its other efforts, that community had rendered past service on difficult human
problems for the Defense Department.  Now it saw a new
set of problems, and it made recommendations to undertake research to solve them, in full confidence that
the research would provide many of the answers.  Some
of these social scientists had been involved in studies
of international problems, with government support or
otherwise.  But the bulk of the research that had
proven so useful for the armed forces was performed in
the areas of selection and training, human factors engineering, and performance evaluation.  A summary of
the history of these contributions and the evolution
of the view of what needed to be done next was prepared
for the formal testimony given before the House Foreign
Affairs Subcommittee under Congressman Dante Fascell,[1]
as a consequence of events that will soon be described.
This presentation still appears to be the best concise
description that can be made available; it is repeated
here, verbatim:

The accomplishment of the DOD mission depends basically
upon how well the people in the Armed Forces do their
jobs.  This implies that they must have the knowledge
and skills required for the jobs and must want to perform them as well as they can.  The behavioral
sciences (which include psychology, sociology, eco-

nomics, anthropology, and political science) are devoted as basic disciplines to the understanding of
how and why people act as they do. As applied sciences,
they are directed to improving man's effectiveness and
so have a direct input to the DOD mission.

The number and variety of jobs in the Armed Forces is
almost as great as in the country at large. They
range from simple, low-level tasks such as washing
vehicles to those of the highest complexity such as
commanding large combat organizations.

The Defense Department, through recruiting and the
draft, must staff these jobs with capable people at a
minimum waste of time, money, and human talent. Individuals who cannot do even the simplest of the Armed
Forces tasks become a financial and managerial burden.
They must be identified and rejected before entering
the service. Beginning with World War I, this process
has been performed with ever-increasing accuracy
through the use of tests and procedures developed by
mental measurement psychologists. The savings made
by these are certainly in the millions of dollars per
year.

Among those who are admitted to the Armed Forces there
are, of course, people capable of doing a large number
and variety of jobs. Some can do even the most complex
and it is of primary importance to identify these and
make sure that their potential is used. But practi-
cally everyone is better suited for one kind of job
than another. He is better off and the efficiency of
the Department is increased if he is trained for and
assigned to the kind of job he can do best. It was a
standing, only half-joke for decades that the Army
makes cooks out of college professors and instructors
out of high school dropouts. This charge has sub-
stantially lost its basis as the result of classification test batteries now used in all of the Departments.
The worth of these was demonstrated dramatically during World War II by the Air Force Air Crew Classification Battery. Studies performed at the end of the war
conclusively demonstrated that, without this aid for
separating men who were well-qualified for pilot train-

ing from those whose chances of ever qualifying for
wings was low, the Air Force would have been required
to put close to twice as many men into training in
order to produce the same number of pilots obtained
from the smaller but qualified group...

Once the individual has been properly screened and
classified, he must be given the knowledge and skills
necessary to do his job.  It is probable that the
Department of Defense is the largest training establishment in the world.

Estimates vary but no one would deny that $3 billion
is a minimum figure for the annual DOD expenditure in
education and training.  The efficient investment of
these funds is possible only if our training methods
and procedures produce proficient people for the least
amount of time and money.  Research on how to identify
the knowledge, skills, habits, and attitudes required
to perform a particular job competently and to instill
these quickly and permanently has paid off in many
ways.  Courses have been shortened or completely
altered by removing unrealistic, "gingerbread" content
which was not really required for job performance.

Large sums of money have been saved by substituting
inexpensive training simulation for expensive and rare
operational equipment.  The demand for hard-to-get
instructors has been kept in bounds through the use of
new and more effective aids and methods.  Most important is the fact that the training end product in doing
the real world job has been improved.

There are outstanding examples of payoffs of research
in this large field.  One is the Army's modernized
rifle marksmanship course, Trainfire I, which trains
the soldier to shoot in combat rather than on a rifle
range.  Another is the Air Force work in programmed
instruction which has produced time savings in the
neighborhood of 33 percent in a wide variety of courses
with no loss and frequently a gain in graduates' proficiency.  Here again, business and industry have
capitalized on this pioneering work by the Defense
Department.

Understanding what a job requires and training men for
it, demands knowledge of how men use their senses and
their muscles to get it done.  Furthermore, some jobs
place very high demands on the senses and may even
damage them.  This has produced a requirement for increased understanding of sensory and motor processes
acquired through psychophysics and psychophysiology.
The recent walk in space would not have been possible
had it not been for the studies of weightlessness performed by the Air Force psychologists at Wright Field
and studies of balance made by the Navy psychologists
at Pensacola.  Navy work on night vision and dark adaptation  increased our effectiveness on land and sea
long before the physicist made his contribution of
infrared scopes.  The Army's studies of the effects of
loud noise and blast have saved the hearing of large
numbers of men.

In addition, psychophysiological information coupled
with job analysis and the study of how various motor
skills are developed and maintained has made it possible to design jobs and, indeed, entire systems to
ensure the best use of man's sensory and motor capabilities.  With the increased complexity of our weapons
systems, has come a recognition that man and machine
must be fitted together if they are to operate effectively.  The design of equipment ranging from shovels
to display and control panels on our most sophisticated weaponry is now performed with the help of the research generated by human factors engineering psychologists in all of the military departments.  Indeed,
without this kind of know-how, some of our present
systems could not possibly be manned.

An example of the kinds of savings resulting from this
type of work is the $3 million saved through early de-
sign changes in the Pershing missile system and a 50
percent reduction in the number of operators required.
Another is the reduction of 25 percent in the loading
time of the Sergeant missile while reducing the required number of men from 11 to 6.

Having the right jobs and equipment correctly designed
and the right men properly trained is not enough to

guarantee efficient manpower management.  It is also
necessary to assign the properly classified and trained
men to the jobs they were trained for.  The importance
of this step was highlighted by the recent study of
the draft which showed that even slight decreases in
assignment "slippage" could result in substantial im-
provements in the overall effectiveness of our forces.
With the availability of computers and the development
of highly sophisticated statistical theory about ways
of achieving maximum use of personnel, the Departments
are now in a position to insure against malassignment
or costly and harmful pooling of idle men.  An example
of the kind of breakthrough which can result from this
type of research is the Pensacola Personnel Appraisal
System in which, at any desired time during a pilot's
training, his progress and achievements can be reviewed and his chances of successfully completing the
course can be determined.  The resulting elimination
of further investment in 'bad bets' has already resulted in savings in the millions of dollars.

Men forget as well as learn.  The Department must,
therefore, concern itself with the maintenance of
proficiency after formal training is completed.  It
is also vital to have a continuing and accurate appraisal of the competence level of our forces.  For
both these purposes, job proficiency measures are
necessary.  Such measures have become more numerous
and more realistic because of the years of research
on how performance can be most accurately and reliably
assessed.

We are basically interested in performance when the
chips are down.  Frequently this means performance
under the kinds of extreme stress generated in combat.
We know that effectiveness is greatly reduced by
stress.  What we must know more about is how to design
jobs and equipment and train men to be more resistant
to stress effects.  Our success in this basic research
effort may be crucial for our national strength when
it counts.

A large proportion of the jobs in the Armed Forces
involve teamwork.  Furthermore, some of the newer and

most important tasks must be performed by groups of
men who are isolated under difficult conditions for
considerable periods of time. The astronauts in a
manned-orbiting laboratory  or men in an armored personnel carrier during nuclear warfare  are cases in
point. These conditions and, indeed, any conditions
which demand cooperation introduce a number of problems.

Research is, therefore, being directed to improving
teamwork, lessening frictions, and increasing the
compatibility of men assigned to a group. Some of the
earliest work of this kind was done in composing SAC
air crews and resulted in clear gains in their efficiency. Subsequently social psychologists and sociologists have been working on similar problems for sub-
marine crews, infantry squads, missile teams, etc.

Our personnel must not only work together but, under
the present concept of worldwide Defense Department
activities, they must also work with both military and
civilian foreign nationals...

Since World War II, the foreign relations of the
United States have increasingly involved the developing nations of Asia, Africa, and Latin America.  In
all these areas countries have been struggling against
great odds to establish stable governments, to maintain their independence and to improve their standards
of living--efforts the United States has supported.
The major Communist powers have, on the other hand,
sought to exploit the instability and economic problems in these nations to expand their control over
large parts of the world.

Khrushchev's January 6, 1961, statement that the Soviet
Union will support so-called "national liberation wars"
has been often reaffirmed by the Soviet Union, even
as recently as June 28, 1965, in Pravda.  On December
31, 1962, the Peking People's Daily stated that:  "The
Communists of all countries...must...resolutely support wars of national liberation..."  Evidence of this
"support"--which includes instigation--has been obvious in Laos, Vietnam, and recently in Thailand.
Communist machinations, directly or through proxy

countries such as Cuba, have also threatened many
countries in Africa and Latin America, and have disrupted their internal affairs.

The State Department, the Defense Department, and key
agencies such as the CIA, AID, and USIA have increasingly had to turn their attention to meeting this
threat.  Because of its involvement in military assistance activities in these nations, and because of the
all-encompassing nature of the threat--in the political, economic, social as well as military spheres--
the Defense Department's missions in this area have
been viewed as broader than the traditional mission of
providing U.S. Armed Forces for the national defense...

Events in Vietnam and elsewhere have made it clear,
however, that while improved military hardware can
make a very important contribution to the defense
against Communist subversive warfare, this by itself
is not enough.  In fact, proper use of "nonmaterial"
tools represented by sound knowledge and actions in
the nonmilitary sphere can obviate the need to involve
large military forces.

Moreover, whether the military is involved in direct
conflict or in preinsurgency military assistance, U.S.
military people all over the world must work with and
help local military personnel at all levels plan and
implement the counterinsurgency programs.  The war itself revolves around the allegiance and support of the
local population.  The Defense Department has therefore
recognized that part of its research and development
efforts to support counterinsurgency operations must
be oriented toward the people, United States and
foreign, involved in this type of war; and the DOD has
called on the types of scientists--anthropologists,
psychologists, sociologists, political scientists,
economists--whose professional orientation to human
behavior would enable them to make useful contributions in this area...

There had been a gradual buildup to this latter
view, with accompanying evolution of the details.  In

the few years prior to 1960, a research group examining
the problems of social science applied to Defense problems, under the auspices of the Smithsonian Institution,
had made recommendations for work in an area which they
called "persuasion and motivation." In a later publication, the leader of this study explained it as
follows:[2]

The topics of persuasion and motivation refer to
methods of influencing people by means which are
short of force, or authoritative command, or other
direct incentives, on the one hand, and short of formal education or training, on the other hand.

Persuasion is exercised for the purpose of motivation;
it shapes expectations, molds opinions and attitudes...
Persuasion characterizes the normal, everyday means of
social intercourse, engaged in by everyone. The military services constantly use persuasion to motivate
and influence their own people and those people outside the services with whom they interact. The military services are regularly used in indirect ways by
the government to influence foreign peoples and foreign states... In any future war of significant length,
there will be "special warfare," guerrilla operations,
and infiltration. Subversion of our troops and populations will be attempted and prisoners of war will
be subjected to "brainwashing." The military establishment must be prepared to assist in promoting re-
cuperation and cohesiveness within possibly disorgan-
ized civilian populations, while attempting to shift
loyalties within enemy populations... The military
establishment needs to know all that can be known
about persuasion (including) the processes of persuasion; group relations and persuasion; the relation of
cultural differences to persuasion; persuasion and
social change...

Another way to approach the interaction of values and
persuasion is to study in greater detail the methods

of persuasion and indoctrination used by the Chinese
and other Asian people in comparison with our own attempts to build favorable attitudes in these countries.
Still another is to study the effects of our own military postures in different countries.  From such testing of theories of persuasive processes can emerge a
systematic classification of the value systems, stereo-
types, and national images of the chief cultures with
which the military establishment is likely to have extensive contact...

On several occasions our representatives have seemed
to be caught unawares by revolutions, when, with no
warning, rioting mobs have boiled up around our bases,
reflecting a state of public opinion and anger which
previously seemed not to exist...

The primary need is to create a small number of
stable, permanent centers of research on persuasion
as related to politico-military needs... Military
support should seek to integrate basic and applied research in the pursuit of a technology of persuasion...

In the present structure of research support, and because of its deep technological needs, the Department
of Defense is the logical source of this new type of
support for the systematic, long-range study of human
behavior.

Shortly after the issuance of this report, Dr.
Harold Brown became the Director of Defense Research
and Engineering (DDR&E).  At President Kennedy's request in 1961, Congress had appropriated approximately
$120 million for expansion of research and development
programs having to do with limited war.  To obtain
some better perspective than then existed about how
the money could usefully be spent, Dr. Brown established a committee of eminent scientists and high-
level DOD civilians and military people, including

those on his own staff chiefly responsible for this
area of work, to explore the nature of the limited-war
problem and recommend how these and subsequent funds
should be spent.  In addition to hearing briefings in
Washington from both the Defense and the State Departments about strategy, tactics, the military forces,
and the relevant research and development programs,
the group travelled extensively to developing coun-
tries--where the United States was involved in military
assistance programs, and where we were attempting to
help the local governments prepare to face the approaching conflicts.

This study group, which included physicists, engineers, generals, and admirals, was largely concerned
with problems of military hardware, weapons systems,
and military tactics and strategy.  But it recognized
that there were broader human problems involved, and
a subcommittee, including some of the members of the
Smithsonian group who had worked on the report quoted
above, was convened to look at these questions.  The
subcommittee's recommendations reinforced observations
made by the main group in its travels and briefings
overseas.  A substantial portion of the final study
report was devoted to the problems of what came to be
called "non-materiel research."  It was recognized
that although weapons systems could and needed to be
created to help the United States match its own military forces and its military assistance to the kinds
of problems then emerging in the world, these would

not provide all of the answers. How governments could
organize to combat guerrilla warfare and insurgency,
how to meet the insurgents' psychological offensives,
how the "static" armies of the developing countries
could be motivated to fight, and how these governments
could better relate to their people, were pointed out
as the most important questions facing the nation's
military assistance programs. A number of specific
recommendations, based on the contribution of the
social science subcommittee, were made for expanding
research in this area. In briefing the results of the
main study group's work to Secretary McNamara, the
chairman of the limited-war study group, a world-
renowned physicist, commented that while World War I
might have been considered the chemists' war, and
World War II was considered the physicists' war,
World War III, which we might already be in, might
well have to be considered the social scientists' war.

The Smithsonian group, after its first report, re-
constituted a group of politically oriented social
scientists to explore in greater detail the problems
of the national defense in terms of America's problems
overseas. A study under Ithiel de Sola Pool of MIT
led to another report, in 1963, which became much more
specific about revolutionary warfare, insurgency and
counterinsurgency, and the research that was needed to
help the United States cope with such problems in its
overseas relations. This later report[3] set the tone
for much of the effort that followed.

It is worth quoting extensively from it, because it
illustrates many important aspects of the advice the
Defense Department was getting.  It is, first, quite
lengthy; ideas are explored in depth and at leisure,
in the sometimes abstruse language that, later, was
often to make it difficult for the action-oriented
parts of the Defense bureaucracy to understand, accept,
and implement the results of studies by social scientists.  Second, it illustrates the kind of thinking
about the problems that, if it may have been subject
to disagreement on the part of some social scientists,
was at least widely enough accepted to evoke no great
hostility.  And third, it demonstrates plainly one of
the lines of thinking that died only very hard over a
long period of time:  that the Defense Department
should study problems of social change very broadly,
and that this was a perfectly legitimate activity.  The
following paragraphs may seem closely connected, but
they are drawn widely, although in sequence, from the
250-odd pages of the report:

The objective of this book is to consider what social
science can contribute to more effective conduct of
the free world's defense effort.  It does not aim to
be exhaustive but rather to spot significant topics on
which social science has heretofore been too little
used.

Our chapters skip over those fields in which the military establishment has already made extensive use of
the new technology of human behavior...

As the Advisory Panel reviewed the outcome of its efforts it came increasingly to realize that it had in-

advertently focused on one aspect of the Defense
Department's problems, namely the management of its
own establishment.

With the partial exception of the report on persuasion
and motivation which concerned itself extensively
with psychological warfare, all of the reports dealt
with the expansion of social science knowledge of a
kind that could be used to make the manpower of the
military establishment more effective...

But there is also an entirely different domain of
Defense Department problems which, the research group
recognized, had not yet been considered. To it, too,
the social sciences might make a contribution.
[emphasis added]

This other domain of problems may be roughly characterized as the operations of the Defense Department in
relation to the external world...

It is thus not in criticism but simply in candid observation that one must recognize that the defense establishment was early eager to accept the aid of social
science on its vast management problems but less willing to concede that social scientists might have something to contribute to those decisions which constitute the crux of military planning and operations...

In many places the military job can only be accomplished by a process of nation building... Success
in counter-insurgency outflanks a stalemate in the
field by concentrating on actions which will in two
to five years' time establish stable communities in a
progressing nation, with the surviving guerrillas
quietly returned from their hide-outs...

Until 1961, when this study was written, the United
States has communicated through its postures and
strategies a resolve to deter and contain--to deter
the Soviet Union from a nuclear attack and to contain
the communist forces within their borders. At the
same time, it communicates an intention to help the
new and poor countries make a free choice politically
and economically...

These questions also arise with respect to the policy
of commitment. Where are we prepared to draw the line?
Where do we use our troops? Where, if at all, and how,
do we defend against the internal subversion and revolution which is the communist pattern?... It is entirely possible that the Soviet blueprint calls for no
invasion at all by communist troops of one of these
countries...if we defend only against invasion, we may
never have a chance to strike with either the left or
the right hand.

This is one implication of our military posture...
Another is the fact that our opponents seem so free to
exploit all the revolutionary movements and expressions
of mass discontent in the developing countries and the
colonial states. We, on the other hand, have been cast
in the role of defending the status quo...

There is another reason for making a special plea on
behalf of the study of internal wars at this time...

Much is in doubt about the causes of internal war, as
we shall see, but of one proposition we may be certain:
internal war is closely connected with social change...
from this basic assumption it follows that one should
expect internal political violence to persist, perhaps
to increase... The tremendous number of internal wars
in the period 1946-1959...--and in other "transitional"
periods, such as late antiquity, the Renaissance and
Reformation, and the early nineteenth century in
Europe--is evidence of this...

It is particularly likely today that the communist
states will use internal wars as tools of international
politics. They have already done so frequently in the
postwar period and are likely to do so frequently in
the future. Communism--especially the present-day
Chinese version--is a militant messianic creed, and
such creeds always tend to produce expansionist zealots.
If the use of conventional warfare is closed to the
communists as a means of exporting their utopia they
will try other means to the same end, and the means
most readily available is the instigation and clandestine support of internal violence. Furthermore, communism places no immediate normative prohibitions on

political violence; on the contrary, communism justi-
fies and glorifies violence. In communist doctrines,
of course, violence is purely instrumental to other
ends...communists have available in other countries
much material for fashioning internal wars:  much des-
perate discontent, many sublime and frustrated hopes,
and much anachronistic hatred of non-communist Western
systems. Most important of all, the communists have
an enormous lead in the experience of and reflection
upon internal war. If we are far ahead of them in
deterrence theory, they are immeasurably farther ahead
of us in revolutionary theory...

At present, the most probable kinds of internal war,
once started, are difficult, if not impossible, to win
by those on the defensive. Above all is this likely
to be true of guerrillas fighting in favorable terrain
...if the noncombatant population is well-disposed
toward the guerrillas and the incumbents have any sort
of scruples...

All this gives added point to the frequently repeated
statement that internal war adds a new dimension, a
political dimension, to the problems of warfare. Internal war is a struggle for political loyalties no
less than military victories, a struggle requiring
intense political consciousness on both sides.
Indeed, the political art of detecting internal war
potential must have priority over the military art of
fighting it.  This applies to military policymakers no
less than civilian ones.*  In a world of alliances,
foreign bases, and far-flung power blocs, detecting in
advance the instability of regimes and knowing how to
shore them up with fair chances of success are among
the most urgent imperatives of the military as well as
the political arts...

Under the discussion of internal wars, a number of
topics for research were presented and elaborated:

---

*Emphasis added. From this statement, as will be
 seen, can be traced the genesis of Project
 Camelot.

...Analysis of the uses of internal war situations.
Since internal war situations are often largely incoh-
ate  in their initial stages; since they are very difficult to anticipate correctly under the best of circumstances, owing to the role of ephemeral precipitants
in bringing them about and the complexity of their preconditions; and since they are particularly difficult
to anticipate correctly with the knowledge presently
available; nothing would seem to be more urgently
necessary than knowing how to use them for one's own
policy purposes once they have occurred.  We live in
a revolutionary world in which internal war is a basic
fact of life.  In such a world even conservative
powers need conspiratorial theories; they can hardly
hope to contain the tide of revolution everywhere,
especially while being in the dark about the forces
causing it.  Studies of the techniques by which internal wars can be molded and channeled are therefore of
the utmost importance.  The Machiavellian overtones,
the apparent cynicism, may make such studies repellent,
but that cannot be helped.

...Studies of communist theories of internal war.  No
doubt we can learn a good deal about using internal
wars from the communists, who are masters of that unattractive art.  But this is only one of many reasons
for studying communist ideas about internal war.
Without subscribing to the theory that communists can
make internal wars under any and all conditions, or
the view that modern internal wars are all communist-
inspired, one can nevertheless argue that knowledge of
communist ideas about the preconditions of internal
war is indispensable at present for anticipating particularly crucial internal wars--those in which communists are in fact involved...

...Studies of the efficiency of certain policy responses to internal war potential.  Here the most important subjects are to determine the optimum uses of
repression, diversion, and concession, or combinations
of the three.  Each of these responses to internal war
potential is potentially useful and potentially dangerous.  Each has worked and failed in certain situations.
Under what conditions, structural and behavioral, are

they likely either to work or to fail?  How far should
they be carried?  What kinds of repression, diversion,
or concession work best in what sort of situations?
How can one policy response best be combined with
another--repression, for example, with concessions or
diversions?

...Studies of the internal war potential of critically
sensitive areas.  In general, the systematic study of
internal war potential must be a long drawn-out process;
there are no short cuts to knowledge as inherently
complicated and difficult to acquire as knowledge of
this subject.  In certain countries, however, we can
hardly await fully adequate theoretical knowledge to
carry out concrete appraisals.  Such countries are
those in which the security of important military bases
might be imperiled by internal war or countries in
which internal war might imperil our fundamental international designs...

As for other projects relating to the problem of anticipating internal war, these can easily be derived
from the text of the study...

...(there is) one other topic for research, to illustrate the kind of general-purpose inquiry requiring
large resources which might be particularly useful at
this stage of inquiry.  This topic involves inquiring
very broadly into what might be called 'symptoms' (or
'indicators') of internal war potential...

In the next few years it can be expected that there
will be a growing interest among social scientists in
the problems of guerrilla warfare and counter-subver-
sion.  It is, indeed, not impossible that this area
may prove to be a more fruitful one for social scientists than many other aspects of military strategy.
This is because the problems posed by such forms of
warfare and violence are intimately related to questions about the social structure, culture, and behavior
patterns of the populations involved in such conflicts.
Without question, social science research is in a
strong position to contribute useful knowledge in
designing and developing internal security forces
[emphasis added].  Indeed most of our understanding

about communist strategy and tactics in guerrilla warfare and subversion and of their basic appeals in
underdeveloped countries has come out of the works of
social scientists...

In the last few years social scientists have become increasingly interested in the political and administrative roles which armies can play in the nation-building
process... There is in addition a long tradition of
historical analyses of the domestic political role of
military leaders, but unfortunately most of the work
in the field of civil-military relations in the West
has only marginal application for understanding current
problems in the newly-emerging nations...

Clearly, the research administrator who wanted to
base a specific program on these recommendations had
some work to do.  Later, recommendations by social
scientists as to the research that was needed would
become more precise.  But it is obvious that the
government and important members of the social science
community were converging on both the definition of an
important problem for research and on acceptance of
the premise that it was "researchable."

## 3  A SYSTEM OF ETHICS AND VALUES

In both the government's and the scientists' views
there were some implicit assumptions about the legitimacy of the activities in question.

First, there was the question of counterinsurgency
(or "internal war") as a matter of interest for
scientific investigation.  In the current view of
much of the intellectual community, as a result of our
problems in Vietnam and the opposition of that community to the war, the term "counterinsurgency" has
taken on the connotation of suppressing "legitimate"
revolutionary social developments in the third world
(or even at home).  This interpretation of the term
was stressed by Senator Fulbright, as well as by many
of those in our universities who increasingly voiced
their opposition to American overseas involvements in
such conflicts.  But in 1960-1964, "insurgency" was
viewed in relationship to the Soviet and Communist
Chinese approaches to protracted warfare, for influencing countries and changing their governments to be
more sympathetic with the "socialist" countries and
"progressive forces all over the world."  We in the
United States viewed "wars of national liberation" as
a polite term for "communist takeover" using terror,
guerrilla warfare, coercion, and suppression of freedom.  We were still sensitive about the problem of
"brainwashing" with communist techniques generally--
for example, Viet Cong methods of indoctrinating their

adherents, thereby making them dangerous and effective
insurgents.  Such terms as "unconventional warfare"
and "special warfare" were used to describe both what
the revolutionary forces and the defenders against
them were doing, but these terms either had specialized
military definitions or did not seem to cover the complete gamut of activities--military, civil, political,
and economic--that had to be undertaken to defeat "wars
of national liberation."

Thus, while those who were defining what research
needed to be done in this area were not unaware of the
other possible connotations of the term, at this time
the term "counterinsurgency" came to serve as a convenient shorthand for American resistance to communist
takeovers of weak countries through "wars of national
liberation."  The term didn't change its complexion
until our efforts in Vietnam faltered and turned the
American intellectual community sour on the idea of
America being "the world's policeman."

A related semantic-cum-philosophical problem, which
was to come on stronger later, was whether research on
another country's problems constituted undue political
interference in that country's internal affairs.  Even
at the time of the growing Defense Department interest
in such research there was sensitivity on this point.
It is well known how the arguments about Vietnam began
around the issue of whether this was, in truth, a civil
war or an attack from the outside, and the United
States Government took great pains to prove the latter

view through State Department White Papers[1] and even
remarks by the President at his press conferences.  A
later article in Foreign Affairs by George Carver[2]
traced the North Vietnamese involvement in the South
from the beginning.  But it seems in retrospect that
none of this convinced anybody, and the opposing sides
held to their views.  Of course, well before this issue became important and gained added poignancy from
direct American participation in the war, military
and economic assistance programs had acted as instruments of foreign policy, through which we hoped to
influence the path of economic and political development of many nations of the world.  Even then we were
confusedly aware of the problems of reconciling the
many uses of such assistance with our public policy.[3]
In addition, as illustrated by the many arguments and
discussions in Congress and the general sensitivity,
at home and abroad, on the issue of aid "with strings
attached," we were torn between the motives of
altruism and extraction of maximum value from the expenditure of American dollars.

As far as the Defense Department was concerned in
the early days of the Vietnam War (and since, for that
matter), not much further rationale was needed than
that the United States had been asked for help by a
beleaguered "allied" government, and the whole official American policy from the President on down was
oriented toward providing it.  So this was not viewed
as interference so much as assistance, and from the

research point of view there was even less concern
because the research was in support of the quest for
knowledge, understanding, and greater effectiveness
in the overseas activities of the United States Government. The main question that was asked by the researchers was whether these could be provided. The
Harvard research groups studying the USSR and the
Chinese Peoples' Republic in the early fifties, as
well as others, had shown ways of doing research about
countries on the opposite side without access to much
more than was published by those countries or could be
gleaned by visiting scholars. As for research on the
problems of friendly countries, the question "Is it
polite to study friends?" was raised in the second
Smithsonian report (see n.3, Ch. 2), and was answered
as follows:

Research on political matters is a neighbor of intelligence. Perhaps this is the reason why a reluctance
to study political conditions in friendly nations, or
to be studied by friendly nations can be detected...
Another reason for reluctance to conduct certain types
of research in friendly nations may be that this kind
of activity can be taken as indicating distrust of the
government of that nation... There is often something
faintly ridiculous about the inhibitions applying to
research among allies. Furthermore, the United States
in particular, and to an only slightly lesser degree,
Great Britain, France, and West Germany publish about
themselves large amounts of information in categories
that are useful in connection with the functioning of
alliances. It is not, therefore, as though any of
these nations were seeking about others information
that they are not willing to disclose about themselves.
Nevertheless, the existence of suspicion about some

kinds of research, especially among emerging nations
without fully democratic governments, should be recognized and faced as one of the problems besetting researchers in this field...

Two measures for dealing with this suspicion are suggested for further exploration.  One would involve
having alliances themselves sponsor research... It is
probable that alliance-sponsored research would not
only overcome a large part of the resistance to studies
in friendly countries  but would also make it possible
to benefit from better cooperation on the part of significant groups in the country being studied.

A related suggestion is that greater use be made of cooperation between private American social science
research organizations and research groups in friendly
countries... Many of them, both within and without the
universities, have traditions of cooperating with
American research institutions and have been willing
to cooperate in sponsoring and executing studies of
mutual interest.

That is, the general idea was put forward that by enlisting the support and collaboration of researchers
and government in the country under study, the work
could be undertaken and would, in fact, be welcome.
We were to learn over the years that the problem was
not so simple, for many reasons; but that, too, lay in
the future.

It is clear, however, that as the Defense Department,
in its efforts to learn more about its military problems in the developing countries, followed the strong
and consistent advice given it by the scientific community, the members of that community who were involved
and the government in general held a group of premises
and a set of values in common, without which the re-

search effort could never have been initiated.  In
1963 and early 1964 they were, in summary, as follows:

- The problems of the United States' relations with
  the developing countries were important and contained many unknowns of a cultural, philosophical,
  strategic, and operational character.
- There was deep concern about communist expansion
  via communist groups within the developing
  countries, supported by China or the USSR and ex-
  ploiting the difficulties faced by these countries.
- If this expansion were successful, it would be
  detrimental to American interests everywhere.
- The communist instrument of expansion was the
  "war of national liberation"--internal war, or
  insurgency.
- Assistance to the developing nations in counterinsurgency was the American national strategy for
  preventing this expansion, and was a legitimate
  form of expression and implementation of American
  foreign policy.
- The armed forces had a major role in counterinsurgency, not only in the military sphere but
  in such areas as local economic development,
  psychological warfare, and internal security.
- Research was needed to help solve the many problems associated with the provision of assistance
  in counterinsurgency to foreign countries.  The

unknowns needing research included the processes
of social change, revolutionary organization,
guerrilla and counterguerrilla warfare, the role
of the military in the development of new nations,
the uses of "persuasion and motivation" in the
advisory processes, and cultural factors that
would increase the effectiveness of advisors.

- Research in the social sciences had helped solve
  "internal" problems for the Defense Department,
  and it could help solve these "external" problems
  as well.

- It was acceptable and desirable for the Defense
  Department to provide the funds for this research
  because it had the resources, the mission, and
  the necessary extensive contacts within the countries concerned.

- It was acceptable to perform research in allied
  foreign countries about their problems, and the
  sensitivities involved in such research could be
  overcome by enlisting the support and participation of local foreign governments and scholars in
  the research.

It would be an exaggeration to say that these premises and value orientations were universally held. To
the extent that the key figures in the Defense Department thought about social science research in this
context there was a good admixture of suspicion, or
skepticism, about its value. The social scientists

involved would have attributed this to lack of understanding rather than pointed hostility.  These social
scientists did not feel especially inhibited by
ethical considerations or the possibility of sanctions
by their peers for their involvement.  The professional organizations were permissive if not apathetic;
only the American Psychological Association had a
code of professional ethics, and this dealt with personal behavior on the part of psychologists rather than
with the kind of work they might undertake to do or
their relationships with or choice of clients.[4]  The
whole was pervaded by the atmosphere of intellectual
excitement and inquiry stimulated by the Kennedy presidency, an atmosphere whose momentum was to continue
for another year, still.  It would not have been difficult to obtain a majority opinion within the government community and the community of scholars most concerned with the pertinent research in the social
sciences that this was a valid set of premises on
which to build government research and action programs.
We shall examine, later, the transformation that was
to overtake these premises.  The reader who is skeptical of them now might note how difficult it is to project backward from the mid-1970s through the bitterness
of the late sixties to that earlier, more innocent,
time.

# II  THE BUREAUCRACY

<u>Prefatory Note:  A Personal Prologue</u>

How did an engineer become deeply involved with the
social sciences?  As these things usually happen, almost imperceptibly.  Much of my career had been spent
on defense problems, and I had developed a strong personal and professional interest in military affairs,
strategy, and the problems of the operation of American military forces on the world scene.  I joined the
Institute for Defense Analyses in 1960, had become
involved in studies of tactical weapons systems and
limited war, and participated as Executive Secretary
of the group performing the limited-war study for
Harold Brown, mentioned in Chapter 2.  These studies
all showed the difficulty and complexity of the military problems inherent in our foreign policy, and led
to the conviction that most of the contemporary
theories of military strategy developed by the early
1960s did not lend sufficient structure and clarity
to the difficult tasks of creating military forces
able to meet the realities of the world political
scene outside the nuclear standoff.  This appeared
especially important at the time, since President
Kennedy and his Administration seemed, finally, to have
discarded the unworkable doctrine of massive retalia-
tion and were changing the form, functions, doctrines,
and missions of the armed forces.  I expressed my
views in a book, <u>Limited War and American Defense
Policy</u>, written during 1962 and 1963.  Through the

work on this book and my work at IDA I became acutely
aware of the growing problems the United States faced
in Vietnam, and of the difficulties of building the
bridges between American and Vietnamese cultures and
politics that would be essential if those problems
were to be solved.

The problems of military equipment, tactics, and
strategy in the particular kind of warfare fought by
the Viet Minh seemed important (and they still do), but
I felt that, as I had observed in my book, "the application of hardware and strictly military techniques...
can obviously be of great assistance, but it is equally
obvious that (they) cannot offer the entire solution.
The technical parts of the problem emerge as ancillary
elements of the entire process of societal revolution
that reflects itself in the outbreak of subversion
and guerrilla war."  When I was asked in October of
1963 to join the Office of the Director of Defense
Research and Engineering as his Special Assistant for
Counterinsurgency programs, I told Harold Brown and
his Deputy for Tactical Warfare Programs, Dr. John
McLucas (to whom I would report), that I believed many
of the important solutions to problems such as we were
facing in Vietnam would have to be sought through research in the social sciences.  Dr. Brown agreed, and
also indicated his desire that I draw together and
create an orderly research and development program
out of the many scattered and, in some cases, duplica-
tive and conflicting efforts having to do with counter-

insurgency in general and Vietnam in particular that
were being undertaken by the Military Services and
the Advanced Research Projects Agency.  I therefore
had a charter to try to start an effort that appeared
important and interesting, and I accepted the position
offered in the expectation that I would be able to
help the Defense Department in ways that I thought
would make the help count.

4   THE SCENE

The position of Director of Defense Research and Engineering (DDR&E) was established by the Defense Reorganization Act of 1958.  Having a rank just below that of the Service Secretaries,* the DDR&E was charged to "supervise all research and engineering activities in the Department of Defense; and...direct and control (including their assignment and reassignment) research and engineering activities that the Secretary of Defense deems to require centralized management."  Thus, DDR&E was responsible for initiating, reviewing, passing judgment on, and assuring the budget for any research within the Defense Department's mission that appeared essential to the national interest.  There was, of course, a staff organization reporting to the DDR&E (known as his "Office," or ODDR&E).  While the precise form of this organization might vary over time, it generally included a principal deputy (who in 1964 and 1965 had the rank of Assistant Secretary of Defense), and a number of subordinate deputies for areas such as strategic weapons, "tactical warfare programs," (that is, attack aircraft, artillery, tanks, aircraft carriers--virtually all the major weapons systems in the armed forces except the nuclear

---

*Strictly speaking, the Army, Navy, and Air Force are "Military Departments," while their operating arms (the troops in the field) are the "Military Services." As a matter of convenience, the term "Services" will be used to refer to either.

strategic offensive and defensive systems such as Polaris, Minuteman, or the Anti-Ballistic Missile System), communications and electronics, and "science and
technology," or basic and applied research programs.
The deputy for science and technology had, reporting
to him, a director of behavioral science research programs.  The Director of the Advance Research Projects
Agency* also reported to the DDR&E; but the latter had
no cognizance over the Assistant Secretary of Defense,
International Security Affairs (ISA), who reported directly to the Secretary of Defense.  ISA was responsible for reviewing the international implications of
military affairs, and for coordinating Defense with
State Department activities; such coordination on
State's part was effected through the Director of the
Bureau for Political/Military Affairs.

The work of ODDR&E centered around the annual budget cycle.  Starting in the summertime, the defense
budget was prepared, to be reviewed by the Secretary
of Defense in mid-fall.  This preparation included all
necessary coordination with the Services, whose inputs
were requested, discussed, argued, and sent to the
Secretary of Defense (Robert S. McNamara, at that time)
as issues to be resolved if necessary.  The Secretary
decided what major items or groups of items would be
included in the budget and the level of funds that

---

*Established by Congress after the first Sputnik, to
  accelerate the research and development necessary to
  improve America's position in what became the "space
  race."  ARPA later came to perform many other tasks
  assigned by the Secretary of Defense or the DDR&E.

should be assigned to them. The "presidential budget"
would then be sent to the White House at the end of
December for incorporation in the federal budget and
presentation to Congress the following spring.

Another part of the cycle occurred in June in connection with congressional appropriation of the money
for the Defense Department's operations based on the
previous budget request. The Department then went
through an "apportionment review," in which further
decisions were made about allocation of funds, taking
account of the actual monies appropriated rather than
those requested, and incorporating changes in programs
that might have been found desirable in the meantime
or been instructed by Congress during its deliberations. Between these two periods (the fall budget
preparation and the spring apportionment review) there
were, of course, the congressional budget hearings.

For each part of the budget cycle, the deputies in
ODDR&E reviewed all of the Service programs, decided
whether to recommend approval of the Service budget
proposals or to propose alternative allocations, and
negotiated with the Services to resolve the large
number of issues that would inevitably arise. Under
the law, the DDR&E himself had the responsibility for
ultimate approval of Service Research and Development
(R&D) expenditures. This meant that final approvals
of projects or programs, and instructions to the Services, were signed by the DDR&E, although the necessary
documents might be prepared and recommendations made

by the deputies and their immediate staffs. Generally, each deputy would be responsible for a large block of the entire $6-8 billion worth of Defense R&D, with each block adding up to hundreds of millions, or billions, of dollars worth of effort. Each subordinate staff member would be responsible for a group of programs decided partly on the basis of how large a program an individual could effectively oversee, and partly on the basis of coherence of projects within a functional area. Only rarely were programs arranged such that one program, or one group of projects in a particular subject area, was handled by an individual solely because of its importance, if the associated funding were very small. The size of the organization simply didn't permit this as a standard procedure, however desirable it might be. But the position of "Special Assistant" offered this kind of flexibility, and such a position could be created when, as in this case, the DDR&E deemed it necessary.

There existed for the DDR&E staff (including the deputies) no real power over the Services, and a great deal of power, at one and the same time. While only DDR&E could legally give official instructions to the Services, the Services knew very well that if a member of the DDR&E staff were negotiating for a certain budget level on a project, or to have a certain project established, this could become an "instruction" if DDR&E wished it to become so. Much of the staff work revolved around the preparation of such instruction

documents, with their attendant discussion, negotiations, and coordinations almost ad infinitum.

Lyons,[1] in an important book on government support
of the social sciences, has noted that the Defense
Department, at the DDR&E level, had only part-time
help to pay attention to the social sciences. This
is true, but it tells only part of the story. My own
work with the social sciences required only a fraction
of my time. Most of my time was spent on problems of
military technology, systems research and development,
analysis of operations in the developing war, and on
organizing and coordinating a fast-growing Defense
Department program that included all manner of things,
ranging from studies of Viet Cong motivation, to the
M-16 rifle, new helicopters, aerial ordnance, or night-
viewing equipment for infantry. As will be seen, the
nature of getting any one task done at that level of
the bureaucracy is to initiate an action, talk with
many people, hold meetings, write papers--and then
wait; much time is spent waiting for other people to
do or decide something in any one program area. Therefore, I found that I had all the time necessary for
the social science research efforts I wanted to initiate, when the time was needed.

The part-time nature of DDR&E's attention to the
social sciences as science lay in the intermittent
occupation of the position of responsibility for the
social science programs under the Deputy for Science
and Technology, rather than in the intentional assign-

ment of the responsibility to someone who held another job simultaneously. This was due to the reluctance of social scientists to give up their academic positions and freedom to take on this important position, rather than to the Defense Department's intent to give the area short shrift, although the conditions under which the job would have to be undertaken, reporting to hardware-oriented engineers and physical scientists, made for an interesting social dynamic not calculated to encourage social scientists' interest. But there did happen to be, during the critical first two years of my involvement, a full-time social scientist in the Office of the DDR&E,* responsible for overseeing all of the Defense Department's work in the social sciences, and I worked with him very closely. In addition, the military departments and ARPA had full-time social scientists responsible for their social and behavioral research programs.**

---

*Dr. S. Rains Wallace, a psychologist whose career was devoted to various aspects of measuring human performance, selection and training of personnel for specific job skills, and related matters. In addition to his work for the DOD, Wallace had been Chairman of the Psychology Department at Tulane University, Vice President for Research of the Life Insurance Agency Management Association, President of the American Institutes for Research, and Chairman of the Psychology Department at Ohio State University. Dr. Wallace died of cancer in August, 1973.

**At the time of the events to be described, these positions were held by: Dr. Lynn Baker and Dr. Ken-

As Special Assistant for Counterinsurgency I did
not interact with the social scientists in the DOD
totally as a novice.  In the course of my work at IDA,
I had come to know some of the social scientists in
the outside community who were advising the Defense
Department on how social research could be helpful
relative to the problem at hand.  I had come to know
the Service and ARPA social science program directors,
as well.  Therefore, in addition to a personal, avoca-
tional interest of long standing in social research I
had had a rather extensive exposure to the pertinent
social research problems and to the people involved in
them.  I had had many discussions with these people,
and with my close friend, Dr. Jesse Orlansky,* at IDA,
about what social research might be expected to accomplish in this area.  When I entered the Pentagon,
Orlansky pointedly reminded the social science program
directors in the Services and ARPA that despite the

---

neth Karcher in the Army Research Office; Dr. Richard
Trumbull and Dr. Luigi Petrullo in the Office of
Naval Research; Dr. Charles Hutchinson in the Air
Force Office of Scientific Research; Dr. J.C.R. Lick-
lider and Dr. Lee Huff in the Advanced Research Pro-
jects Agency.

*Dr. Orlansky is a psychologist who has specialized in
human factors engineering, measurement of human performance, and other problems in the application of
the behavioral sciences to defense systems.  He was
one of the founders of the behavioral research firm
of Dunlap and Associates, and has been a member of
the IDA staff and management since 1960.  He has also
been a member of many scientific advisory committees
for the Military Services and NASA.

fact that my background and responsibilities dealt
primarily with hardware, someone in ODDR&E with my
orientation to and hope for the social sciences presented a rare opportunity for them to implement some
of the things "the community" had been urging on the
Defense Department. I did not feel that my own membership in a different discipline would interfere,
since there were obviously many sources of expertise
and help.

So the atmosphere in the bureaucracy was hopeful,
and it appeared that the chance had come for the social
sciences to help with the difficult problems of overseas conflict facing the Defense Department and the
country.

When the Defense Department--which from here on will
be called by its familiar acronym, the DOD-- undertook
in 1964 to enlist the social sciences in support of
its expanding foreign operations, it was not starting
from a zero level of effort.  There were already a
number of research programs underway intended to improve the U.S. government's knowledge about foreign
countries and their peoples, the behavior of foreign
governments, causes of revolutions, and cultural factors affecting relationships between the United States
and other countries.  The thrust of the recommendations
previously described, when translated into action, was
to build on this base, to add work seeking the particular knowledge and understandings for which the need
had become apparent, and to increase the level of
effort to meet the newly emerging, newly emphasized
problems.

Before describing this existing research base, it
will be useful to digress into a brief discussion of
what is meant by "a million dollars worth of research,"
in terms of effort applied, since the question of
money available to the DOD but not to others, such as
the State Department, for such research was to domi-
nate later discussion of the propriety of the work.
By the time the researcher was paid his salary, his
"fringe" benefits were added, his secretarial help and
travel to Washington and overseas were paid for, and

other "overhead" expenses--for example, general administrative support of his organization, and the mortgage
or rent on their buildings and facilities--were covered,
it cost (during the 1964-1969 period covered by this
book) an average of roughly $50,000 per year for one
professional researcher, outside the government, to
work on a problem for the government.[1] This might
vary, depending on the organization. The cost at some
universities might be as low as $35,000-$40,000 per
year; but often many overhead items were covered in
other accounts encompassed by a variety of grants from
many sources. Moreover, the university researcher
received his teaching salary from the university, and
the research grant was used to cover his time only
when he was not teaching. He could be assisted by
graduate students who received minimal compensation.
Thus, a man-year of effort in a university could be
stretched farther than in a contract organization.
On the other end of the scale, some non-profit or
profit-making organizations who had to charge all their
expenses to contracts (in addition to a management fee,
which might vary from 4-10 percent and was used for
organizational development, such as exploratory research in new areas or continuing staff education)
might require $50,000-$60,000 per year for a professional researcher in the continental United States.
The cost could go as high as about $70,000 per year
for a researcher moved overseas and living there with
his family for a period of two, three, or four years.

Since most Defense Department work in this subject
area was done by contract, the money to support this
research had to be shown in the Defense budget explicitly, under the particular research subject "line item,"
and appropriated by Congress each year.  Therefore, it
was highly visible.  Some work by social scientists in
other subject areas, such as the studies of human resources and performance undertaken for the armed forces,
might be performed "in-house," and the budget would be
covered by a general appropriation for in-house labora-
tories.  But although the items might be distributed
differently, and the accounting categories might not
be the same (for example, such research might be
carried under manpower, operations and maintenance
funds, or facilities, and all might be scattered
through different, aggregated budget line items), the
total cost for a year of work by a professional researcher within the government was not very different.
Even the State Department, which had at the time only
about $150,000 for "external" contract research, did
much related analysis in its Bureau of Intelligence
and Research, which had a budget and staff whose
overall "professional man-year" costs did not depart
far from this average figure.

Thus, regardless of the source, whether the research
was contracted out or performed in-house, "a million
dollars worth of research" meant about 20 professional
social scientists, or analysts, working on the government's problems and paid for by the government.  A DOD

budget that went from about $5 million to about $8 million for this work (about the range that was covered,
although many higher figures were quoted, incorrectly,
as we shall see) meant increasing the number of professional social scientists engaged in this area of research from about 100 to about 160. In the DOD case,
since most of the pertinent research was performed by
contract, these researchers were largely outside the
bureaucracy. The analytical staff of the State Department's Bureau of Intelligence and Research came to
roughly the same numbers, although they were almost
exclusively within the organization.[2] The additional
60-odd people would be drawn from a professional social
science community that, including all social scientists,
numbered over 50,000 during that period of time.[3] At
the same time, thousands of professional engineers and
physical scientists were working on research and development to solve weapons and equipment problems associated with or related to the Vietnam war alone, and the
number working on all Defense Department research and
development was obviously far higher. While it later
became obvious, and was in fact understood at the time,
that a very few people performing research relating to
foreign social problems could be in a very sensitive
position, the numbers talked about were never very
large, and only a few of these people--perhaps 10 percent of them--ever went overseas to do research on the
problems in the field under DOD auspices.

The sponsorship of DOD programs in the areas associ-

ated with overseas conflict and counterinsurgency was
divided, in 1964 and subsequently, among the three Services, the Advanced Research Projects Agency (ARPA),
and the Office of the Assistant Secretary of Defense
for International Security Affairs (ISA). The patterns
of work among these varied. Such research in the Air
Force and the Navy was funnelled through or initiated
by, and monitored by, the Air Force Office of Scientific Research (AFOSR) and the Office of Naval Research
(ONR), respectively. They worked largely through a
system of research grants to university scholars. The
offices were under the general supervision of the military, but essentially operated with a fair degree of
independence under the control of civilian division
directors within the offices (see notes, p. 53). The
grantees worked as individuals and had great freedom
to travel, contact American and foreign officials, and
to undertake their work and publish their results with
no restraints on academic freedom. The work was usually not classified, although the scholars might need
access to classified sources. But the work might be
quite sensitive, especially if the scholars had to
contact American or foreign government officials or
study government papers. AFOSR and ONR relied upon
the good sense and circumspection of the scholars to
protect their sources and not to upset the delicate
matters of foreign relations.

Work for AFOSR and ONR was undertaken largely through
the mechanism of unsolicited proposals sent to these

organizations by the scholars. Generally, relationships existed between the Service organizations and
the universities, which would allow the scholars to
learn what problems were of interest. But except for
specifying general areas of interest to encourage proposals, the thinking about problem definition and
specific research subject matter and format was performed by the grantees. The research projects then
were molded into final form through discussion between
the scholars and the government "program managers."
Some work for the Air Force in this area was also performed by the RAND Corporation, a nonprofit Federal
Contract Research Center (FCRC) which had a style and
a reputation for scholarliness that rendered it not
much different from the university community in important respects, and which gave it the same kind of
access and freedom. Some studies oriented primarily
toward naval strategy but possibly having social
science components might also be performed by another
FCRC,[4] the Center for Naval Analyses, again under similar conditions.

The Army's research operations in these areas were
quite different. Behavioral and social science research at that time was conducted for the Army primarily
through one in-house and two contract organizations--
respectively, the U.S. Army Personnel Research Office
(USAPRO), the Human Resources Research Office (HumRRO),
and the Special Operations Research Office (SORO).
USAPRO concentrated largely on the kinds of human fac-

tors and testing problems described in the statement
for the Fascell subcommittee (pp. 18-24). The other
two organizations, which had been established for the
Army by George Washington University (HumRRO) and
American University (SORO), were at that time captive
Federal Contract Research Centers, obtaining their
funds exclusively from the Army and working on problems
largely prescribed by the Army. These organizations
were supervised by the Army Research Office, and in
some cases parts of their programs were monitored by
a representative of the Army Deputy Chief of Staff for
Operations (DCSOPS), a primary "user" of the results.
ARO was essentially a _military_ organization, although
it employed civilians. Its Human Factors and Operations Research Division, headed in 1964 and 1965 by
the late Col. William Sullivan, had two civilians--
Dr. Lynn Baker and the late Dr. Kenneth Karcher--both
psychologists, who provided technical supervision over
the work of SORO and HumRRO and who were to play an
important part in later events.*

Each year SORO and HumRRO had to work out with the
Army detailed agreements for their individual work

---

*This office also supervised the work of the Research
Analysis Corporation (RAC), another FCRC which performed operations and systems analysis work for the
Army. RAC became deeply involved in counterinsurgency
research under the auspices of ARPA; social scientists
were involved in some of this work, but it was opera-
tionally rather than social-system oriented. The Army
supported little counterinsurgency research at RAC.

programs. While management responsibility was vested
in ARO, DCSOPS made its formal "requirements" for outputs known and played an important part in shaping the
program. The organizations were assigned formal tasks
by, and prepared reports for, the Army. The reports
were published only after Army (for example, DCSOPS)
review and approval. There was close supervision by
the Army not only of the work but of the salary structure, travel, contacts with Army officers in the field,
and contacts with others for the purposes of gathering
data. Thus, whereas the Air Force and the Navy hired
top talent at universities--that is, supported scholars
in their own areas of expertise, largely doing work
that the scholars proposed to do--the Army-supported
organizations had tightly structured programs representing largely what the Army wanted them to do, and
for which professional researchers were hired to work
as assigned, first on one task and then on another,
away from any close contact with university colleagues.

It is implicit, first, that there was a division
among the Services between "basic" and "applied" research. The university scholars supported by the Air
Force and the Navy were searching out and exploring
basic phenomena--why did certain human events or interactions take place; what were the pressures for social
change in a society; what were the underlying mechanisms of human behavior and interaction therein; what
were the differences in such behaviors in different
cultures? Thus their work was along the lines of the

fundamental studies called for by the Smithsonian reports. But the Army contractors worked on applications of social science knowledge, and followed more closely the applied directions recommended in the report of the limited-war advisory group for DDR&E. In HumRRO, peopled largely by psychologists, the program was oriented toward problems of troop training and behavior, and performance under stress. This included some study of language training and of cultural factors in contacts between American Army personnel and foreign military personnel. Beyond this, HumRRO's program did not get much involved in the counterinsurgency questions. Rather, their cross-cultural research fed and was picked up by the others.

SORO was the organization that concentrated on studies of foreign areas and revolutionary war. SORO had been established by the Army in 1957 to serve the needs of the Army's psychological warfare directorate, which did not find the special skills needed either at HumRRO or the Operations Research Office (RAC's predecessor organization). Its mission and level of effort were expanded in 1962, with increased interest in the Army Special Forces and counterinsurgency operations. This was part of the Army's response to President Kennedy's call for increased effort in such areas.

SORO's work included analyses of how communist party organizations worked; case studies of revolutionary warfare, such as Cuba, Algeria, and Vietnam; and, for DCSOPS who wanted to use them in preparation

for Special Forces operations, descriptions of tribal
groups in various countries. Also under DCSOPS auspices they engaged in preparation of "area handbooks"
--unclassified books that described, in detail, the
history, culture, and societal structures of diverse
foreign countries in the "third world"--to be used for
educating officers assigned to overseas duty. These
handbooks were also in great demand by other parts of
government, such as the State Department or AID, who
regularly sent people to overseas assignments. By the
nature of the research or study assignments, while the
people supported by ONR and AFOSR used basic data
sources, or performed field and laboratory research,
SORO used secondary sources and did much library research. As an organization, they were inexperienced in
field work, although (with HumRRO) they had small field
offices working under the respective military commanders in Korea and Panama on specific problems of the
relationships between American troops and the local
populations.

The research programs of the Services were thus different in quality and responsiveness to Service needs.
It was my view then that the Air Force and Navy programs could be undertaken by the best people but the
work was generally oriented to subjects the scholars
wanted to explore, while the Army could much more
easily initiate work on problems that appeared important to the Services but it could not always have such
work performed by the best available expertise. This

dichotomy underlay much of the later difficulty that
the entire DOD program encountered.

The ISA- and ARPA-supported work (see p.60) followed
a different pattern still. ISA needed strategic and
policy-oriented studies--what, for example, might
happen in various areas such as NATO or Communist
China, under various international conditions, and
what were the policy implications of such events for
the defense of the United States? ISA, often working
through ARPA for administrative arrangements (since
both were part of the Office of the Secretary of Defense) let contracts with Federal Contract Research
Centers such as RAND or the Institute for Defense Analyses (IDA); with nonprofit organizations such as the
Stanford Research Institute (SRI); and on occasion,
they might be able to undertake a study contract with
a well-known university scholar. The work supported
by ISA, essentially a civilian organization, was under
much less rigid control than the Army's, but research
differed from that at universities in that much of it
was classified. However, at this time, before the
campus turmoil engendered by Vietnam, the universities
had no trouble accepting classified research; often it
was embraced as a source of steady support. Thus,
since such work was usually undertaken by mutual agreement between the organizations and their sponsors, the
conditions for ISA's contractors were generally similar
to those at universities, with the additional advantage
for the government that teams of two or more research-

ers could work full-time on a problem without diversion
for teaching or to administer other grants necessary to
support graduate students.  These research organizations were able to attract scholars and experts from
universities and government, and to turn out studies
of high quality, depth, and perception, more or less
at a predicted time, which was not always the case with
university research.

RAND and a number of other organizations such as
RAC and SRI also worked for ARPA (sometimes, as in the
RAND studies of Viet Cong prisoners which will be described later, jointly with ISA).  In 1963 ARPA had
initiated a basic research program in the behavioral
sciences associated with advanced information proces-
sing technology, under the direction of J.C.R. Licklider, a well-known psychologist who had taken leave from
the consulting firm of Bolt, Beraneck, and Newman to
help implement some of the recommendations of the first
Smithsonian report.  ARPA, after helping to start a
U.S. space program, had by this time become a more
generally applied DOD instrument for starting new,
experimental research and development programs that
entailed more technical risk than the Service budgets
could tolerate.  Licklider's program represented the
kind of advanced work that ARPA could undertake; at
the same time he was available, as a member of the
agency, for consulting on the counterinsurgency studies just being initiated under ARPA's Project Agile.

Project Agile, which came, along with "counter-

insurgency" and "the CIA," to symbolize all that the
Students for a Democratic Society and others found
reprehensible about American overseas operations,[5] had
been established by ARPA in 1961, in response to
DDR&E's instruction which resulted in turn from recommendations contained in the limited-war study group's
report. The name "Agile" was selected to signify the
project's ability to respond rapidly to urgent requests
for research. Its assignment was to perform research
and development in the counterinsurgency area, largely
in support of American activities in Southeast Asia.
It had, early in its history, concentrated on counterguerrilla hardware systems and equipment. In late
1963 and early 1964, it was beginning to become concerned with the human problems of such warfare.

After Licklider's departure from ARPA in 1964, and
under stimuli which will be described in detail shortly,
Agile increased its effort in the so-called "soft"
sciences related to Vietnam and counterinsurgency. In
1965 this area of work, and some basic social science
research that had been initiated by Licklider, both
came under the direction of Dr. Lee Huff, a political
scientist who had worked for ARPA in Thailand. One
of the first such efforts undertaken by Agile, under a
contract to the RAND Corporation and jointly sponsored
with ISA, was a program of interviewing Viet Cong and
North Vietnamese prisoners and defectors in Vietnam,
to explore the factors of motivation and social cohesion that bound cadres to the Communist side in the

Vietnam war. Also through RAND, ARPA initiated a
study of the relationships between U.S. military advisors and their "counterparts"--those they advised in
a one-to-one relationship--in Vietnam. Agile had had
studies performed of the effectiveness--or reasons for
the lack of it--of the strategic hamlet program in
Vietnam, and in 1964 Michael Pearce, a young RAND
social scientist under Agile sponsorship, who spoke
Vietnamese and lived in a village some thirty miles
from Saigon, was studying the dynamics of the interactions among the Viet Cong, Vietnamese government
officials, the Vietnamese army, and the people, in a
Vietnamese village. A study of village security in
Thailand was also initiated in 1963, and an evaluation
was soon to be made of the Thai Government's Mobile
Development Units, which were designed, as part of an
effort to counter communist infiltration and propaganda, to help integrate the villagers in Northeast Thailand better into central Thai society. The ARPA program was much freer than that of the Army because individual contracts were let with many different organizations, so that the best available research quality
could be sought.

The total DOD program of nonhardware research that
could be considered directly relevant to counterinsurgency problems in 1964 came to about $5 million,
divided as shown in Table 1. Table 2 lists the titles
of typical study projects from each of the sponsor's
subprograms. The breakdown into four categories was

Table 1    Support for work in the Social Sciences
           Related to Counterinsurgency, FY 1964
           (Thousands of Dollars)

|  | Amount | Equivalent Professional Researchers* |
|---|---|---|
| a. By Sponsoring DOD Component: | | |
| Army | $2,305 | 46 |
| Navy | 280 | 7 |
| Air Force | 393 | 8 |
| ARPA | 2,200 | 44 |
| Total: | $5,178 | 105 |
| | | |
| b. By Orientation of Work: | | |
| Political studies | 562 | 11 |
| Operations research, systems analysis, economics | 1,841 | 36 |
| Persuasion and motivation, psychological operations | 1,617 | 34 |
| Manpower, selection, and training research | 1,158 | 24 |
| Total: | $5,178 | 105 |
| | | |
| c. By Organization Conducting the Research: | | |
| Universities | 455 | 9 |
| Nonprofit organizations | | |
| SORO | 1,180 | 24 |
| RAC | 691 | 13 |
| RAND | 542 | 11 |
| HumRRO | 845 | 18 |
| Other | 529 | 11 |
| In-house, government | 455 | 9 |
| Industry | 472 | 9 |
| Foreign universities | 9 | 1 |
| Total: | $5,178 | 105 |

*Based on $50,000/man-year

Table 2   Illustrative Projects Supported, by Sponsor, Program Area, and Type of Contractor, FY 1964

POLITICAL STUDIES:

| Army | Navy | Air Force | ARPA |
|---|---|---|---|
| None | USSR-Chinese relations (university) | Patterns of national development and implications for military planning, Africa and Latin America (university) | Studies of Northeast Thailand (nonprofit) |

OPERATIONS RESEARCH, SYSTEMS ANALYSIS, ECONOMICS:

| Army | Navy | Air Force | ARPA |
|---|---|---|---|
| Studies in counter-insurgency (nonprofit) | Research implications of naval counterinsurgency and unconventional warfare operations (nonprofit) | None | Republic of Vietnam Air Force after-action study (nonprofit)<br><br>Railroad security (nonprofit)<br><br>Ambush patterns and counteraction techniques (In-house) |

Table 2 (continued)

PERSUASION AND MOTIVATION, PSYCHOLOGICAL OPERATIONS:

| Army | Navy | Air Force | ARPA |
|---|---|---|---|
| Psychological operations guides (nonprofit) | Delineation of the naval role in psychological operations (for-profit research org.) | Military power and persuasion (nonprofit) | Analysis of mobile development unit operations (nonprofit) |
| | Inducing cooperation between adversaries (university) | Measurement of attitudes and attitude change (university) | |
| | Small group coalitions (university) | | |

MANPOWER, TRAINING AND SELECTION RESEARCH:

| Army | Navy | Air Force | ARPA |
|---|---|---|---|
| Development of concepts and techniques in area training (nonprofit) | Development of culture-free tests (industry) | None | Advisor-counterpart communications (nonprofit) |

Table 2 (continued)

MANPOWER, TRAINING AND SELECTION RESEARCH:

| Army | Navy | Air Force | ARPA |
| --- | --- | --- | --- |
| Procedures for increasing the effectiveness of small infantry-type units (nonprofit) | | | |

Note: All projects not included; represents a sampling to convey the flavor of work supported by each sponsor.

derived later, when we started to work at expanding the program; it will be described in some detail in Chapter 7.

We have already alluded to the processes by which "quality control" was exercised over the work. AFOSR and ONR generally maintained contact with their grantees and reviewed their work periodically with them, but the drives toward high quality were largely those of scholarship exercised within the university community. The Army reviewed meticulously the products of the work it supported, and through this review process affected both its quality and its orientation toward the Army's areas of concern--at least as interpreted by the reviewing officers. The program directors in the Office of the Secretary of Defense--ISA and ARPA--generally worked through "agents" in the Services; that is, their money was transferred to the Services, which let the contracts for research. But responsibility for technical review and supervision of the work was retained by the initial sponsoring organizations, and quality control was left at least as much up to the contract organizations as to the sponsors. The sponsors could, of course, exercise the sanction of not extending, renewing, or giving further contracts if work was found to be below par.

This, then, was the basic program material to which the DOD, while I was in the Office of the DDR&E, had decided to add, and the organizational structure we

had to work with.  It might be commented about the
shape of this initial program, that its size and the
studies and subjects included in its description reflect, to a certain extent, judgments that were made
at the time about what information to include in
assembling the program data.  The counterinsurgency
problem was so complex, and touched on so many different aspects of human behavior and social structure,
varying from the military to the economic to the political and the cultural, that a separate decision had
to be made for almost each individual project regarding whether it should be included or not.  Since the
intent was to understand the phenomena in all their
broad aspects, and since the boundaries of the DOD
role were quite fuzzy, the judgments were almost invariably made to include more that might appear relevant rather than less.  In the words used at the time,
we tended to "cast the net wide."  These judgments
were subsequently refined by a study undertaken for
the purpose; but this is jumping ahead.  After the
events of Project Camelot, with the attending reaction
by Congress and the press, this tendency to encompass
as much as possible became more and more constrained.
Ultimately, with Senator Mansfield's amendment to the
1969 Defense Authorization Bill requiring all DOD work
to be directly and obviously relevant to purely military matters, almost everything that the DOD might do
in relation to foreign areas that would use the contri-

butions of social scientists came to be included, so
that, ironically, the act of making judgments about
relevance became irrelevant.

The report to the government by a group of experts who
make program or action recommendations in a particular
area, which then languishes because the recommendations are conceptually or bureaucratically difficult
to implement, is a familiar phenomenon in American
government life.  Given a set of recommendations that
read, roughly, "increase social science research on
counterinsurgency, and here are some general subject
areas of interest," and assuming that the government
is positively motivated to follow such recommendations,
how does one go about doing it?  There are no rules
except that one has to work within the bureaucracy.
The task becomes purely a matter of matching the elements of the bureaucracy and their interrelationships
to the components of the problem and their interrelationships, and trying to launch new ideas and new budget assignments over the usual bureaucratic inertia
and resistances.  We needed to learn what was going on
currently in the DOD's programs, to establish a measure
of control over those programs, to decide where to go
next, and to start the process of instruction and coordination that would initiate the travel of the new
program from conception to implementation.  All this
came to be encompassed in a set of five actions, which
evolved as the effort went along as much as they were
planned long in advance:  the establishment of an in-
house DOD working group; a more or less regular series

of meetings with the research directors of the other departments of government; a review of past history, new program proposals, and the DOD's research instruments by the Defense Science Board; negotiation and issuance of appropriate instructions for budget actions and program changes; and, subsequently, meetings with the staffs of the responsible congressional committees to explain the new funding requests.

From all the previous work of the social science community, we had a fair idea of what needed to be done generally. But the need now was to make the ideas very much more specific. An ad hoc committee of those responsible for this area of research and development in the Services and ARPA was convened, with myself as chairman. The committee first met on February 7, 1964, and agreed that it would serve as a channel for informal communication of ideas and "trial balloon" instructions between DDR&E and the Services, and as a vehicle to discuss and agree on purposes, definitions, and specific projects. The questions of defining counterinsurgency and judging the relevance of individual projects were among the first discussed. The work of drawing together and collating lists of "relevant" ongoing projects was initiated. It was agreed that these would be grouped in the four categories (which, by themselves, illustrate the scope of the research being considered) mentioned earlier: political studies; operations research, systems analysis, and economics; persuasion, motivation, and psycho-

logical operations; manpower training and selection
research. In addition, a first step was to be taken
toward listing additional work that the participants
desired to undertake for two years ahead, assuming that
additional funds would be available.

From these discussions I gained the impression that
not all the members of this ad hoc committee were exactly eager to bring their work together under one set
of headings for later exposure. As is natural in
bureaucratic affairs, the coming together for a common
task began the exposure of divergent points of view
and self-protection for the different agencies. The
resulting conflicts, friendly and low-key though they
were in committee, had much to do with the shape of
the final program plan. Since the Director of ARPA
reported directly to DDR&E, he would have no trouble
in protecting his efforts; but ARPA was concerned
about whether the committee's deliberations would
lead to an altered pattern of control. The Army
viewed the subject as very much within its mission
and responsibilities, and was anxious to get started;
but the committee's work would shake its established
patterns and exacerbate the then-quiescent conflict
between the Army's R&D and DCSOPS organizations about
what SORO should be doing.

The Navy and Air Force representatives indicated,
more by attitude than words, that they foresaw a number of problems in the offing. They had had enough
trouble obtaining support for their programs from the

professional military officers who were really more
concerned with hardware, weapons systems, and studies
of tactics and operations, and anticipated more critical reviews as visibility and pressure to change were
increased. The relationship with the university community would always include some sensitivities, and
would need protection. The gathering together of a
list of all their projects, which would then become
part of a different sort of program than the basic research efforts within which they were then imbedded,
made those projects in the aggregate much more visible
and therefore much more vulnerable to adverse action,
both within the Services and by Congress. Thus it
took some time over several meetings and a considerable
amount of discussion and negotiation to agree that all
the information would be drawn together and that the
program would be considered in the aggregate for this
particular purpose. But all of this was quite straightforward in concept and didn't present more than the
expected number of bureaucratic difficulties.

At almost the same time I initiated an effort to
examine in relation to each other, and if possible to
tie together, the efforts of the DOD and the other
interested government departments. This was a much
more complex problem, since there was not, among the
various departments, nearly as much unity of purpose
and of methods as there was among the disparate parts
of the DOD--and even the latter were different enough
from each other. A meeting was held on March 20, 1964,

with representatives of State's Bureau of Intelligence and Research; the research director of USIA; one of the men in charge of a part of AID's research and evaluation program (there was more than one program); and a representative of the CIA R&D community.

The purpose of the meeting was stated, first, as information exchange on "non-materiel research of interest to all the departments with respect to the counterinsurgency area," and then to explore the possibility of improving coordination of this research among the departments. Again, we ran into the definition problem and, again, decided to leave it broad and up to the judgment of the individuals as to what might be included in such a program. But it was decided that the scope should encompass research in the "political, behavioral, economic, life sciences, and operations research associated with areas of psychological operations and civic action."

I outlined the developing DOD program objectives and gave a preview of our intent to expand this area of research. These plans received universal blessing from those attending the meeting. They agreed that the problems were of importance and universal interest. Of course, shadings of differentiation within this general agreement were to appear soon enough. We discussed the potentiality of conflicts between this particular attempt at interdepartmental coordination and the efforts of other coordinating groups, such as the Federal Council of Science and Technology and the

State Department's Foreign Area Research Coordinating
Group (FAR), which was just being formed. The latter
was especially important because all the principals in
the DOD ad hoc committee were eventually to become members of FAR (along with representatives of any other
government department that might be supporting work
having to do with a foreign area--even the National
Science Foundation and the Department of Agriculture).
FAR was to play an important role in the later bureaucratic infighting between State and Defense over Project Camelot.

The group agreed to meet again soon and to exchange
information on the departments' respective research
programs, following which we would discuss where to go
from there. The possibility of exchanging funds,
whereby one agency, such as DOD, could contribute to
support of work more appropriate to the mission of
another, was also explored. It was noted that this
might not sit well with Congress, but that the idea
warranted exploration in any case. We did meet again
on May 8, 1964, with some new faces as interest and
responsibility were sorted out. In particular, William
Nagle, Director of External Research in the State Department's Bureau of Intelligence and Research, came
himself, and thus began a  year-long interaction that
was to have important consequences for the DOD's program. The respective research programs were discussed,
and for the first time each department obtained a coherent and comprehensive view of work done by the

others in this area, and of the relationship of its
work to that of the others. None of the departments--
even DOD, at the time, except for the Army and ARPA-
Agile work--had as specific an orientation to the subject of counterinsurgency as was being contemplated by
the DOD for the future. Thus, the work bore generally
on internal economic and political development of the
developing nations, but not specifically on the human
problems of revolutionary events that were boiling up
in American consciousness and foreign policy.

AID's program included such things as country-
oriented economic modeling, studies of the diffusion
of innovation, studies of the economic aspects of
cultural change, and studies of socioeconomic problems
such as land tenure (but, in the last case, not as
used by revolutionaries such as the Chinese Communists,
the Viet Minh, or the Viet Cong). Despite the large
AID responsibility in Vietnam and elsewhere, there was
no research associated with the economic problems of
that country at war, or with AID's public safety program and its operations in Vietnam. (This came much
later, about 1967, when AID established a Vietnam
bureau.) It became apparent also, from this and other
"two-sided" discussions, that the "formal" research
program of AID was not all of AID's research, since
evaluations of overseas economic programs, a key part
of AID's job, were performed by the "desks"--those
offices responsible for administering and overseeing
action programs in specific countries or regions--

using AID program funds; these studies were not under
the control of AID's research director. The AID research program, exclusive of the "desk" evaluation
programs, came to about $12 million annually.

USIA had about $300,000 per year, generally devoted
to survey research--the impact of information programs
overseas, views of the United States by foreign populations, attitudes and aspirations of populations in
foreign countries toward whom our information programs
were directed. The USIA representatives made the point
that they had the facilities and know-how for such
work, which could make an important contribution to
understanding the overseas social and attitudinal
problems associated with counterinsurgency, and that
these could be available to other agencies for their
use if appropriately funded. Again, they had no research supporting their operations in Vietnam, although
USIA had the responsibility for all information and
psychological operations programs in Vietnam, and were
soon to be joined with the military in a USIA-directed
organization in Saigon (the Joint U.S. Public Affairs
Office, JUSPAO). They agreed that much work was needed in Vietnam, to understand the outlooks and aspirations of people on both sides in the conflict, and the
impact of the war on the Vietnamese people--a need
ARPA was later to fill. USIA either couldn't get, or
didn't ask for, the research budget--I never found out
which, but in their case as well as State's, the two
possibilities obviously interacted to establish a

pattern.

CIA stated that they had no general research program
in the social sciences, but that they performed ad hoc,
in-house studies in support of their immediate operational needs. The meeting and the DOD work, current
and proposed, were of great interest to them for what
they could learn from them.

In this and in many subsequent meetings, I learned
much about the State Department's research structure
and attitude. They took a dim view of contract research. They felt that research into subjects relating to foreign affairs, or studies that might support
policy-making in foreign affairs, had great sensitivity
and was best done in an atmosphere of secrecy with
respect to "outsiders." Their attitude was that they
would rather not have the outside world know they were
studying subjects that might be of immediate operational importance, and clearly this couldn't be avoided
if they hired people on contract. Ergo, outsiders
could simply not study important affairs of state.
State did have about $150,000 for contract work, which
they tied to the problems of the "country desks" and
which might be used, as examples, for studies of
elites in Africa or estimation of the long-term consequences to Panama of a second canal. But most of
State's study or research was performed in-house and
was not discussed by this group. Later views of this
work that I obtained showed such results as narrative
descriptions of events like the rebellions in the

Congo of the early 1960s, which might contain some
"inside" information but little analysis of causes and
effects, and which struck me--a purely personal view,
and, of course, I don't claim to have seen all of
their work--as not much different from the analytical
dispatches by well-informed correspondents that one
could have read in the newspapers.

By the time of our second meeting, State had also
formally established the Foreign Area Research Coordinating Group, which was to serve as a clearing house
for all information on foreign area studies--drawn
together from all government-supported contract work,
summarized, and disseminated to all departments. The
impression I had at the time was that this effort represented the primary occupation of the External Research Group in the Bureau of Intelligence and Research.
The State attitude toward research became important
because it affected how the DOD and the social scientists interested in work overseas were to view the
State Department when State was given government-wide
responsibility for reviewing research having to do with
foreign areas.

State's attitude toward counterinsurgency was, at
the time, also interesting, and especially frustrating
in view of our involvement in Laos and Vietnam. They
appeared to consider problems of internal conflict a
diversion from their normal areas of concern, outside
the main interest of foreign policy and diplomacy, and
something that would, if played down long enough,

eventually be resolved in the normal course of international relations.  This was not because of any expressed aversion to the conception of counterinsurgency
as a method of countering Communist activities such as
those in Vietnam, or because of any unhappy connotations that the term might have--possibly some such
attitude existed, but I didn't detect it at the time.
Rather, the attitude of those in the State Department
with whom I spoke was that events in foreign countries
were all interrelated with each other, and it was not
State's "style" to single out some sequence of these
events for special consideration.  Events in Vietnam
would be handled in due course by traditional methods,
and it didn't seem that even a burgeoning war would
disturb their system, cause them to establish a
special effort, or require coordination and research
planning outside the "normal," diffuse channels they
had established.

State's attitudes toward research at the time are
summarized by Lyons' statement that "the Foreign Service.....leans almost exclusively on the traditional
historical and institutional analyses favored by the
political realists, when it does not proceed simply on
the basis of intuition....The conservative attitude...
its recruitment policies, its emphasis on short-term
goals, its limited research system--all tend to discourage acquaintance with recent trends in social
science."[1]   Their response to the war evoked the
following from a wholly different source.  Cooper, who

worked on the problems of Vietnam in the CIA, the
White House National Security Staff, and, later, Ambassador Harriman's negotiating staff, has written:[2]

...But time after time during 1964 and 1965 McNamara
and his subordinates seemed to be crying for political
guidance and leadership from the State Department.  It
was slow in coming.

The State Department seemed resigned to playing a reactive, even peripheral, role during the early '60s.
The war in Vietnam, it was felt, was Pentagon business...

By and large the non-defense elements of the government
were neither psychologically nor organizationally able
to come to grips with an insurgency that was quickly
getting out of hand.  None of the courses given at the
Foreign Service Institute, and none of the experiences
of AID specialists and Foreign Service officers elsewhere, seemed relevant to what was going on in Vietnam.

Thus, Nagle, as a member of the State Department bureaucracy, was reflecting what seemed to be the general
climate of opinion and attitude at State.

My own graphic illustration of these attitudes,
other than that received during the Camelot crisis,
occurred in two related incidents.  Early in 1965,
after the Defense Science Board's report recommending
certain research was sent to the State Department, I
suggested to Nagle that some subjects had arisen during
the course of that work that appeared to be of interest
and importance to the United States but were really
beyond the scope of DOD's direct concern.  Among these
was the question of understanding the political groups

we undertook, implicitly or explicitly, to support or
oppose by our policies in the developing countries.
Another subject which seemed important was that, since
events in Vietnam were obviously not going as smoothly
as the early predictions might have led us to wish
(this was the period of unstable government under the
"generals" after Diem's overthrow), one should undertake some studies leading to understanding of feasible
"fallback" positions in Southeast Asia in case things
in Vietnam did in fact not work out as then planned.

I offered to have the funds made available and the
research undertaken in such a way that State could
formulate the problems and participate in the general
direction of the work. State's answer, as I remember
it, was that the State Department didn't believe that
such work should be done under contract. I later
probed quite deeply to find out whether the work was
being done by State in-house. Eventually I came to
believe that these were long-range, "iffy" sorts of
problems which, since they did not present themselves
for immediate decision, were simply deferred in the
analyses State was performing to support its own policy-
making. State was concerned with much more immediate
futures and problems. One can suppose, also, that the
thought of seeking alternatives in Vietnam was bureaucratically and politically unattractive in 1965.

In another case a year later, I asked a high State
official whether any study was under way on the problems of the growing rebellions in Portuguese Africa,

to help build an understanding of the forces at work there so that if we were forced into a policy crisis by some future events we would have the knowledge needed to formulate the policies wisely. The response was that this subject was too sensitive to study--"if it even became known that this was under study..." They may have been right. The subjects were certainly sensitive ones to study; and there are similar ones today. On the other hand, I haven't observed recently that we are necessarily developing the best knowledge and expertise for formulation of policies about such problems (although it must be admitted that our policy of no action in that area seems to be working reasonably well, thus far).

It became apparent as a result of these interchanges that with a serious war building up in Southeast Asia, the DOD, rightly or wrongly, appeared to be the only government organization that saw the need to undertake research on problems associated with that war and was gearing up to try to meet them. But the others were interested, and they faced budget problems and political problems; so that they were glad to let the DOD take the lead, and they encouraged us to do so.

At the May 8, 1964, meeting, an idea was born that was to persist or be rediscovered often in various forms. This was to establish a formal, high-level interagency coordinating group to review research needs in this general area, propose projects, and see that

they were undertaken. It was suggested at the time
that this group might report to the Special Group, CI,
and it was agreed that this would be worth further exploration. Again, problems of budget exchanges were
discussed. We confirmed our earlier intuition that
neither the Budget Bureau nor Congress would be especially happy to have money that was appropriated for
one department transferred to another. On the other
hand, it seemed that each department could let contracts in its mission area at the others' request, and
that each could work with and advise the DOD if the
DOD with its larger funds were to let such contracts.
Thus, the problems were not viewed as insurmountable,
even though "clean" exchanges didn't appear to be in
the cards.

And so, while Congress and the news media were later
and continually to deplore the lack of interdepartmental coordination on research having to do with foreign
policy matters, and were to call for more and more coordination, those most deeply and directly involved
had initiated the coordination at an early date.    It
is ironic, too, that at these meetings AID and DOD,
rather than State, were the ones who raised questions
about the sensitivity of performing research in and
about foreign countries, and initiated discussions
about ways in which these sensitivities might be respected and the research prevented from causing problems
between those countries and the United States. Of
course, while "the DOD" on one level had such concerns,

on another level and independently "the DOD's" actions
were to lead before too long to just the kinds of problems that were feared.

It is almost axiomatic in the American system that an idea welling up from the bowels of a bureaucracy needs the recommendation and approval of an outside, respected advisory group before it can receive the official imprimatur. Despite the fact that these new ideas originated virtually at the top of the DOD research leadership, and that they were based on recommendations contained in a series of studies by recognized experts in the field, the decision to increase social research on counterinsurgency problems, which would involve budget changes and specific contracts, started a whole new ballgame. It is perhaps proper that the opinions of the experts who were responsible for social research within the DOD couldn't be accepted at face value, since the nonexperts in the Department couldn't know how these opinions were colored by past prejudices and current bureaucratic constraints. And when the work is to begin "at eight o'clock on Monday morning," the specific problem is not the same as that contained in the reports of the more generally concerned study groups. So a new study group was formed.

To obtain expert advice on specific work to be done in the expanded program and about what would seem to be a reasonable rate of expansion, and to obtain the advice from a level and source that would carry the weight and authority of "the best people in the field" with the upper structures of the DOD and the Services,

and with Congress, DDR&E turned to the Defense Science
Board.  The Defense Science Board was created in 1956
in response to a recommendation of the Hoover Commission "that the Assistant Secretary of Defense (Research
and Development) appoint a standing committee, reporting directly to him, of outstanding basic and applied
scientists.  This Committee will canvass periodically
the needs and opportunities presented by new scientific
knowledge for radically new weapons systems."[1]  From
this beginning the scope of the board's membership and
studies came to encompass all of the DOD's technical,
scientific, and associated management efforts.  In 1964
and 1965 it consisted of 28 members, eight of whom were
drawn from public bodies such as the Atomic Energy
Commission, the National Academy of Sciences, National
Science Foundation, National Bureau of Standards, and
NASA.  The others were selected on the basis of their
eminence in any of the fields of scientific research
and engineering with which Defense Research and Development might have to be concerned.  Study tasks were
assigned by DDR&E, who might be acting on his own or
on behalf of the Secretary of Defense.  The board's
chairman and vice-chairman were appointed by the
Secretary of Defense on the recommendation of the
DDR&E, and very often its reports were addressed to
the Secretary of Defense "through" the DDR&E.  Eminent
scientists, not members of the board proper, could be
added to special subcommittees or "panels" of the
board to carry out specific studies.

At the time of these events, Dr. Frederick Seitz,
who was the president of the National Academy of Sciences, was also the chairman of the Defense Science
Board. (Although this connection between the National
Academy and the DSB no longer exists, it was not as
tenuous as might be thought at first glance. The
Academy was formed by an act of Congress in 1863, in
part because eminent scientists of the day were seeking
an organized way to contribute to the Union war effort.)$^2$  A Behavioral Sciences Panel was appointed,
under the chairmanship of Dr. Lyle H. Lanier, a member
of the board and the executive vice-president and pro-
vost of the University of Illinois. The panel included,
besides Lanier, Ithiel de Sola Pool, who had participated in the Smithsonian studies; Dael Wolfle, the
Executive Director of the American Association for the
Advancement of Science; and Thomas Caywood, one of the
founders of the Operations Research Society of America,
and a leader in the field. On April 21, 1964,
Harold Brown initiated the work of the panel with the
following charge:

conduct a study and evaluation of research and development programs and findings related to ethnic and other
motivational factors involved in the causation and
conduct of small wars among the peoples of Southeast
Asia.

It was usual for a member of the DDR&E staff to work
with a Defense Science Board panel performing a study
requested by DDR&E. In this case, I worked with the

Behavioral Sciences Panel as executive secretary, and
Rains Wallace, who joined the Pentagon as Director for
Behavioral and Social Sciences under the Deputy DDR&E
for Science and Technology in August of 1964, participated in the panel's meetings and helped write the
report.

The work of collecting information on ongoing programs and planning for the future, which had been initiated with the ad hoc DOD committee, met an immediate
need; the DOD committee became in effect a supporting
group for the DSB panel.  The panel heard from the
Services and ARPA about what work was being supported
and what they thought the needs were.  They met with
the major contractors and scholars who were doing the
work.  In addition they were briefed by the military
commands, from overseas and Washington, who represented
potential "users" of the research results, on how they
viewed the developing problems overseas, and on the
problems they were encountering in trying to provide
military assistance in Vietnam and elsewhere.  Particular attention was given to the special needs and problems arising in the course of the Vietnam war.  Rather
than taking the position that they would solve the
problems with tactics and hardware, and yet without
dismissing those as unnecessary, the military "users"
reiterated their view of the importance of understanding the people in the countries where they were working;
of understanding the motivations to fight or not to
fight of troops on our side and on the other side; and

of what makes a good advisor, able to relate to and
work with his counterpart.

I had written to Brigadier General John K. Boles,
Jr., a thoroughly professional soldier who had gone to
Vietnam to head the Military Assistance Command's
Joint Research and Test Activity early in 1964, and
with whom I had a very close working relationship,
about the work of the committee, describing the kinds
of problems it was concerned with, and posing a list
of questions, including the following:

- What capability exists in Vietnam for such
  research now?
- Do opportunities and data exist to explore the
  psychological strengths and weaknesses of the
  Viet Cong?
- Is it possible to work on such studies through
  the medium of prisoner-of-war interrogation, as
  was done in Korea?
- Has the South Vietnamese government ever carried
  out opinion surveys in the cities and villages?
- What studies of the kind I had outlined did he
  feel would be necessary and feasible?

In response, Boles said that "Generally, I think that
the studies cited in your letter are excellent, and,
if performed successfully, would go far toward helping
us get a handle on defining our CI problem--something
which we really have not succeeded in doing yet.  Unfortunately, the war here greatly complicated the

problems involved in conducting such research;  it is
a great pity that these studies were not carried out
in Vietnam five years or so ago when it was more peaceful, because the results would certainly have been most
helpful then and now....It is generally acknowledged
that insurgent movements can be successful only where
the established government has lost, or failed to gain,
the support of its people.  If....research techniques
could be applied in a given country to determine the
degree to which the people....support its established
government, we would have an extremely valuable tool
for evaluating the real danger represented by an insurgent movement.  This tool undoubtedly would help
us in advising a friendly country...." He then proceeded to answer the questions, generally to the effect
that there was no research capability in Vietnam; that
the South Vietnamese government had been very sensitive about the performance of research there, but that
this sensitivity was evaporating under the increasing
pressure of the war; that MACV (U.S. Military Assistance Command, Vietnam) and the Vietnamese government
would therefore cooperate in the performance of research, but that research would be difficult because
of the insecurity in the countryside. Of the possible
subjects for research mentioned (to be described shortly) the two most important were viewed as the problems
of advisor/counterpart relationships, and the psychology and motivation of the Viet Cong as they might be
explored through interviews with prisoners and defec-

tors.

Boles later visited Washington while the panel was
in session, and spent a day discussing with them the
problems and needs of research on the insurgency and
counterinsurgency in Vietnam.  He stressed the relative
failure of the "hardware approach" in solving the problems of insurgency.  Although not deprecating those
efforts, and recognizing the contributions that they
were making, Boles reported that it was generally
recognized by the military in Vietnam that hardware
research would not provide the answers to the struggle
in Vietnam.  He felt this general recognition had improved the climate for research, and indicated that
this was reflected in, among other things, General
Westmoreland's frequent comments in staff meetings on
the need for and desirability of social science research.

Other high-ranking military visitors to the panel--
men such as Air Force Major General Anthis, who had
been in command of U.S. air operations and advisory
efforts to the South Vietnamese Air Force--added to
the list of specific questions.  These encompassed such
problems as teaching American advisors more about the
nature of the task they had to do, especially to keep
it from being viewed as solely a military job; assessing what aspects of American counterinsurgency advisory
programs should be emphasized for the greatest effect;
and studying the problem of grassroots leadership in
Vietnam in order to be able to advise the government

on how to strengthen such leadership, which seemed at
the time to be the exclusive property of the Viet Cong.
The problems of knowing how one was doing against the
adversary in the counterinsurgency conflict and of obtaining data for evaluation and planning, loomed very
large in all these discussions.  Further, a number of
difficulties in performing research in the field, including those of assuring the understanding of the
American military below the very top levels; of obtaining the support and cooperation of the South Vietnamese government; taking the time, against political
pressures for great speed, to evaluate long-term social
programs properly; and the sheer difficulty of being
able to take systematic data in the field under adverse
conditions--all problems which were to come to plague
the DOD's field research efforts later--were brought
out.

At the same time that it was concerned about what
work needed to be done, the panel started to explore
the capability of the research community to undertake
that work.  It was concerned with what the "state of
the art" might be.  A study by the Institute for
Defense Analyses of the materials being gathered by the
Services was commissioned to ascertain the then-current
status of the ongoing programs and the availability of
qualified research organizations and personnel.  What
had previously been in the category of rather vague
generalities now received much more careful definition.
The work categories which the ad hoc committee of the

DOD had decided to use for organizing the project list-
ings were defined more precisely:

(1) Political studies:  Analyses of national or
international political interrelationships,
looking toward the qualitative elucidation of
counterinsurgency problems.

(2) Operations research, systems analysis, economics:  Operations-research or systems-
evaluation studies related to specific operational problems in Vietnam or elsewhere;
generally, but not necessarily military oriented;
possibly including problems of tactics and doctrine, but not selection or evaluation of hardware equipment or systems.

(3) Persuasion and motivation, psychological operations:  Studies of attitudes; social, economic
and political behavior; motivation of individuals and groups; interpersonal and intergroup
relationships and responses to various stimuli
in such relationships.

(4) Manpower, training and selection research:  Research into requirements for training programs;
preparation of standards and tests for personnel
selection; development of criteria for measuring
the effectiveness of selection and training
procedures.

The problem of relevance, which had earlier been dealt

with but not resolved, was explored much more deeply.
Still another group of research experts* was convened
and asked to review the ongoing and proposed DOD
studies, expressing their opinions as to their relevancy to counterinsurgency in two categories: directly
relevant studies; and supporting studies, which were
not specifically relevant to counterinsurgency but
which would give useful information concerning methodology or general behavioral processes. Thus, while
the problem of relevancy was always a troublesome one,
there came to be some expert judgment about the appli-
cability and utility of individual projects from outside the operational community that was responsible
for undertaking the studies. Detailed information on
who sponsored work within the DOD, the kind of work
sponsored, contracting patterns, and the research organizations was compiled, and the dollar allocations
within the program were listed according to subject,
sponsor, country of interest, organization performing
the work, etc. For the first time there was a clear
view of the DOD's efforts and immediate plans in this
area. Some of the results are shown in Tables 3, 4,
and 5, which follow. Note that the plans for Fiscal
Year 1965 even at this time included higher expenditures than FY 1964, partly as a result of the Services'

---

*Joseph E. Barmack, City University of New York; Alex
 Bavelas, Stanford; Launor Carter, Systems Development
 Corporation; Max Milliken, MIT; and Jesse Orlansky
 and Alfred Blumstein of IDA.

Table 3    1964 Program Distribution and Planned Increases for Following Year
           (Thousands of Dollars)

a. By DOD Component

| DOD Component | FY 1964 | | | FY 1965 | | | Change (%) | | |
|---|---|---|---|---|---|---|---|---|---|
| | Direct | Support | Total | Direct | Support | Total | Direct | Support | Total |
| Army | 2305 | 1899 | 4204 | 3106 | 1798 | 4904 | 35 | -5 | 17 |
| Navy | 280 | 280 | 560 | 560 | 313 | 873 | 100 | 12 | 56 |
| Air Force | 393 | 209 | 602 | 724 | 382 | 1106 | 84 | 83 | 84 |
| ARPA | 2200 | 437 | 2637 | 3477 | 437 | 3914 | 58 | 0 | 48 |
| Total: | 5178 | 2825 | 8003 | 7867 | 2930 | 10,797 | 52 | 4 | 35 |

b. By Area of Work

| | Direct | Support | Total | Direct | Support | Total | Direct | Support | Total |
|---|---|---|---|---|---|---|---|---|---|
| Political studies | 562 | 145 | 707 | 813 | 195 | 1008 | 45 | 34 | 43 |
| Operations research, systems analysis, economics | 1841 | 1788 | 3629 | 3301 | 1869 | 5170 | 79 | 6 | 5 |

Table 3 (continued)

| Technical Area | FY 1964 | | | FY 1965 | | | Change(%) | | |
|---|---|---|---|---|---|---|---|---|---|
| | Direct | Support | Total | Direct | Support | Total | Direct | Support | Total |
| Persuasion & motivation, psychological operations | 1617 | 574 | 2191 | 2151 | 649 | 2800 | 33 | 13 | 28 |
| Manpower, training & selection research | 1158 | 318 | 1476 | 1602 | 217 | 1819 | 38 | -32 | 23 |
| Total: | 5178 | 2825 | 8003 | 7867 | 2930 | 10,797 | 52 | 4 | 35 |

Table 4    Average Size of Studies

| Contractor | FY 1964 | | FY 1965 | |
|---|---|---|---|---|
| | No. of Studies | Average No. of People | No. of Studies | Average No. of People |
| Universities | 30 | 1 | 34 | 1 |
| Nonprofits | | | | |
| SORO | 20 | 1 | 22 | $1\frac{1}{2}$ |
| RAC | 15 | 3 | 15 | 3+ |
| RAND | 7 | 1+ | 4 | $2\frac{1}{2}$ |
| HumRRO | 13 | $1\frac{1}{2}$ | 13 | $1\frac{1}{2}$ |
| Other | 7 | $1\frac{1}{2}$ | 6 | 2+ |
| In-house government | 4 | $2\frac{1}{2}$ | 9 | 2 |
| Industry | 5 | 2 | 4 | 3 |
| Foreign universities | 1 | 1 | 1 | 1 |
| Unknown | - | - | 6 | 3 |
| Total: | 102 | $1\frac{1}{2}$ | 114 | $2^-$ |

Table 5   Distribution of Funds, by Country Studied

| Country | FY 1964 | | | | FY 1965 | | | |
|---|---|---|---|---|---|---|---|---|
| | Direct | Support | Total | Direct (%) | Direct | Support | Total | Direct (%) |
| South Vietnam | 1211 | – | 1211 | 24 | 1571 | – | 1571 | 20 |
| Southeast Asia | 388 | – | 388 | 8 | 617 | – | 617 | 8 |
| Asia | 25 | 15 | 40 | 0.5 | 66 | 16 | 82 | 0.9 |
| Latin America | 417 | – | 417 | 8 | 685 | – | 685 | 9 |
| Africa | – | – | – | – | – | – | – | – |
| Middle East | 80 | 156 | 236 | 2 | 30 | 181 | 211 | 0.4 |
| Multiple countries | 1716 | 256 | 1972 | 34 | 2305 | 180 | 2485 | 30 |
| Overseas, not specified | 399 | 91 | 490 | 8 | 1068 | 98 | 1166 | 14 |
| USSR and Communist China | 160 | 260 | 420 | 3 | 160 | 275 | 435 | 2 |
| Europe | – | 105 | 105 | – | – | 110 | 110 | – |
| United States | – | 544 | 544 | – | – | 544 | 544 | – |
| Not country-oriented | 642 | 1398 | 2040 | 13 | 679 | 1446 | 2125 | 9 |
| Unknown | 140 | – | 140 | 3 | 686 | 80 | 766 | 9 |
| **Total:** | 5178 | 2825 | 8003 | | 7867 | 2930 | 10,797 | |

responses to the urgings of the Smithsonian reports,
and partly as a result of the work of the ad hoc DOD
committee that I had convened prior to the DSB panel's
study.

The DSB panel report was positive and reflected
acceptance and elaboration of the previous ideas on
what was needed and how it should be obtained.  Further, there was some very specific advice on where to
go next.  The assignment to study "small wars among
the peoples of Southeast Asia" had been stretched considerably, but no one objected.  After reviewing the
post-World War II world situation, the report stated:

This world situation has added an essentially new dimension to the responsibilities and requirements of
the Department of Defense (DOD).  In addition to dealing with problems associated with the confrontation of
nuclear powers in this space age, the Department must
now assess the potentialities for internal conflict
and subversive revolution in underdeveloped countries
and take appropriate steps to help prevent insurgent
movements in those areas from growing into communist-
dominated governments hostile to the United States.
Obviously, this broad mission must be carried out within the general framework of U.S. foreign policy, which
is established by the President and implemented primarily through the Department of State.

In recognition of the growing seriousness of the inter-
nal-war problem in developing countries, in August
1962 overlapping operational responsibilities were
assigned to the government departments concerned.
Thus, it is required that DOD activities be closely
coordinated with those of the State Department, especially with programs of the Agency for International
Development (AID).  With regard to the collection,
evaluation and dissemination of information, the DOD

shares the mission with the State Department's regular
foreign-service agencies and also with the U.S. Information Agency and the Central Intelligence Agency.
Effective interaction among all these agencies is
essential to the successful conduct of this country's
foreign relations--in the broadest sense of that term.

It is significant that the Department of Defense is the
only agency assigned explicit responsibility for carrying out research and development in support of the
internal defense of developing countries friendly to
the United States. This does not mean, of course, that
the other agencies are prohibited from doing research
bearing upon this general problem. AID, for example,
has research funds and is planning a considerable expansion of its research effort; but its studies would
not be concentrated upon social conflict and insurgency. An adequate research program with this focus would
have to be conducted mainly by the Department of Defense.

The ongoing DOD programs were evaluated and criticized
quite severely:

(1) The overall level of effort is seriously inadequate to meet the DOD's need for knowledge
about incipient and active insurgency in critical areas of Africa, Asia and Latin America.
The small amount of work being done overseas
is oriented toward Southeast Asia, chiefly
South Vietnam. There is little research regarding Latin America and other parts of Asia,
and there is none on Africa. Accentuating the
meagerness of this Defense effort is the dearth
of overseas research in the behavioral sciences
by other organizations. University research,
for instance, by no means fills the gap.

(2) Specifically, there is a great need for up-to-
date basic information about the major cultural
and political groupings within the developing
countries that are of special significance to

the United States.  The ethnic, religious, economic and political conditions conducive to
social conflict can be adequately understood
only through intensive, systematic research performed within each country....

(3) Since most of the current research consists of
comparatively small, unrelated projects, the
overall program needs better focus, greater con-
tinuity and a more systematic structure in all
its aspects--including basic research on relevant behavioral and social processes, applied
research on the phenomenology of insurgency
and counterinsurgency, policy studies, and an
evaluation of the effectiveness of counterinsurgency operations.

(4) Most of the programs are of a unidisciplinary
nature, although an adequate attack upon the
problems of social conflict and insurgency would
involve several different disciplines.  The
major programs, at least, should be multi-
disciplinary--involving not only different kinds
of behavioral scientists but also specialists
from the information sciences and operations
research.

Specific areas of work were recommended in some
detail:

1. Political Studies

...Over the range of research in this area,
from policy studies dealing with the effects of
alternative governmental actions to the examination
of the characteristics of insurgent populations,
there is an urgent need for substantive information
to improve the planning and execution of policy.
Political action must be planned, coordinated and
integrated with military action; otherwise, there
is a risk that counterinsurgency operations...will
fail.

Research on fundamental sources of stability and instability in emerging nations, as well as more nearly applied research on the characteristics of specific political systems, is desperately needed... In a case of current importance in Southeast Asia, we appear to be in deep trouble partly because there has been no systematic political research in Vietnam.

In the politics of revolution, overt political behavior is drastically different from that in stable democratic or totalitarian systems...Experience gained in a more stable political environment is probably not directly applicable. Suitably posed research questions, on the other hand, can lead to the successful development of improved descriptive and analytic information for operational problems...

Systematic research is needed, not only on the internal politics of revolutionary political behavior but on the international analogue...the conflict between the Soviet Union and Communist China may well have important implications regarding future communist support for wars of national liberation...there is a need to explore the political alternatives open to the United States regarding international intervention of a different type than was used in Vietnam, along with implications of the possible success of national liberation movements in other areas with respect to U.S. policy.

Examples of the type of studies suggested are as follows:
- Exacerbation of insurgency by communist countries
- Vulnerabilities of political systems to infiltration and exploitation
- Characteristics of insurgent populations
- Types of insurgency and internal violence
- Impact of civic action on local politics
- Impact of large-scale foreign support of indigenous governments on the structure of local support

- Differences between urban and rural insurgency
- Political implications of military counter-insurgency operations
- Political role of indigenous military institutions
- Political effects of alternative government policies
- U.S. foreign-policy equivalents to communist national liberation movements
- Political indoctrination and organization in Viet Cong-controlled villages

## 2. Operations Research, Systems Analysis and Economics

...Since extensive commitments in the field of counterinsurgency are relatively recent undertakings by the Department of Defense, not much prior work is directly applicable. Little of the research reported reflects a systematic program in operations research related to counterinsurgency. A more serious deficiency is that inadequate consideration is given to variables of behavior...the character of counterinsurgency operations is such that behavioral aspects are often critical...behavioral variables be used to a greater extent in operations research and systems analysis.

In addition to the economic analysis of production and distribution systems under conditions of insurgency, research on the operational and economic consequences of civic-action programs is needed.... We need to devise basic strategies concerning the application of civic-action resources with a view to....desired effects and the relationship....to long-term programs of political and economic development.

...it is necessary to study para-military forces supporting the internal-security mission of the regular military services. Most of the pertinent research done so far has emphasized the regular military mission, to the exclusion of the parts played by the police and the militia...

The following list illustrates the types of

research problems that the Subcommittee believes
are appropriate topics for systematic operations
research:
- Information requirements for counterinsurgency
  planning
- Modeling of the counterinsurgency environment
- Analysis of indicators of potential insurgency
- Analysis of behavior as an indicator of atti-
  tude
- Use of Vietnam Data Base for indication of
  progress in the war
- Studies of food-distribution system in Vietnam
  and how it feeds the Viet Cong (or other in-
  surgents elsewhere)
- Analysis of Viet Cong logistics
- Analysis of Viet Cong tactics and operations
- Research on telecommunications in counter-
  insurgency environment
- Research on the economic infrastructure of
  village environments

3. Persuasion and Motivation, Psychological Operations

...The direct measure of success is the extent
to which the control of people, not the destruction
of armies, is achieved. With this object in view,
the motivation aspects of the conflict become far
more important in counterinsurgency than in conventional warfare.

In the existing program, it is apparent that
there is little systematic research in (1) the
sources of political power in rural environments,
(2) the types of motivation for granting or with-
holding political support, (3) traditional patterns
of communication in general, and (4) the sources of,
and reasons for, behavior destructive of the existing society. This information might be obvious in
a totally repressive society, but in the mixed
milieu of a typical under-developed country it is
not so easy to determine....

...There is an important need for quantitative
data on the anthropological, sociological, political and psychological aspects of societies in which

insurgency is a threat.  In Vietnam, we now appear
to be in a difficult situation because our decision
to commit ourselves to a certain kind of counterinsurgency action was based on insufficient knowledge of the sort of people we were dealing with
and the way they might react to our efforts and
those of their own internal groups.

The following list represents only a small por-
tion of the studies that would compose an adequate
research program:
- Dynamics of village counterinsurgency:  bases
  of village support for one side or the other
- Viet Cong motivation
- Use of traditional religious beliefs by
  counterinsurgents
- Systematic study of elite and mass beliefs,
  behavior and interactions
- Potential sources of support for insurgency
- Outlets for aggression and antisocial
  behavior
- Response of the passive villager to insurgent
  terror
- Patterns of insurgent recruitment
- Rural intervillage and intravillage communica-
  tion and influence patterns
- Influence of traditional elite-peasant
  relationships on feasibility of successful
  rural counterinsurgency

## 4. Selection and Training of U.S. Advisers

Until very recently, the primary emphasis of
social-science research on our military operations
in the developing nations has been on the indigenous
peoples, despite the fact that an interaction between the indigenous population and U.S. military
personnel is involved and the success or failure of
this interaction may facilitate or prevent the
attainment of U.S. objectives.  It seems probable
that we have concerned ourselves least with the
side of this interaction we should know most about--
the U.S. adviser....anecdotal evidence indicates
that the performance of many advisers has been

dramatically unsuccessful.

...Psychology has contributed greatly to the
selection and training of many kinds of people in
widely varying jobs.  There is every reason to expect that the use of psychological research techniques would considerably improve the military adviser's effectiveness.

...In brief, it will be necessary to:

(1) Study the relationships of U.S. and indigenous people and the factors that may increase or lessen the effectiveness of cross-
cultural interchange.  This may be done
through studies in the field, the systematic
debriefing of returned advisers, and the
study of research findings already in existence.

(2) Define the objectives of the military-
adviser system, and set up methods for
determining the degree to which these objectives are being achieved in specific
situations.

(3) Develop proficiency measures that may be
applied to military advisers who are still
in the field or have recently left it.  Then
combine these measures to serve as criteria
in evaluating various selection instruments
and alternative training procedures.

It should be noted that these tasks imply a
need for closely and continuously observing military
advisers in the field--in this case, not for the
purpose of rating individual performance....Opposi-
tion to allowing this observation will be great,*
particularly on the part of higher level personnel
in foreign areas, who tend to perceive such evaluation as invidious or threatening.

...research that is not based on (realistic performance) criteria may actually result in selection

---

*As, indeed, it was later found to be -- SJD.

and training procedures worse than those that have
grown up informally.

As soon as some reasonably reliable criteria
are available, work should begin to develop a procedure for selecting individuals who are likely to
perform well and rejecting those whose chances of
performing successfully are low....*

It is unfortunately true that procedures for
training military personnel who must develop relationships with foreign nations have been constructed
in an informal, hit-or-miss, nonuniform manner...

It is generally assumed, for example, that the
highest priority should be given to teaching the
potential adviser the language of the country in
which he will serve.  This assumption may be correct, but it is possible that a man who has only
the rudiments of the language but possesses other
useful knowledge, skills or attitudes might, in
fact, be more effective than someone who can fluently reveal his inadequacies or prejudices....

Finally, there is little point in having effective selection and training procedures if they are
inappropriate to the personnel-assignment system or
if they are emasculated by a bureaucratic system.
For this reason, an immediate and continuing operational analysis of the system by which personnel
are assigned to counterinsurgency activities is
required....

In addition to its specific research recommendations
the report took account of some other special areas of
concern.  First, the suggestion was made that the
"soft" sciences be "hardened" by combining operations
research and social science research techniques.  Par-

---

*Note the intended extension, to this area of perfor-
mance, of a technique that was eminently successful
in connection with hardware (pp. 19-23)--SJD.

ticular study areas where it appeared that such combination could be useful included the development of indicators of potential insurgency, indicators of progress in counterinsurgency, and, particularly in the
last case, improving the operational data base being
built in Vietnam (work in this area was later to lead
to the Hamlet Evaluation System, which became, for
good or ill, one of the foundations of the government's
assessment of progress in the war). The report recommended that in areas of active or threatened insurgency
the military commands organize operations research
units with behavioral scientists as participants to
help in analysis of ongoing operations. (There was
precedent for this in earlier British operations in
Malaya.) It pointed, also, to the army's Camelot
project, which had started some time before the report
was written, as an example of research in which systems research techniques could be applied. It noted
also that ARPA was thinking tentatively about a feasibility study to find whether it might be possible to
obtain sufficient data on a social system to be able
to describe it quantitatively and simulate its behavior on a computer. (This program never started,
having come to a halt when Licklider left the Pentagon
in 1965.)

Secondly, the report recognized that few people
were appropriately trained to perform competent research in the area of counterinsurgency. It recommended that the underlying foundation of behavioral sci-

ences research personnel be built up, through support
of multidisciplinary centers for basic research in selected universities. These centers, of which perhaps
five were visualized, would have both an "area" focus
(for example, Asia, Africa, Latin America), and a
"comparative international" orientation (for example,
the world communist movement and its methods in the
developing countries, and comparative studies of stability and internal conflict in the developing countries). Specific criteria to make such centers as
effective as possible were prescribed. These included
commitment to a college "degree program"; avoidance of
the usual loose conglomeration of separate departmental
efforts under a "study center" label; availability of
interested and suitably oriented faculty; and willingness to base the program primarily on field research.

Thirdly, the report noted that two specially oriented programs merited particular attention and support.
The first was that of SORO, which was viewed as the
"principal large-scale effort supported by the Department of Defense in the field reviewed." The second was
Project Agile, which was recognized as the Defense
Department's only program specifically and wholly
oriented toward the problems of counterinsurgency.
With respect to Agile, the report had this to say:

These small-scale AGILE projects have been essentially
exploratory in nature; for example, studies have been
made of adviser-counterpart relations, mainly interviews with U.S. advisers; urban insurgency; and the

anthropology of the Montagnards, tribal groups in Vietnam. They have yielded much useful information and opened up promising areas for investigation, but, with regard to the solution of these important, complex problems, they have barely scratched the surface.

Regarding SORO the report said:

It is recommended that the Department of the Army continue its strong support of the Special Operations Research Office; and that SORO be encouraged in its effort to shift research emphasis from small, library-based projects to more comprehensive programs of empirical research conducted, at least in part, in overseas locations. It should be recognized, however, that an organization whose capability was developed for the first type of work will not necessarily be adequate for the broader research. SORO's staff as a whole is seriously deficient with respect to mathematical-statistical capability, and it includes no professional economists....

Assuming that SORO can expand and strengthen its staff in the directions indicated, it should probably be recognized as the principal DOD agency for behavioral-science research directed specifically toward the Defense mission of counterinsurgency and special warfare. Furthermore, SORO should probably become the primary point of focus within the DOD for studies of socio-economic and political conditions in the developing countries. By its contract, SORO should be permitted to conduct a reasonable amount of basic research related to its area of cognizance (e.g., in the form of "institutional" funds) without having to secure specific Army approval of each project. More generally, with regard to terms of reference and administration, SORO's contract should be appropriately broadened so as to allow the kind of flexibility in planning and conducting research that seems essential to ensure productivity.

Thus the DSB panel entered directly into the conflict

that had been going on within the Army regarding whether
SORO should undertake research or continue to provide
the library-search-service kind of activity that DCSOPS
felt was necessary to support its training and orientation programs. The panel recognized the essential weaknesses of this key link in the entire research program
that it was proposing, and made sensible recommendations
for strengthening it; these, as will be seen, could not
be carried out in time to avert disaster. And it subtly exacerbated the conflict between the Army and ARPA
views of the role each should play. But the recommendations that had emerged from the internal and interacting dynamics of both the DDR&E "shop" and the panel's
study efforts were viewed in ODDR&E as exactly the
right prescription for the further development of the
program.

The Defense Science Board effort consolidated the
results of all the previous studies and planning efforts that had recommended and started to implement an
expansion of social research to help the United States
in its growing struggle against the "war of national
liberation" strategy of the Soviet Union and Communist
China (see Table 6). It critiqued the ongoing DOD
program, isolating inadequacies and opportunities. It
surveyed the capability available, what it could do
and what it needed to be made to do, and it made very
specific recommendations regarding subjects and areas
for study, who should undertake the work, and how they
should go about doing a creditable job of it. The re-

Table 6    Summary of Impetus toward Increased Social
           Research by the DOD on Problems of Counter-
           insurgency

Studies:

| Study or Planning Effort | Date | Auspices |
|---|---|---|
| First Smithsonian report | 1960 | DOD (Office of Naval Research) funding to Smithsonian Institution |
| Limited War Task Group | 1961 | DDR&E, "in-house" |
| Second Smithsonian report | 1963 | DOD (ONR) funding to Smithsonian Institution |
| Defense Science Board | 1964 | DDR&E |

Internal DOD Programming Efforts through 1964:

| | | |
|---|---|---|
| Modest budget increases and "getting organized" | 1962–1964 | Self-generated by Services, with guidance from ODDR&E |
| Ad Hoc Committee on Counterinsurgency Research | 1964–1965 | DDR&E, Special Assistant (CI) |
| Increased budget proposals | 1964–1965 | Self-generated by Services and ARPA |
| Ad Hoc Interdepartmental Coordinating Committee | 1964–1965 | Initiated by DDR&E, Special Assistant (CI) |

port accepted the idea that the Defense Department needed, and had, the mission to do the work, and that it would do the work because it had the dollars to do so; the change in values that would subject the whole premise to question had not come about yet. In general, the panel made an effort to relate its recommendations to the DOD mission, and it noted the need for coordination with and dissemination of results to other departments of government who were concerned with the same problems. This report was thus the culmination of several years' evolution of a set of ideas. It focused them, and turned vague and shifting conceptualizations into concrete program ideas that could be funded.

The DSB report was published and distributed within
the DOD and the other departments on January 30, 1965.
While the panel was doing its work, the normal cycle
of program review, preparation of budgets, and planning ahead for new programs was continuing with its
inexorable momentum.  In order to incorporate the new
program in the budget for Fiscal Year 1966 (July 1,
1965 to June 30, 1966), we had to instruct the Services
regarding what was needed, receive their initial proposals, negotiate differences of opinion and conception, incorporate the results in the draft of the budget and the written justification for the budget requests, recoordinate the draft, and send a final draft
of the "presidential budget" to the Secretary of Defense by the end of November 1964.  Then, he would
review it as necessary with the offices of the Comp-
troller and the Systems Analysis group (the latter,
who originally earned the name "whiz kids" when Secretary McNamara established the group in 1961, played
no role in the events described here; the money involved was too small for their notice, although several years later, in 1967, they became involved in
analyzing "progress data" from Vietnam).  The Comp-
troller and the Systems Analysis group would have been
working to clarify various major issues for decision
throughout the year; the Secretary would make decisions
involving budget issues; he would iron out any remain-

ing differences with the Services and DDR&E (who could appeal, or "reclama," an initial decision); prepare his "posture statement" (which had also been "in work" for some months); and send the budget to the White House in time for review and incorporation of major new ideas (this one was not "big" enough to receive such separate attention) in the State of the Union message on January 1.

It sounds slow, involved, and tedious, and it was. If we wanted to increase the social research program associated with counterinsurgency by additional funds to be expended during the year following July 1, 1965, we had to start thinking in August of 1964--about a year earlier--about how much money we wanted, for what it was to be spent, and how it would be distributed among the Services and ARPA. The time lag until there were actually people working on the problems with the new funds might be as much as two years, since once money was made available it might take most of FY 1966 to define individual projects precisely enough to specify contract work statements and go through the red tape of soliciting proposals, evaluating them, and negotiating and signing contracts. The bureaucratic process thus required that if we wanted to see any new effort at all before July of 1966, we had to start in the middle of 1964 to pave the way for it. Some small starts could be made earlier through modest "reprogramming," but it would be difficult to rob Peter to pay Paul when both were already doing much of what was wanted but had insufficient funds in the first place.

The expanded DOD program was intended to rely heavily on the DSB report. The DSB panel, which had started its periodic meetings in April of 1964, was planning to complete its work and write its report in the
fall and winter of 1964-1965. Since we in ODDR&E had
to start working on the budgeting problem in August
1964, we were in the position, not for the first or
last time in government program planning, of having to
start a program before we had done our homework, and
with ideas only half formulated.

But this was not as bad as it sounds. By late summer of 1964 the DSB panel, and therefore Rains Wallace
and I, had a fairly clear view of what was in the existing programs and the shape of the recommendations that
would be made, although the details and specific issues
remained to be worked out. In August of 1964 the preparation of an "interim" guidance memorandum from
DDR&E to the Service Assistant Secretaries for R&D and
the Director of ARPA was initiated. This became the
first formal document relating to the expanded program,
and was issued on September 2, 1964. The "covering
brief" transmitting the memorandum to DDR&E for signature explained its purpose and summarized its contents: . provision of guidance to the Services and ARPA;
affirmation of the Defense Department's mission for
such work; asking that the military departments and
ARPA make a coordinated review of their plans and
programs with a view toward expanding the effort; ask-

ing that appropriate resources be provided in the respective FY 1966 budgets; and indicating that more specific and detailed guidance would be forthcoming upon
completion of the DSB study. The Services and ARPA
were asked to submit their preliminary plans by October 15, 1964.

The pattern of responses differed only in program
details from the more definite plans that were made
after the DSB report was published, and it followed the
positions that began to emerge in the early deliberations of the ad hoc DOD committee. The Air Force proposed almost to double its relatively small program of
research at universities. Since their budget for such
work had in the past been consistently reduced from the
AFOSR requests by the upper echelons of the Air Force,
this amounted essentially to a very modest expansion
from the work they were actually trying to undertake
in any case. The Navy was cautious, expressing the
opinion that with some very small expansion they were
doing about the right amount and kind of work. ARPA
proposed to expand behavioral sciences research, including a separate counterinsurgency-oriented behavioral research program in Project Agile, from about
three-quarters of a million dollars per year to $5
million over the following five years. This included
a substantial ARPA contribution to the Counterinsurgency Information and Analysis Center at SORO (on
which more, shortly), which would absorb about three-
quarters of a million of this budget. ARPA's proposal

included a combination of individual research projects;
regional research centers based on universities overseas to undertake research in those areas with locally
trained social scientists; and the attempt to assess
the feasibility of computer simulation of behavioral
patterns for predictive purposes.*

ARPA anticipated major problems in the latter program arising from the scarcity of reliable data, and
from differences between the value systems of the
builders and interpreters of the computer programs and
results, and the groups being simulated.  More generally, they anticipated that it would be difficult to
identify individuals both qualified and willing to
do original field work.  The host nations would be
sensitive about such research and would have to agree
to it before any could be done.  They foresaw administrative, security, and language barriers to conducting
research in such areas as Vietnam.  In all this ARPA
was prescient; their reservations were not unfounded.
However, the reservations were presented in terms of
problems to be solved, rather than reasons not to pro-

*It has come to be both unfashionable and even gauche
 to think about computer simulation of something so
 subtle, delicate, and complex as a society.  The
 reader must remind himself that consideration was not
 being given here to doing it, but to exploring whether
 it should even be thought about seriously.  In another
 context, society accepts the simulation of urban evolution (by Forrester of MIT)[1] with equanimity and
 even interest, even though this is at least as difficult and uncertain as what we were considering.

ceed.

The Army proposed roughly a $2 million per year in-
crease in their programs for FY 1965 and FY 1966, but
noted that it would be very difficult to increase expenditures at a rapid rate, so that the expansion might
be delayed. They proposed a detailed research plan
which included what appeared to be carefully thought
out programs in six areas:  research studies of counterinsurgency policy and planning; research on requirements for social science information and area studies;
research on military psychological operations, and the
information and communication process within developing nations; research on the design and impact of
civic action and military assistance efforts for
counterinsurgency; research on relationships between
Americans and local officials and populations in military operations in the developing nations; and "counterinsurgency single-country studies." They expected
their total program to reach a level of about $5 mil-
lion per year in about three years. Other than their
concern about the rate of expansion, they expressed no
reservations.

By the beginning of 1965, the DSB report was near
completion, and we started to work on the draft-
coordination-redraft cycle of the final guidance memorandum that would launch the expanded program.  This
memorandum was issued by DDR&E on March 24, 1965.  It
tried to deal with all of the problems highlighted by
the DSB report, and followed closely from the recommen-

dations in that report. The general nature of the
work desired was reviewed. It was noted that areas
such as Africa and Latin America, about which there
appeared currently to be little knowledge of the kind
needed, and virtually no research, required further
attention in the DOD's study programs. Problems associated with military civic action, internal security,
and constabulatory operations (all of these in countries receiving U.S. military and security assistance)
were identified as areas virtually neglected in the
existing research program.

Attention was given to the problem of research
quality. It was pointed out that behavioral and social
science research applied to Defense's problems other
than personnel management and human factors engineering
were still viewed with suspicion and had yet to prove
their worth conclusively. There followed recognition
that the creation of high competence on the scale demanded would have to be a long-term proposition, with
an admonition not to support work of poor quality with
unqualified researchers solely for the purpose of expansion. For specific program guidance, the DSB report
was transmitted to the Services and ARPA. The Navy
and Air Force were instructed to elaborate the individual university and contract research studies that
were characteristic of their current research efforts.
ARPA was assigned the responsibility for creating a
university-center program having the general characteristics and objectives described in the DSB report.

The work it had proposed to undertake through Project
Agile was encouraged.

The Army was singled out for major responsibility.
This followed from the nature of the Army's program and
from the magnitude of its responsibilities overseas.
The Army had been responsible for much of the applied
behavioral sciences work that had to do with troop performance in the field and troop training and proficiency. Of all the Services, the Army was most heavily
engaged in Vietnam (at that point, with Special Forces
and many thousand additional military advisors) and
had the most intimate contact with Vietnamese forces
as well as with the Vietnamese people in the countryside. Major responsibilities for advisory assistance
in the use and maintenance of equipment; for training
large numbers of troops; and for counterinsurgency-
oriented programs such as psychological operations and
military civic action, as well as counterguerrilla warfare, fell on the Army's shoulders. The problem of
transforming research results into policy, training
programs and curricula, and doctrine to which the Services adhered, was always a difficult one, and the Army
as a user would be in a far better position to do this
than ARPA, which had no "troops in the field" and was
viewed with suspicion by those who did. It was therefore logical that the Army should be assigned the responsibility by DDR&E, who supervised all DOD research
under the law, for a major applied research effort in
the counterinsurgency area.

From the research plan that they had proposed the
previous fall, the inference that they understood the
problems and could undertake the work seemed reasonable.  They were directed to establish, in the Washington, D.C. area, a "centrally coordinated applied research effort" which would build on their five-year
program plan.  They were specifically assigned responsibility for the major aspects of research on selection
and training problems, and those associated with
"special warfare."  Their responsibility included the
establishment of a coordinating office, which would
not strictly supervise but would help keep related to
each other all of the other Service and ARPA programs.
In addition, the guidance memorandum pointed out that
coordination would be necessary with the State Department, AID, USIA, and CIA.  The Army was instructed to
invite representatives of those agencies to work in
residence with the headquarters of their effort, and
to work with participating government organizations
and research contractors.  The general funding levels
that had been proposed in the response to the earlier
guidance were accepted, and the Services and ARPA were
instructed to adjust their FY 1966 budgets accordingly.

As I worked closely with ARPA and the Services to
try to assure a coherent program whose parts were properly interlocked and coordinated, it became apparent
that ARPA, which had planned expansion of the work
under Project Agile, and the Army, which was moving
forward with its own expansion plans revolving initial-

ly around Project Camelot, were coming into conflict.
In response to the March 24 memorandum, the Army had
proposed to assume the total responsibility for at
least the applied research part of the overall program,
and this had been granted by DDR&E. ARPA was unhappy
that the responsibility for coordination was assigned
to the Army, because it appeared to them that this in-
fringed ARPA's independence as an agency reporting
directly to DDR&E; and they feared it would retard
the expansion of Agile's work in Southeast Asia, which
was already underway, while they might have to wait
for the Army to come up to speed. The proposed Agile
work was not in conflict with what the Army was planning from the duplication point of view, but it was
clear that the Army and ARPA, if they both expanded
rapidly and simultaneously, would compete for the same
limited talent, and this would be no help at all to an
orderly expansion of the program. It became apparent,
therefore, that further guidance was necessary to try
to resolve this conflict.

We built on a proposal that had been made by the
Army in response to the March 24 memorandum, by preparing another, much more specific, instruction, to
which ARPA and the Army agreed. The Army would create
a new office reporting directly to the Director of
Army Research (a "short-circuit" of the bureaucratic
system not often used in the Service bureaucracy). It
would be staffed jointly by representatives from all
the Services and ARPA, as well as representatives of

the outside agencies having an interest in the work.
It would be responsible for direct supervision of the
Army's work, but only for coordination of the efforts
of other agencies.  It would also be the responsible
point of contact with overseas commands having to
clear the work a priori, and for translating the research results into language and plans appropriate for
the "user" community.  This joint office, which would
in fact be little more than a coordinating committee
chaired by the Army, would be responsible for future
planning of research efforts and, through recommendations to its constituent agencies, helping to assure
that a coherent and useful program was undertaken.  It
was explicitly stated that while the military departments and ARPA might continue to undertake individual
applied research efforts, these would be coordinated
within the joint organization and would therefore become an integral part of the planning done by that
body.  At the same time that this memorandum was prepared, letters were drafted to be sent to the Secretary
of State, the Administrator of AID, the Director of
the USIA, and the Director of the CIA, explaining what
was being planned and soliciting their support.  The
"package" was to go out formally in June, but its
progress was interrupted by the explosion over Project
Camelot.

At this point we had entered the indeterminate region
between planning and implementation.  At some time in
any effort such as we are describing, some of those
who have been involved in the preparation of plans,
being aware that they will have implementation responsibility, shift their efforts gradually from planning
to action.  Events develop slowly, even under pressure,
so that the exact point at which the boundary between
talk and action has been crossed is difficult to define,
although it can often be identified in retrospect.  In
this case, the shift was in two stages:  from relatively generalized DOD planning involving all the relevant
agencies to specific plans made by one of the action
agencies--the Army--for its own efforts; and thence to
action by the Army, undertaken before either its own
or the DOD's plans had been fully formulated.

This transition took place in a complex bureaucratic
environment with developing crosscurrents of interrela-
tionship and conflict among parts of disparate agencies, and between some of those agency "offices" and
the individuals who served them under contract or as
advisors.  The external environment was also in a dynamic state, with the increasing war in Southeast Asia
lending a sense of urgency while associated tensions
at home and abroad began to intensify.  Let us recapit-
ulate, briefly, before proceeding.

The Defense Department offered the essential lure,

in effect a pot of gold in the form of resources for
potential support of social research in connection with
Vietnam and other "wars of national liberation"; and it
lent to the attraction of the resources a sense of mission reinforced by the President and many of those he
had brought into his Administration--in the White House,
the Defense Department, and elsewhere.  A number of in-
fluential members of the social science community,
aware of their past successes with DOD-supported research in the behavioral sciences, encouraged the DOD
to believe that the kind of research they advocated
could be equally useful in the world of international
affairs--a world partly outside the DOD, but connected
with its assigned tasks.  Those tasks, in Southeast
Asia, were related to an unfamiliar kind of war, of
which the only apparently "known" quality was that it
posed a danger to the United States because it was
being encouraged and supported by nations we considered
our adversaries.  Members of the DOD hierarchy, civilian and military, who exerted influence and control
over the available resources accepted the advice of
the social scientists.  They believed it had merit
since they perceived that much of the problem of Vietnam and similar conflicts lay in understanding societies, cultures, and relationships among people, rather
than in improving weapons and military equipment (or,
at least, in addition to those more familiar activities).

The President had assigned responsibilities for

counterinsurgency operations overseas to several agencies.  These were overlapping responsibilities, pre-
senting opportunities for both productive cooperation
among the agencies and conflict between them.  The DOD,
having become accustomed as a general matter to undertaking research and development to solve its problems
and to expanding the relevant R&D when the problems
became pressing, turned its attention with the same
reflex to the specific problems developing in Vietnam
and Southeast Asia.  In this, it was encouraged by the
presidential assignment of responsibilities, which included "relevant research and development."  The other
agencies, some without research resources of their own,
reacted positively to the invitation to participate
with the DOD, but with no resources and, in the State
Department's case, with reservations.  State met the
DOD's offer of research support and cooperation with
overt cordiality but, it turned out later, deep misgivings as well as an apparently irresistible bureaucratic interest in the opportunity to expand its span
of control in the research field.  The response seemed
to reflect State Department attitudes that included
reluctance to accept the character of the Vietnam conflict as it was perceived by the DOD, and fear of
studies that were not performed by their own personnel,
because such studies were sensitive.  While State had
virtually no resources to support contract research,
they had a substantial in-house study staff.  However,
the linkage with DOD was left to the part of the Bureau

of Intelligence and Research that was responsible for
spending State's minuscule contract research resources,
rather than the part that did the substantive research.

Within the DOD, the situation was similarly mixed.
There had been, earlier, no especially strong support
for social research beyond that essential to improve
the functioning of the Services' men and equipment.
Now, the horizon was being expanded, and this expansion, pressed by a few individuals on his staff, was
being supported by the third-ranking official under
the Secretary of Defense.  In the Navy and the Air
Force, those responsible for such research were cautious, and saw mainly the opportunity to expand the
work of individual scholars that they supported in
several universities.  Wanting a more massive and
centrally coordinated effort, with greater orientation
to operational problems rather than underlying social
and political phenomena, the ODDR&E staff turned to the
Army and ARPA.  Both responded positively, but they
came into conflict with each other and with ODDR&E as
a result of the Army's ambition and ARPA's desire to
preserve the independence of its control over the work
it funded.  An uneasy compromise was worked out, and
it was also decided that the interested agencies outside DOD would be invited to join in the coordination
and planning.  Thus, any coordinating group, when it
was established, would be composed of individuals
having mixed motives and organizational loyalties, and
having diverse understandings and attitudes about re-

search and the real-world problems that were to be the
subjects of research.

Those problems, in March through May of 1965, were
becoming more urgent. The United States was beginning
to bomb North Vietnam and Marines were landing at
Danang, in South Vietnam. The United States had rejected U Thant's offer to help make peace. The antiwar
movement in the United States was beginning to become
more vocal; "teach-ins" and demonstrations centered in
and around the universities were growing in number and
intensity. Many social scientists were involved in
and helping to organize the antiwar protests, and their
numbers would increase. The war protest movement was
strong overseas, as well, exacerbating sensitivity to
"American foreign intervention"; and there was tension
in Latin America over American counterinsurgency policies as reflected in Vietnam, and over America's expressed perception of rising communist revolutionary
agitation in Latin America (which was believed by many
in the United States government to originate in Cuba).

Into this maelstrom the Army's early start toward
implementing the new DOD social research policies
gradually began to intrude.

About August of 1964, the Army had started to plan
a large expansion of its counterinsurgency-related
study effort. Its nature was described in the research
plan submitted in response to the September 2 guidance
memorandum from DDR&E. Initiating some aspects of the
plan, the Army joined together with ARPA to establish

a Counterinsurgency Information and Analysis Center
(CINFAC) at SORO.  This center would draw together
available information about tribal groups, developing
societies, and social systems in various parts of the
world, using library sources generally, but adding
first-hand information culled as needed from consulting experts who had performed research in these areas.
It started with the information base that already existed to support the preparation of SORO's Area Handbooks, and would grow from there.  Any government
agency that needed information about a foreign country
or area in the "third world," for purposes of training,
policy making, or what-have-you, could query the center
and expect, within a few days or weeks, depending on
the amount and complexity of the information that had
to be assembled, an answer reporting the current state
of knowledge.  The center was not a new idea, but
rather the extension of an existing pattern to a new
subject area.  Other such centers operated by appropriately qualified organizations, such as the Battelle
Memorial Institute, had been established by the Defense Department to make available to the scientific
community the accumulated knowledge of years of research in a variety of technical fields.  The pattern
was part of an attempt to deal with the well-known
"information explosion."

The work of the center was to include reports on
such diverse subjects as the progress of economic
development under the AID program in South Korea, and

the history of the village council in South Vietnam. Another question that the center's workers answered, which we shall discuss in due course, figured large in Senator Fulbright's later attacks on DOD social science research. Typically, CINFAC might receive 100 to 200 questions a month, about half of them from DOD components and the others from scattered agencies of government.

While CINFAC was being established, a document began, also in August 1964, to float up into the Army "system" for approval, requesting allocation of funds to SORO for a project which was later named Camelot and which had as its objective:

...to test in one country the feasibility of designing and developing, for strategic planning and other Army use, an advanced system of early warning of internal conflict or its increased likelihood in foreign nations, together with concepts for early Army reaction systems requirements.

The scope of the project was to develop means for measuring "conflict potential," estimating "posture effects," and establishing information collection and handling systems to feed data into the first two efforts. The request for funds noted that "the study here proposed is a high risk, high pay-off feasibility study."

The genesis of the idea of measuring "internal war potential" is clear in the words of the second Smithsonian report (Chapter 2), and elaboration of those

ideas continued in the Camelot documents, as will be
seen. However, this statement of a desired project
seemed a far cry from the subtle kind of social research that was called for in the reports by the scientists. It illustrates well what happens when an operating organization tries to incorporate results from research into its action capabilities. It was not so
much that the action part of the Army did not understand the subtleties of the research or the scholarly
aspects of obtaining results; it was, rather, that in
general the Army had to interpret the knowledge gained
in terms of its mission, as it understood that mission.

If the policy of the government, illustrated by our
entry into Vietnam and by the organizational changes
and mission assignments that had continued throughout
the Kennedy and the beginning of the Johnson Adminis-
trations, was to lend assistance to countries threatened by "wars of national liberation," and the U.S.
Army was assigned a role as one of the instruments of
this policy, then the Army had to glean what knowledge
it could to prepare itself to carry out this mission.
In fairness, it must be noted that the popular conception of the Army going off on its own to carry out
nefarious foreign policy activities far beyond the
scope of its military assignments, which became common
after the Army was attacked for the Camelot project,
was simply false. The Army was preparing itself to
carry out a mission that the President had ordered it
to be ready to carry out, with the approval and know-

ledge of Congress. The fact that important segments
of Congress later acted to change Congress's granting
of this approval does not obviate the fact that, at
the time, the Army was operating within the context
of national policy agreed upon between the executive
and legislative branches.

However, the Army was certainly in sympathy with
the assignment. The terse and insensitive military
language of its request for funds reflected the beginning of this "user's" translation of the language of
the scientists into the operational language necessary
for its application of the research results, and the
translation reflected the Army's view of what the
scientists' language was all about.

The project funding request was signed by Colonel
Sullivan, Chief of the Human Factors and Operations
Research Division of the Army Research Office, whom we
have met earlier. Colonel Sullivan was an infantry
officer with a "can-do" outlook. In my years of working closely with him, I came to feel that he understood
full well the broader sensitivities and implications
of the social research that was being proposed; but he
was not one given to questioning the aspects of the
program that might cause difficulty. From his point
of view as a soldier, if the job was assigned, he expected that there would be problems and troubles
(every assignment had them), and his overriding motivation was to overcome them in the best way he could.
Because we had worked together, he had been aware of

the directions being taken by DDR&E thinking in this
program area, and he had had a preview of the instructions to come.  He concluded that the Army should "move
out smartly," without waiting for explicit direction
from above.  He received tentative approval from the
Director of Army Research, Brigadier General Walter
Lotz (an electrical engineer), and from the Chief of
Army Research and Development, Lieutenant General William Dick.  By about December of 1964, the project idea
described in the August memorandum had evolved into
Project Camelot, which was to be assigned to SORO.*

From later task statements and documents describing
the evolution of the research plan, the idea that the
predicting mechanisms would be developed through research in one country had developed into a much broader
study plan.  There would first be an attempt to gather,
in many countries, various kinds of data describing
the nature of the societies and how violence might
erupt and affect social change in those societies.
These data would then be used to develop a "model" of
a society in conflict, and to select, from among the
various existing but untested theories of social

---

*SORO had the habit of naming all of its projects.
This made subsequent attacks on them easier, and in
the case of Camelot added a new connotation to an old
concept in the English language.  In the words of Dr.
Vallance, the Director of SORO, later testifying before the Fascell Subcommittee: "The label 'CAMELOT'
simply emerged from the basic intent of the story....
that is the development of a stable society with domestic tranquility and peace and justice for all." [1]

change, those that appeared to be valid.  The consultants working with SORO had catalogued, from the literature, about 800 hypotheses about internal war.  Almost all of them appeared plausible, but many appeared
to be in direct opposition to each other.  For example,
some economic theories stated that (a) internal wars
are generated by growing poverty, and others stated
that (b) internal wars result from rapid economic progress.  Social theories postulated that (a) internal war
is a reflection of disorder resulting from great social
mobility, and also that (b) internal war is a reflection of frustration arising from little social mobility.  Political theories said that (a) internal wars are
responses to oppressive government, or that (b) internal wars are due to excessive toleration of alienated
groups.  It was first seen as necessary to sort out
some of these theories and try to decide which ones
had real validity based on historical data.  Possibly
many did, depending on the culture and the circumstances, and it would be necessary to establish these cor-
relations empirically.  Then a detailed description,
or model, of social change in diverse societies would
be constructed.  From this model--and there could be
more than one--the "indicators of internal conflict
potential" would be developed.  Finally, using the
models, the events in a single country would be examined in depth to ascertain whether the predictors
were, in fact, valid ones--that is, whether they would
indeed predict.  From here, it might be relatively

straightforward to apply the verified theories to strategic planning.

To run the project, SORO hired the late Dr. Rex
Hopper, an expert on Latin America from Brooklyn College, New York,* and assigned a few staff people.  I
met Hopper only once; he appeared to stay very much in
the background.  He did not, for example, testify before the Fascell Committee.  Aside from Vallance and
Bill Sullivan, our main contact with the project was
through a young political scientist, Ted Gude, who was
very bright and who appeared to do the organizing, much
of the writing, briefing, and contacting of external
consultants.  SORO planned the work so that it would
remain unclassified and could involve many members of
the scholarly community.  They planned to rely heavily
on outside experts, and enlisted many consultants who
were well known in such fields as anthropology, psychology, and political science.  During the spring of 1965
a number of these consultants formed a working group
that met one day a week with the internal staff, helping to draft preliminary documents, research plans,
and generally to describe what the project was supposed
to do and how it would go about doing it.

SORO had planned to complete, in the United States,

*Dr. Hopper was Chairman of the Sociology Department.
He had explored the sociology of social movements,
particularly of Latin America, and was co-author of
a book,   The Seizure of Power:  A Century of Revolution.   He died of a heart attack not long after the
Camelot events described in the following chapters.

its preliminary thinking and library research on
theories of conflict, revolutionary warfare, and processes of change in diverse social systems, during the
winter and spring of 1964 and 1965, focusing on several
societies at a time.  Overseas research was planned to
begin--again, largely library research--by September
of 1965.  It was intended that such research would be
undertaken almost simultaneously in some 21 countries--
an expansion of overseas research of unprecedented ambition and scope.  Following from SORO's previous work
on case studies of revolution, they built their planned
research around such conflicts, and planned to examine
such historical or current events as:  the Argentina
revolution of 1943; the Venezuelan revolution of 1945;
the Peruvian coup of 1963; Colombia since World War II;
the Egyptian coup of 1952; the Iranian coup of 1953;
the Korean revolution of 1960; and Greece in the context of the cold war.  As rather remote possibilities
which might later be found interesting, they also considered, in a very tentative way, the Algerian independence struggle, the Congo since 1960, the French-
Canadian separatist movement, and some others.  Chile
was not mentioned as one of the possibilities, although
it figured very much in the news later on.  The amount
of money to be spent was never very certain.  Ultimately, the Army allocated about half a million dollars
for the first year (only about half of which was spent),
and then planned to spend about a million dollars per
year for three to four years thereafter.

Despite these ambitious plans, the project never really got off the ground during the fall of 1964. The full project staff was never assembled or fully organized. There were many meetings, but the output consisted of generalities, never becoming specific about research hypotheses and how they would be tested; what data would be gathered; what the social system models would consist of. That is, the "research plan," without which a study in the social sciences (or in any other scientific area) cannot be undertaken, remained vague and formless. In its report, the DSB took note of Project Camelot, saying:

...Presumably, as Project CAMELOT gets under way, there will be such (i.e., systems-oriented) staff additions (at SORO) and a corresponding methodological reorientation, but this matter should be kept under continuing review by the ODDR&E.

By January 1965, Rains Wallace and I were quite concerned about, and discussed with Lyle Lanier and Harold Brown, the increasing evidence that the SORO management might not be up to the broader tasks being planned for it. We considered the possibility of asking the Army to change the management of SORO, but this seemed inappropriate at the time. The evidence was still largely in the form of random observations, unformed fears, impressions, and hunches; it was insufficient to justify broaching this delicate question to the Army, and it was never raised outside the circle of those most concerned in ODDR&E. Several times later during that spring I had talks with social scientists who were not involved in Camelot but who visited SORO and discussed the project with its staff and management. Uniformly, they reported that they believed that SORO did not know what it was doing. These inputs served to reinforce the concerns reflected in our subsequent actions.

We had several talks with Colonel Sullivan, who then put more pressure on SORO to prepare and present a firm research plan. About the time we were preparing the March 24 guidance letter (in February), we received a document from SORO entitled "Project CAMELOT: Design and Phasing." Among the most important problems the document presented were these:

● diffuse wording, still not pointing toward specific research tasks and problems. For example,

> Since it is not possible to specify a priori the exact form of possible models of internal conflict and internal war, it is necessary to develop a broad range of information requirements for the case studies so that many types of models can be developed and tested with the data.

> The initial models developed in the theoretical design effort will have as a primary objective the specification of the types of models that may prove valuable to the project.

> The research design for the individual analytic case studies and the individual social systems studies will be planned to include the information requirements for all of the various models.

Clearly, the thinking was circular. Which models?

What would they look like? How could they plan to
get data to construct models of which they had not
yet conceived? What data would they seek? Would
they randomly amass data on all conceivable subjects and then try to process it? A disastrous
end for such an undertaking could be readily predicted.

- This led, of course, to more specific concerns
  about the data problem per se. The general tone
  of the discussion was that they would have more
  data than they would know what to do with; but
  there was no indication that they would know or
  try to determine a priori what data were needed,
  whether they might exist or be available, how they
  would be obtained, how SORO would obtain access
  to sources. None of this had yet been explored,
  after six months' "work," nor did it even appear
  to have been recognized as a problem.

- There was a section which talked about small
  group experimentation "particularly as concerned
  with concepts such as cohesion, control, sociali-
  zation, goal development, and motivation in primary groups." The purpose of such experimentation, the validity of its results in terms of
  large social systems, or the possibility of doing
  it in the cultures and situations they would be
  concerned with, and how it would relate to the
  objectives or final results, were not dealt with.

- The plan still read as though the program would
  be done primarily by outside consultants, with
  little effort by the SORO in-house staff except
  loose coordination.  In our view, systems analysis of questions of this kind required that the
  technical work be tightly coordinated, carefully
  planned, and divided into subtasks to be performed
  by a cohesive, in-house research staff.  Consultants could help, but they couldn't do the job
  themselves.  Thus, this was not shaping up as a
  coordinated program, but rather as a loose conglomeration of somewhat related studies by individual
  scholars who had their own diverse interests in
  the general area, and who were, it seemed, to do
  the Camelot tasks, when those were defined, as
  spare-time jobs.  This moved opposite to the DSB
  recommendation for improving social science research methodology.

- Finally, the rush to go overseas about six or
  eight months after publication of this "plan,"
  in view of the state of disarray of the plan, was
  frightening.

Wallace and I called for a meeting on the subject,
and met with Sullivan, Gude, and Vallance at ARO in
early March.  We discussed in detail the problems we
saw, and Gude responded by describing the thinking of
the group of consultants then meeting periodically
with the staff, and promised to pay more attention to

the specific research questions in future writing.
(They later did prepare a very detailed document of
information requirements which, when it surfaced in
Chile, made it look as though this were a strictly in-
telligence-oriented operation by the U.S. Army.  The
relationship between intelligence and research in this
area had been recognized by the Smithsonian panel, and
was a troublesome one, which I will come back to in
some detail much later.)  Gude noted that there was to
be a meeting of the key consultants and a number of
distinguished scholars, forming a technical advisory
group, in August.  Then, the detailed and final research plan would be worked out, the staff would be on
board, and, he assured us, we would be satisfied with
the project.  After the meeting Wallace and I decided,
privately, that if the August convocation did not produce these results the project would be cancelled.

We were now in a dilemma.  DDR&E was preparing to
issue a guidance paper giving the Army major responsibility for the total program, and the Army capability
seemed to be weak, indeed.  But all of the programmatic
results of the previous year's bureaucratic work had
evolved in directions desired by both the DOD and many
members of the social science community.  The Services
and ARPA, despite their diverse concerns, were responding positively, making plans and allocating budgets.
At various points in previous years, the organizations
directly responsible for research in the social sciences within the Services had also responded to recommen-

dations for increasing the work by requesting the budgets, which then nad been turned down at the top Service
levels.  This was not happening now.  The question was,
should we at this point call a halt until the Army
could solve its problems of management and research
capability, and risk losing credibility and the ability
to restart afterwards; or, should we go ahead, and try
to fix the Army's problems as we went along?  Inevitably, bureaucratic momentum won out.

After the flurry of activity involved in getting
Although in retrospect this was obviously a mistake,
it seemed a reasonable risk at the time.  SORO was
still working in-house and unobtrusively (we thought).
Money was not being spent at a high rate because of
the small staff.  We had the ultimate control of the
Army's budget to use as a club.  Therefore, we decided
to go ahead with the guidance, but we retained our
private determination to have Camelot cancelled, while
the Army might be allowed to go ahead with the other
parts of its six-point program, if the project did not
shape up in August.

After the flurry of activity involved in getting
the March 24 guidance letter out, I had another inconclusive discussion with Gude and decided to put on
paper what was bothering me most.  Since we were still
trying to get the Army turned around rather than turned
off, the situation appeared to bear handling with kid
gloves.  Being aware of the power of an official com-
plaint to a Service or a contractor from a member of
the DDR&E staff, I wrote a personal letter to Gude

rather than a formal letter to Sullivan or Vallance.
In it, I reviewed the situation regarding Camelot as
we saw it; I pointed out the novelty and difficulty of
taking a systems approach to the study of a major
social problem; and I dwelt on the problem of getting
the idea accepted, both by the social science community
and the operational community.  I noted that just doing
the project could affect the social system that the
project was about, if the latter were defined to include the ambassador, the military commanders, and the
whole U.S. decision-making apparatus as well as people
and government in the country in question.  In effect,
just by the act of undertaking the research we were
effecting social change, and we had to tread very gingerly.  Their plans were as yet imprecise and uncertain.  Therefore, they should not plan to be in 21
countries overseas by September, but rather should
hope to start by then to arrange to do research in
one country over the winter; they could then learn to
test data sources, the climate of acceptance, etc.  If
succesful they could plan, some months later, to start
preparing the way for research in two or three additional countries.  That is, the problem should be approached much more slowly, and the schedule should be
extended considerably.  I did not know when I wrote
this letter that it was already too late, because Rex
Hopper had sent a personal letter to a colleague in
Chile a few days earlier that would literally destroy
SORO's program and seriously undermine the remainder

of the DOD effort.

In the course of my work I had made it a practice
to travel to various overseas commands, especially in
Southeast Asia, to obtain a first-hand view of the
problems of warfare, field operations, hardware needs,
and of doing research in the field.  In late April I
decided to go to the Panama Canal Zone where the headquarters of the United States Southern Command (Comman-
der-in Chief, South, or CINCSO) was based.  With the
growing attention to Vietnam, Latin America, which
seemed vitally important in view of the conflict with
Cuba and Castro's promises to stimulate revolutionary
movements elsewhere, had received little attention.
In the Canal Zone, the Army had a tropical research
center where environmental research and equipment
testing were performed to obtain data that might be
applicable to the jungle environments of Southeast
Asia.  There were training facilities operated by
CINCSO's component commands to train the Latin American
military in such diverse skills as military organization and aircraft engine maintenance.  ARPA and SORO
both had field offices there; and there were other activities relevant to my responsibilities in ODDR&E.  I
would also obtain my first "official" view of the problems in that part of the world, through the eyes of the
U.S. military command, and pave the way for trips I
hoped to make later to countries in Latin America.  At
the same time, I took the opportunity to tell General
Porter, the Commander-in-Chief, about our views of the

FAR was, in fact, briefed a number of times on the DOD efforts. (It was also at about this time that I wrote to State suggesting studies that we would be willing to fund under their cognizance, with results described earlier.)

The discussion was inconclusive, and I had the uneasy feeling that FAR was too tempted by the obvious opportunity for extension of its domain. But when the meeting ended I thought that the position I had stated was understood and accepted. I also believed that our agreement was confirmed in later telephone conversations. I was therefore very much surprised when in late May I received a letter from Nagle which started "I am herewith amplifying the terms of our telephone conversation, in which I was pleased that you so readily accepted my view that any new inter-agency foreign area research mechanism should be under the Foreign Area Research Coordination Group...," and then proceeded to describe how FAR rather than the Army would establish the coordinating mechanism. But since the new DDR&E memo and a letter inviting State to assign a staff member to the Army's new office were in final preparation and about to go to DDR&E for signature, I judged that this would either set the question to rest or provide a high-level forum for arguing it. The package did go forward about the tenth of June for DDR&E signature, and I felt quite relaxed about the whole matter.

I was in for another nasty shock when on June 14 I

received a call from Nagle.  He informed me that State
had just received a confidential cable from Ambassador
Dungan in Chile which said that a communist newspaper,
on Saturday morning, June 12, broke a story under the
headline "Yankees Study Invasion of Chile," subheaded
"Project Camelot Financed by U.S. Army."  The cable
then complained that the Ambassador had not known of
any such research project; he was very disturbed that
this activity should have been undertaken in Chile
without prior notification; and he asked what was going
on.  He considered the effort to be seriously detrimental to U.S. interests in Chile.  With this, Nagle
said he would be in touch and hung up.  I informed
DDR&E and called SORO to find out what had happened.

The next few days were extremely hectic.  The story
was picked up by Radio Havana and then by Radio Moscow,
and then appeared in inner-page dispatches in American
papers.  We were frantically trying to find out what
had happened in Chile, of all places, since there had
been no plans for research there; no visits were authorized, per my promise to General Porter; and this
was the first I had heard of anything having to do with
that country.  Operations in the Dominican Republic by
American troops were still very much in the news, and
the two stories were being linked together in the dispatches.

The dry and concise language of material that was
subsequently prepared for but not presented to the
Fascell committee (we decided to let the Army present

its own story) makes interesting counterpoint to the
confusion of the events:

a) The Chilean newspaper that carried the story was
   El Siglo, the Communist Party organ in Chile.   The
   story was subsequently picked up by Radio Havana,
   Moscow Domestic Service, and London's Reuters.

b) No research related to Project CAMELOT had ever been
   planned or conducted in Chile.  However, three contacts by Special Operations Research Office (SORO)
   personnel with persons in Chile were identified:

   (1) Dr. Rex Hopper, Director of CAMELOT, had
       stopped in Chile on personal business for two
       days in early April.  He had attended a social
       science research meeting in Rio de Janeiro in
       late March--the meeting being totally unrelated
       to Project CAMELOT.  While in Chile, he infor-
       mally discussed CAMELOT with two personal
       friends.

   (2) On 5 April 1965, Dr. Hopper wrote a letter to
       Dr. Galtung, a Norwegian social scientist work-
       ing with the UN in Chile, inviting Dr. Galtung
       (who had been at Columbia University with other
       members of the CAMELOT staff) to participate in
       a planning conference to be held in Washington
       in August.  A brief description of the project
       was given, including the fact that it was
       sponsored by the U.S. Army.  The letter offered
       a fee of $2,000 for the entire month of August.

   (3) Dr. Hugo Nutini, an anthropologist from Pitts-
       burgh University, had been a consultant at SORO
       on Project CAMELOT during the period February-
       April 1965.  Dr. Nutini, a native Chilean now
       a naturalized U.S. citizen, was scheduled to
       go to Chile on other business in April.  On the
       initiative of the project director he was asked
       to informally assess the interest of academic
       and governmental officials with respect to the
       possibility of doing some related research in
       Chile (apparently, in terms of Chile as an ex-

ample of orderly social change) and to determine what indigenous resources existed to do
the research.  This was to be done in the
"natural course of events" of Nutini's other
business, and he was to be paid as a consultant
when he returned.  A portion of his fee was
advanced to him.  Dr. Nutini talked to approximately 150 persons in Chile, including governmental officials and academic personnel.

As I later reconstructed the story from various sources,
it seemed that members of the Santiago university community had been upset when Galtung, who was very much
opposed to American intervention in Vietnam, had told
them of this new evidence of American military perfidy;
they had contacted Chile's foreign minister, who had
in turn gone to Dungan; while they were trying to sort
the matter out, other faculty members had given the
story to El Siglo.

Two other occurrences from these few days remain
vivid in my memory.  First, when I learned from SORO
that Hopper had sent the formal Camelot task statement
to Galtung as an enclosure with his letter, I checked
back to it.  When I saw the words, "Project Camelot is
a study whose objective is to determine the feasibility
of developing a general social systems model which
would make it possible to predict and influence politically significant aspects of social change..."
(emphasis added), I knew that the whole idea of doing
research in Latin America was in trouble, and possibly
dead.

Second, Wallace and I had been scheduled to meet

with the staff of the Senate Armed Services Committee
as part of our beginning effort to explain the expansion of the social science program to Congress.  We
did have this meeting on June 22, and reviewed with the
staff director all the activities that had led to the
new program plans; the background; why we thought the
research was necessary; what the research might accomplish; the DSB report; and our current plans.  He had
read the Camelot news items, and inquired.  We explained what the project was, what we thought had
happened, and how we hoped to correct the problems.
We expressed our hope that this wouldn't hurt the program plans too severely.  We noted frankly that we
felt it would be hard enough to convince Congress of
the value of the work, and that the Camelot news would
make it more difficult.  We stressed the relatively
modest pace of program expansion and budget, reminding
him of the small number of people the budget represented.  We discussed the continuing coordination we had
maintained with ARPA, the Services, and the State Department.  He seemed to us interested and sympathetic,
but obviously made no commitment.  So, we could see
the beginning of problems that we had believed we
would have to prepare for in any case.  Having done
our internal work in DOD, we now had to face the outside world, which we presumed would want to be convinced, and it looked none too easy even under the
best of circumstances.  The current circumstances were
far from that.

# III DONNYBROOK

Prefatory Note:  A Personal Interlude, 1

The next weekend, June 26, began as a peaceful one.
We hadn't heard much more from the outside world that
week about Camelot, and our investigation of SORO's
jumping the gun in Chile was proceeding.  As the chronicle of their stumbling unfolded, we made plans to
assure that they couldn't do that again; and next week
we would decide what to do about the project.  On
Saturday my wife and I drove a 500-mile round trip to
take our two girls to summer camp in Pennsylvania.  We
returned, dead tired, at about midnight, looking forward to seven weeks of relative quiet.  For the first
time in ten years, we were going to be alone together
for more than a few hours.  At about 8:30 Sunday morning, we were awakened by a phone call from Colonel
Sullivan--had I seen the Washington Star that morning,
and what time could I come to a meeting at his office?
He sketched out the problem briefly, we arranged a
time, and I rushed out for a paper.  On the front page,
again in the dry language of the brief later prepared
for the congressional committee:

On 27 June 1965, an article appeared in the Washington
Star alleging that Department of the Army and Department of State were feuding over the unauthorized intrusion of DOD into the field of foreign policy matters
and that Department of the Army was conducting research in Chile without letting the State Department
know about the project.

The consequences were to be great, and to unfold over
the next five years or more.  Not the least of the
casualties, but perhaps not large in the general scale
of things, was our peaceful summer.

The Camelot news was to send a shock through the American social science world, starting a period of self-searching, questioning, and witch hunting that was to disrupt both the established value system and relations between social scientists and the government.  DOD research in the social sciences became big news, and for a time it seemed as though hardly a day could pass without a story about another DOD probe into areas that were coming to be deemed "none of its business." The State Department "moved in," to broaden its scope of control over all such activity, and in particular to exercise control over at least this part of DOD research; this created a countercurrent of concern in the social science community.  While the DOD tried to put its house in order, Congress took a closer look at what it was up to and, as the record will demonstrate, didn't like what it saw.  In the next fiscal year the program was cut back essentially to where it had been before the new efforts were started.  But, more important, it seemed to me that Senators McCarthy, Fulbright, and Mansfield took DOD social research overseas as a symbol of what they viewed as the DOD's expanding and improper grasp on foreign affairs, and they used this as one of the elements of what were to be years of opposition to the DOD's more general role overseas.

All of this did not, of course, take place solely because of the misguided actions of a few social scien-

tists in a foreign country.  The news of the Army's
"research project in Chile" broke in a period of
heightening concern about the Vietnam war, when the
further evidence of American interference in a foreign
country's affairs in the Dominican Republic had exacerbated the Vietnam irritation immeasurably and had
confirmed the Administration's opponents' view of what
Senator Fulbright called "the arrogance of power."
American bombing of North Vietnam had started in February, 1965, just about the time the Defense Science
Board's report was published.  The public debate, along
with the demonstrations, teach-ins, and other opposition to American participation in the war were building
up during the spring of 1965, and were to lead to the
first peace march on Washington during the following
November.  "Dissent" was becoming a fashionable word,
and the Camelot news gave many social scientists a
cause célèbre within their own house to add to their
growing dissatisfaction with American behavior overseas.

The sensitivities of all Latin America had been
rubbed raw by the entry of American troops into Santo
Domingo, which was viewed as reversion to the policy
of the "big stick."  It wouldn't have taken much for
any Latin American to have believed any story about
American intervention anywhere on the continent.  The
evidence, as far as they were concerned, existed in
Chile in the form of the Camelot plan's detailed description of the kinds of information the project's

staff and consultants had said they wanted: political
party alignments; social conditions; army and police
organization and roles in the society; economic and
social maldistribution and discontent--as the phrase
goes, "the whole bit." Many other American scholars
were working in Latin America at the time, under
private foundation and university sponsorship, and
all came under suspicion. And before too long were to
come the revelations, starting with the news that
Michigan State University had allowed some of its
staff to be employed under contract to the CIA to
train police in Vietnam,[1] that the CIA had "penetrated"
a number of American universities and the National
Student Association. The American community of students of foreign societies could foresee the end of its
welcome to perform research overseas--everywhere, perhaps, but in sensitive Latin America especially.

Thus the time for DOD to expand its interest in
studying revolutionary war and the structure of foreign cultures turned out to have been inauspicious,
and only a slight misstep was required to shake the
profession to its roots. SORO's contact with social
scientists in Chile was that misstep.

The issues that were raised were relatively few,
but they were fundamental. The legitimacy of counterinsurgency as a strategy for the United States, and as
a subject for study by the American community of
social scientists, was questioned. The word changed
from a name for a strategy to a symbol of all that was

considered reactionary in American foreign, and even
domestic, policy.  The propriety of the DOD's supporting research into the functioning of social systems
was challenged; the fact that the DOD was carrying out
presidential policy was forgotten.  The problem of how
the DOD controlled what went on under its research contracts became a crucial one, involving complex issues
of centralization of research management, political
sensitivity, and freedom in inquiry.  It became an article of faith that the State Department should have
control of anything having remotely to do with foreign
policy or, indeed, with research in or about foreign
countries.  The fact that DOD could get money to support research in these areas while State apparently
couldn't, was deplored but not questioned from the
State point of view; many years elapsed before the
next step--of trying to get the money for State--was
taken.  The further question was raised, and became
ever more persistent, as to whether the Defense Department should display any interest in foreign policy at
all.  On the one hand, the DOD was condemned for trying
to learn something about its task, since if it tried
to do so this implied it was seeking control of foreign policy.  On the other hand, the military were condemned for being insensitive to the nuances of international affairs and diplomacy.  Either way, the DOD
was out of line.

State's attitude toward and ability to undertake
research were never explored, but underlay the uneasi-

ness of the social scientists about the role that was
given to State.  This concern led to the further question of whether any part of the government could support such research without having its motives questioned.  Next in turn came the problem of personal
ethics--whether social scientists could properly lend
themselves to purposes of government--and from there,
full circle, to the growing schism between the scholarly world and the Defense Department.  Issues that
were never raised explicitly but were also of fundamental importance (and remained so) appeared in the
role of the press, with its devotion to a combination
of truth and sensation; in the question of whether
valid scientific research could be performed under the
conditions of public scrutiny and disorder in the field
that obtained; and whether the research results would
be of any practical value in the long run, in any case.

All these issues are easily and briefly stated in
retrospect.  But they developed painfully and over a
considerable period of time, in a jumble of external
events, internal meetings, and bureaucratic infighting
that were emotionally charged and kaleidoscopically
juxtaposed.  The only way to gain perspective and
some sense of logical sequence, even now, is to look
at each of the many threads in turn, showing as the
occasions arise how each interacted with the others.
In doing this, it will be convenient (as it has been
up to this point) to refer to "the press," "the Congress," "the social science community," and others, as

though these were monolithic entities.  But surely the
reader has observed by now that within each of these
entities were diverse individuals and groups, each
with unique motivations that sometimes reinforced and
sometimes conflicted with the motivations of others.
It is, of course, out of the actions and interactions
among these various participants that the evolution of
events developed, as will become clear in the succeeding chapters.

Suppose we start with the press.  Its role was crucial.
It brought the Camelot fiasco to the public's attention and stimulated the interest of members of Congress
in DOD social research.  It fed, if it did not trigger,
the bureaucratic conflict between the State and Defense
departments.  When all was over it could claim much of
the credit for having brought the DOD's supposed mis-
behavior to public account.

But its own behavior was interesting.  Its concern
was with the surface phenomena, and with their more
sensational aspects.  The fundamental issues were almost never raised; but the DOD's efforts to undertake
social research efforts overseas were never lost as
the target.  The background and the reasons for the
DOD's activity were barely explored--although, as we
shall see, that was partly the DOD's fault.  Some of
the press stories were quite accurate, although these
seemed to get less prominence than the others.  Most
of the stories had a few of the facts and wove them
together with half-truths and surmise, so that the output seemed always to be full of distortions or misin-
formation osculating with the truth.  Some of this
could be taken as good, clean fun; some as haste or
carelessness; some seemed calculated.

The story that really triggered the furor was not
the original dispatch that Reuters had picked up from
Radio Havana and the Moscow Domestic Service.  It was

Walter Pincus' front-page story in the Washington Star, on June 27, headlined "Army-State Department Feud Bared by Chile Incident." The article told of "a growing conflict between the State Department and the Pentagon;" revealed that the U.S. Ambassador to Chile had cabled the Department about the "Army-sponsored study begun there without his knowledge" (obviously information leaked to Pincus, because the cable was classified); talked of State's "open-mouthed amazement" at the DOD's growing interest in foreign policy and social science research; and expanded at length on State's view of the foolishness of trying to do research on social systems, and on how the DOD could get research money, while State couldn't. Three days later, Secretary McNamara received a letter from Senator McCarthy, asking for details about the project and the State-DOD conflict.

In a continuing series of articles over the next few days, Pincus described Senator McCarthy's preparations for a Senate investigation, and little by little described some aspects of the Camelot project, making it seem, however, as though SORO were already undertaking research, without a by-your-leave, in Venezuela, in French Canada, and elsewhere. The disparity in funds for research between Defense and State was stressed continuously, at first comparing the $6 million said to have been ultimately envisioned for Camelot* with

---

*But see Chapter 9, p. 145.

the annual $140,000 or so for State's external research,
then pointing out how difficult it was for State to get
its internal $4.2 million INR budget past Congressman
Rooney.  Pincus mentioned DOD studies in the behavioral
and social science field funded at "$20 million, an
amount far above anything that could conceivably be
requested or received for such studies by any other
Federal agency...," without inquiring as to what work
was covered by that budget, and leaving the implication that this was all for "foreign affairs research"
--a misconception that persisted.  Whereas Pincus had
said only that "research in Chile" had been started
without State's knowledge, a Newsweek article on July
5, in the breezy style of the weekly news magazines,
went a step further, stating that "Dungan may be some
time getting a complete answer to his cable.  For one
thing, the Army's Project Camelot seems never to have
been called to the attention of top State Department
officials."  This idea--that the Army had started a
study about foreign policy on its own initiative without informing State--persisted in most later writings,
even as recently as a note in the May 1971 Scientific
American[1] about "a covert research effort in Latin
America financed by the Department of Defense."

As a matter of simple fact, aside from the discussions I had had with the group of Departmental research
directors and FAR, the record shows that the Army had
briefed diverse groups in State on the project at
least a dozen times starting in August, 1964.  A mem-

ber of the INR staff had met with the group of consultants at the weekly SORO planning meetings in the
spring of 1965.  One of those briefed at State was
Walt Rostow, then chairman of the Policy Planning
Council, who was reported by the Army attendees to
have found the proposed research interesting, to have
seen "no objection of a bureaucratic nature" (in the
words of the Army report), and to have expressed his
pleasure that the External Research people had already
assured DOD of interest and cooperation.  (Despite all
the later problems and publicity he never said this
publicly, and Secretary Rusk testified in August that
all Camelot contacts with State were minor and that
the project was never known at the policy level.)  The
SORO team had also briefed a behavioral science advisory committee of the National Academy of Sciences that
had been established at Army request to advise the
project, with State Department representatives present.
As late as May 25, 1965, Nagle had written to Vallance,
thanking him for keeping the State Department so
closely informed of Project Camelot.  Most of this information was made known to the congressional committees having an interest in the problem, and was published in the record of the Fascell hearings later,[2]
but little of it appeared in the press for reasons
which we shall explore shortly and which were partly,
but not wholly, the fault of the press.

The knowledge of SORO's and DOD's efforts to keep
State informed made Pincus's claim that there was

"open-mouthed amazement," as well as a memorandum in
State deploring the project, particularly irritating.
It seemed to me to be obvious that Pincus was being
fed his information from State.  It also seemed obvious
that some people in the State Department, at least, had
reservations about the general area of DOD research and
about the particular project, and were expressing them
privately within the Department.  At no time, although
there had obviously been many opportunities, were such
reservations raised with anyone in the Army or ODDR&E
during all the meetings among Army, DOD, and State
Department representatives during the previous year.
One was led to wonder why, if State were deeply concerned about the potentially adverse impact of such research on American foreign policy (as they later would
claim to be), they did not mention those concerns while
they had the opportunity to prevent the adverse events
from taking place.  Since, as I was told, their representative to SORO knew of SORO's plans to contact
Galtung, and presumably knew that even some of SORO's
consultants had warned against it, a single phone call
would have changed the entire outcome.  It is not surprising that at the time we in DOD attributed a certain bureaucratically oriented malevolence to their
actions; this seemed in keeping with what I had interpreted as a power play in the weeks before the Camelot
story broke, and was reinforced by their subsequent
behavior, as will be seen.  The Fascell subcommittee
was led to remark that, "We cannot condone the type of

interdepartmental rivalry which was evidenced in the
steady stream of "leaks" originating in the State Department, undoubtedly intended to preclude any other
disposition of this proposed undertaking.  This...can
hardly serve to advance the interests of our foreign
policy..."[3]

There followed a spate of articles and interest in
the DOD's adventures with the social sciences in
"trade" magazines, in various newspapers, in Science
magazine (which printed one of the more calm and accurate accounts),[4] and even in Punch, which added a
welcome touch of friendly humor in the midst of all
the sound and fury.[5]  After the Camelot project was
cancelled, in early July, the Washington Star crowed
editorially that, "Thanks to an exclusive article by
the Star's Mr. Pincus...the strange excursion of the
Army into sociology in other lands was brought to
light....this is a rather strange garden path for the
Army to be exploring, and the State Department was
properly outraged....After some behind-the-scenes conferences, the Army decided it might better abandon the
$700,000...."--again, misinformation which the Star's
editorial writer, at least, might have checked with
its own Mr. Pincus; but his outlook was obvious.

Toward the end of July, I was called by John Goshko
of the Washington Post, who was covering Latin American affairs and the State Department at the time.  He
said he had heard about a recent Camelot-type flap in
Brazil, and asked if I could tell him about it.  He

said he knew about a contract ARPA had with a company
to do research on counterinsurgency in Brazil, and
that State had received a message of protest from the
ambassador; and he wanted to know if we had "killed
the contract." I explained to him that nothing of the
kind existed or had happened, and reminded him that
while I would be perfectly willing to talk with him
about it in detail, the rules of the DOD news game at
the moment required that he first direct his inquiry
to Public Affairs Assistant Secretary Arthur Sylvester.
He said he would do that, but, as far as I know, he
never did. I assumed he had to file his story before
some close deadline passed.

The project in question was in the counterinsurgency
area, but was far simpler and more direct than Camelot.
It was intended to explore, from newspaper data available in any library, whether the reported patterns of
violence in a country could be correlated with social
change well enough to serve as an "indicator" of the
onset of violent revolution. Whereas Camelot wanted
to analyze the nature of the illness in detail, this
project desired only to determine whether symptoms of
the illness could reliably be identified from surface
phenomena. Of course, not everyone believed such analysis was necessary, or would be successful, since it
could be argued that an informed and knowledgeable observer could easily describe the condition of a sick
society and predict its convulsions. But the opinions
of "old hands" varied with their antecedents and polit-

ical coloration, and in many countries political and
social violence waxed and waned, without any fundamental social change taking place.  It seemed reasonable to try to use more rigorous analytical methods to
determine whether some patterns of events were more
likely than others to indicate when such fundamental
change was about to take place.  As it turned out, the
study was only moderately successful--but that was not
then, and is not now, the issue.  The real issue was
whether objective analytical inquiry could shed light
on the problem and should be undertaken.

In this case, the study team was originally supposed
to visit some countries in Latin America to gather
data in local libraries.  But when the Camelot news
broke, ARPA immediately changed these plans.  The Ambassador to Brazil had learned of the project through
State and, believing the intent was still to visit
Brazil, which had been one of the countries on the
itinerary, had cabled his concern--and was reassured
by return cable, ending the "flap."  However, the story
by Goshko the day after he called me described the
"Brazil project, like Camelot," as "designed to study
ways of influencing social and political change in
developing nations..."  It then described "the Army's"
(sic) plans to undertake the project in Brazil and
how the Ambassador had stopped them, then saying that
"since last Friday the matter has been the subject of
hurried discussions between State and Defense officials"--an exaggeration bordering on fabrication, to

say the least. Subsequent articles told how the project was "suspended," and an editorial in the Post said
that "the Army, undeterred by Secretary McNamara's
death warrant for Camelot, was blithely moving ahead
with its Brazilian inquiry..." It then castigated the
Army for undertaking research that was "not only gratuitous but grossly insulting." An article in the Star
on the same subject by Walter Pincus carried the mis-
information that "sources indicated the impetus to
cancel Camelot came from the White House," and this
was perpetuated in other, later writings by social
scientists. Again, as we shall see, the facts were
wrong but the orientation was obvious.

It seems, in retrospect, that at least some reporters and editorial writers feel free to weave a tale
creating an impression they want to convey, without
necessarily having, or feeling the need to find, all
the facts in the case. Perhaps many, or for all I
know, most, reporters try to find out as many facts as
they can consistent with having to meet their deadlines.
It does seem difficult for many of them to keep their
value judgments from getting in the way of objectivity.

There had, about this time, also been a Pincus story
about the Navy's "Project Michelson," undertaken at
the Naval Ordnance Test Station in California.[6] This
revealed that the Navy was using money (about $250,000
per year) from its Polaris program for studies by
social scientists of the political aspects of strategic
deterrence. The article quoted the Chief Scientist of

the Office of Naval Research as saying that "as a pioneering venture, it would be a good idea to see what
the so-called soft sciences....could bring to bear on
the....desirable and undesirable features....of sea-
based deterrents." Titillating report titles, such as
"Risk Taking and Risk Avoidance in Soviet Foreign Policy, 1945-62," and "The President's 'Slip-of-the-Tongue'
on Cuba, August 1962," were quoted. Congress didn't
know about the project, and again inquired. This added to jangled nerves in the DOD. Once again, and in
a completely different area, the DOD's attempts to
understand the social implications of military force,
in application and as viewed from various aspects of
public policy, were made to seem somehow improper.

At this point it was decided that something concrete had to be done to terminate State's destructive
campaign of leaks to the press about DOD's study programs. A telephone conversation between Harold Brown
and Thomas Mann, then the Under Secretary of State for
Economic Affairs, resulted in an agreement to limit
distribution of messages about these projects within
the State Department, while DOD would take steps to
change research project titles that could be misleading and damaging when taken out of context. The rationale, on which both the State and Defense officials
at that level agreed, was that the appearance of the
information in the press, in distorted form, was providing every opportunity for the destruction of a research program still deemed important for the national

security.  This was not the only case where the question would arise of how much information about the
government's activities should be made public or with-
held in the interest of furthering those activities;
the Pentagon Papers provided a more celebrated example,
and the issue will surely reappear in the future.  The
more fundamental question, of course, was why the DOD
did not make a public defense of its position and its
program, if the latter were so important.

A number of the social scientists who had contributed to the growth of the DOD effort, some of whom were
beginning to feel repercussions in their professional
lives because they had been associated with Camelot,
pleaded with us to release a full and coherent story
about the project.  The Army did, too, and with good
reason--they were essentially taking the public "rap"
for having carried out a DOD policy they did not originate.  Presumably, if the overall research program made
sense, even though some parts of it might not have
been as well thought out or executed as others, and
if the program were supported by and based upon the
best, most knowledgeable scientific opinion that could
be marshalled to advise the DOD over a period of years,
explaining this to the public would have provided a
better basis for judgment and rational argument than
the flow of fragmentary, incomplete, and inaccurate
stories that actually reached the public.

There were several reasons for the DOD's reticence,
not all based on sound logic.  First, there was the

problem of the acute embarrassment caused by Camelot
itself. The first reaction of a bureaucracy--and most
of those in it--when it feels itself caught out or under fire is protective. Feelings of guilt follow embarrassment, and closely thereafter, the desire to
become as inconspicuous as possible. Then, there was
the context. All the stories, at first, were about
projects having to do with Latin America. In the prevailing atmosphere in that area about American intervention, following on the heels of the landing in the
Dominican Republic and the publication of the Camelot
task statement about predicting and influencing the
course of social change, it seemed impossible to compose a discussion of the rationale for a program involving DOD interest in Latin American social systems
that would not exacerbate international sensitivities
even further. Our feeling in DOD was that anything
that DOD said about such interest would make matters
worse, and that the United States would be better
served if the DOD simply took its lumps, kept quiet,
and let it blow over. (Of course, it wouldn't blow
over, but at that time the dimensions of the problem
were not fully appreciated.) Next, there were social
research projects of much more immediate importance to
the DOD, in Vietnam and elsewhere in Southeast Asia,
that were not getting any publicity, that were classified, and to which it appeared unwise to draw attention under the circumstances. Some of these studies
were discussed before the Fascell Subcommittee, and a

little bit about them became part of the public record.
But that record of closed hearings was not published
until December, and the press had in the meantime
turned its attention temporarily to other matters.

The initial inclination within the DOD was thus to
remain silent. This was reinforced by the general attitude of the DOD's upper hierarchy toward discussions
with the news media. It will be remembered that early
in McNamara's tenure it was easy for any journalist
to talk with any official, and that many leaks of positions opposed to those of his Administration had
plagued Kennedy's early attempts to establish civilian
control over the Services. Tight controls were instituted; the rule became that a reporter who wanted to
interview an official must submit his request to the
Public Affairs Office. If an interview were approved
by that Office (after suitable consultations), a representative from the Office would sit in on the interview. This was undoubtedly intended to assure that
officials did not depart very far from "approved"
policy, but in my years in the Pentagon I never found
it particularly inhibiting. One could always meet the
demand for information by holding a "background discussion," not for attribution. The rule could also be
viewed as a means to help insure against misquotation
or distortion, by the journalist, that could be attributed to the interviewee, to his embarrassment. The
other side was that the rule placed the decision about
what subject matter could be discussed with the press

under strongly centralized bureaucratic control.  This
was part of the pattern that led to the accusation of
"management of the news" by the DOD.

   This issue is more complex than the simple facts
might suggest.  While in a democracy the public is entitled to know what is happening inside government,
the director of a major department of government needs
to assert some policy control over his staff.  If each
member of the staff is free to express his dissenting
or critical opinions on important issues, publicly and
at will, such control can become a shambles.  The
courts have on occasion ruled that the risk must be
taken; but the bureaucracy has shown no signs that
control of public statements on policy is being fore-
gone.  The system of "checks and balances" can be seen
to have many facets.

   Be that as it may, the Public Affairs Office decided
that nothing should be publicly said about Camelot by
OSD, and this was not likely to be reversed at higher
levels.  As had been pointed out in the March 24 guidance memorandum, this area of research had yet to prove
its worth.  In view of the larger foreign policy and
defense issues under debate at the time, such as the
increasing virulence of the war in South Vietnam, the
bombing of North Vietnam, the intervention in the Dominican Republic, and the ever-simmering military force
structure issues such as that over the F-111 airplane,
the subject of social research in foreign areas was
not likely to appear important enough for the leaders

of DOD to rush to its defense against public opposition; and therein lay its greatest vulnerability.
While it was doing no harm, it could be tolerated as
an experiment. More, in the internal discussions between DOD and State the right of the DOD to study the
problems that directly affected it and its ability to
carry out its mission was supported strongly. But if
the work got into enough trouble to warrant a public
attack on it, there were limits beyond which even its
strongest supporters at high levels did not feel they
could go to save it.

Thus the DOD kept quiet and took its punishment
(with the Army bearing the brunt, because it had the
largest program and also was the contracting agency
through which ARPA usually carried out its own work),
while the press helped several more projects to come
apart at the seams over the next several months. The
DOD's silence, it seems in retrospect, probably added
to the appearance of guilt and whetted the appetite of
the press. This was a result that might have been
foreseen; but even if it had been, it probably would
have made no difference in the decision not to respond.

One of the first of the additional projects to suffer was the new journal, Conflict. This was to be a
"Quarterly Journal of Revolution and Change," published
by SORO in their new role at the center of the DOD's
applied research program. Volume I, Number 1, had,
over the previous year, been prepared for distribution
by about July, 1965, throughout interested parts of

the government and the research community. The first
issue would have made a strong beginning. It contained,
among other things, an article about Vietnam by Henry
Cabot Lodge; an article by an eminent China scholar,
William C. Johnstone, about Communist Chinese counterinsurgency in Tibet; a description of the State Department's National Interdepartmental Seminar, by its Director, Ambassador R. A. Kidder; and a section of articles
about the history, geography, and politics of Colombia,
by a list of distinguished scholars as well as the New
York Times correspondent in Bogota, and General Andrew
O'Meara, former Commander of the U.S. Southern Command.
But this section on Colombia, juxtaposed as it was in
July against the background of attacks on the Army's
research interest in Latin America, caused the Army to
have second thoughts. With the agreement of DDR&E and
the OSD Public Affairs Office, it was decided to post-
pone distribution of the first issue of the journal
until a more propitious time. This intelligence was
somehow picked up by Walter Pincus, who used it as the
basis for a story in the Washington Star on August 17.
It was no longer possible to release the journal quietly, and it quietly died. With it died the opportunity
to establish another forum of exchange of information
important to government officials and those who assisted them.

The same article by Pincus mentioned two additional
SORO projects--Colony and Simpatico. The first, which
was being carried out by a SORO anthropologist in Peru

with Peruvian government approval and assistance, had
been under way when Camelot broke. It involved observation and analysis of Peruvian army efforts to assist
the economic development and integration of the Indians
in the trans-Andean highlands into the Peruvian economy
and society. The results of the study were also intended to assist the U.S. Army to develop its "civic
action" doctrines for military assistance to the armies
of the developing nations. It will be remembered that
the 1963 Smithsonian report had recommended, as an important area of research, the study of the constructive
role that the military in developing countries could
play in improving social conditions. "Civic action"
was a fundamental part of the American military counterinsurgency doctrine, but it was generally taken on
faith that it was a good doctrine. It was recognized
that it would be important to obtain some real data to
ascertain whether, in fact, assistance by a country's
military forces in local economic development, education, and technical training did build social cohesiveness and political awareness in a country's outlying
areas.

This, too, is a question of value judgment as well
as objective observation. Civic action could be
viewed as a means by which a military dictatorship can
indoctrinate its population and thereby eliminate opposition to itself. Some of this flavor adhered to the
Army's efforts, in the press reports. The study was
completed prematurely under stringent constraints in

Peru, and was to be continued in Bolivia where a similar Bolivian Army development effort was being planned.
But the American Ambassador in Bolivia became skittish
as a result of the publicity over Project Colony and
the Camelot furor, and although the Bolivian government
and CINCSO had agreed upon and approved the project, it
was cancelled at the ambassador's request.

Simpatico, which had been planned earlier but begun
in the summer of 1965 while the Army was under fire,
had a more spectacular demise. It, too, was concerned
with military civic action--in the strife-torn country
of Colombia. A psychologist and an anthropologist
were working in a remote area of the country, where
the Colombian army was trying to pacify the ubiquitous
banditry and terrorism of many years' standing by gaining the support of local villagers. Using structured
questionnaires and such psychological "instruments" as
the thematic apperception test,[7] the researchers were
trying to learn the villagers' attitudes toward the
government, the army, and the turbulent events in their
society. While questions later arose regarding the
scientific validity of their techniques in that setting,
this was not in question at the time. The Colombian
government was fully aware of the project, having approved and welcomed it, and maintained close contact
with the research results in which it obviously had a
strong interest. The two American researchers had arranged to hire a Colombian research firm to carry out
most of the field work. Thus, the project was follow-

ing the two precepts for study in foreign countries
suggested in the 1963 Smithsonian report:  it had local
government approval and interest, and the local research community was involved.

The trouble arose during an election campaign, when
the Colombian government was attacked by its opponents
for permitting, or perhaps even using, the perpetrators
of Camelot to undertake similar nefarious "espionage"
efforts in Colombia.  The story of the blowup appeared
in the New York Times on February 6, 1966.  According
to that story, the Colombian researchers, who were politically oriented against the government, had objected
to the nature of the information sought in the research
and had taken their complaints to the opposition party.
The Times's news article became the subject of a speech
the next day by Senator Fred Harris of Oklahoma on the
Senate floor; he questioned the propriety and advisability of DOD undertaking social research at all.  Senator Harris was soon to start hearings on the creation
of a National Social Science Foundation to do such
work.  On Sunday, February 13, an article by Dan Kurzman in the Washington Post discussed the question of
DOD social research overseas, based on the Simpatico
news.  In a well-balanced article, Kurzman pointed out
the reasons behind the DOD's stated need for the research, and the fears of opponents of such DOD research
that "the Pentagon hopes to determine the minimum
amount of social and economic support that must be
given the peasants and other lower class groups in

order to avert a revolution." But the more general attitude was reflected by the headline, which said "Hey
Senor! Do You Beat Your Wives Often?" The study did
not survive.

Thus, in the six months or so after Camelot became
a public issue, the press had shown again, as it had
many times elsewhere, that it could raise an issue
that was to change profoundly how the government went
about its business. It became the means whereby Congress became aware and involved. As we shall see, it
stimulated and reinforced discussion among diverse
parts of the interested scientific community, who might
otherwise have tried to resolve the questions raised
in a more leisurely, quiet, and reasoned atmosphere.
It helped establish the relationship between the events
of the DOD social research program and the broader issues that were concerning the nation. It imposed the
reporters' and editors' value judgments on the news,
and thereby initiated reconsideration of the value system under which the DOD was involved overseas and was
undertaking research to support its involvement. It
allowed itself to be used by one part of the federal
bureaucracy to attack another, for reasons that appeared not to have been purely those of high principle.
And, of course, it was the rapid drumfire of press reports, almost universally critical in tone and attitude, that caused the DOD itself to take another look
at what it was doing, and how, and to try to change
its approach.

It is, perhaps, needless to add (but nevertheless too tempting to resist) the personal note that this view, from the "inside," of the functioning of the press on an important issue makes one loth to take at face value any other press descriptions of important issues and events where there is no personal knowledge and experience.

The news stories, the editorials, the congressional
reaction, and the State Department all seemed to convey
the tone that the DOD was a dullard who had somehow
stepped out of line and needed to be prodded and
watched, lest he do so again.  But the DOD was not,
before or after the Camelot story, unmindful of the
problems and the sensitivities involved in the social
research it sponsored.  And before it was prodded, it
moved to try to limit the damage and prevent a recur-
rence.  The sudden realization that faith in the discretion of the presumed experts on social studies
might have been misplaced led to what was consistently
fought by the researchers and research managers as
overreaction, but what the overseers of that research
consistently forced to go further.  The first problem
was to reduce vulnerabilities elsewhere.  In ODDR&E we
started an immediate search to ascertain what researchers were overseas, where, and under what circumstances.
Where their presence was known to local American authorities and local governments--largely in Southeast
Asia--we could relax somewhat.  Where their presence
was not known, the attempt was made to have them come
home.  It had become obvious that ambassadors everywhere had become uneasy and hypersensitive.  From our
point of view in ODDR&E, as well as that of the ambassadors, it wouldn't do to have DOD-supported researchers discovered by the press to be working in "their"

countries.  However, the Service research managers who
had given grants to university scholars to study overseas objected strenuously.  The scholars had been working overseas for years without such problems developing.  They had intimate friends and contacts within
the governments and scholarly communities where they
were doing their research.  Interference with these
scholars' academic freedom was, they said, unwarranted,
and the scholars had given sufficient evidence over
the years that they could be trusted.

This posed, for the first time in this context, an
issue that was not to be resolved until the DOD and
the university social science community separated, by
more or less mutual agreement, and with some considerable trouble for some of the individuals involved.
But this is getting ahead of the story.  The result of
the reflex was the review, on an individual basis, of
each of the few cases where researchers were found to
be overseas.  A decision was made in each case as to
whether the damage--to the project, to the scholar, to
the DOD, to foreign relations--would be worse if the
research were to be interrupted, or left alone with
the risk of surfacing in the press; and a few people
were asked quietly to drop their research and come
home, at least temporarily.

In the meantime, the spate of news stories about
Camelot and the gradual unfolding, in our private
councils within the DOD, of the story of SORO's lack
of discretion had confirmed our earlier fears about

the project and its leadership.  It became clear, as
the days went by, that it could not pick up where it
left off with any semblance of credibility.  What little faith we had had in SORO's ability to do the work
was destroyed as their lack of sensitivity to the ex-
plosive issue of interference in Latin American affairs
became apparent.  The decision was therefore made to
cancel the project, and the discussion turned to how
the other pieces of the overall program might be re-
assembled.  The cancellation became a political issue
when the DOD was notified on July 5 that Congressman
Dante Fascell, chairman of the Subcommittee on International Organizations and Movements of the House
Foreign Affairs Committee, was planning hearings on
the Camelot affair, and inquiring whether DDR&E would
be willing to testify.  Work on the cancellation memo
was rushed, and the memo was sent from Harold Brown to
the Secretary of the Army on July 7.  It stated simply
that the recent events surrounding Camelot had shown
that the approach to research of that type needed modification.  In part, it would have to be handled so as
not to be open to distortion in the communist press
abroad, and not to embarrass the United States if performed on an unclassified basis.  It was clear that
although the type of research represented by Camelot
remained important, the usefulness of the particular
project was destroyed.  Therefore, it was requested
that the project be cancelled, and the Army was asked
to formulate a plan to carry out the research to pro-

vide the military forces with the information they
would need if they were called upon to engage in counterinsurgency assistance abroad.  It also suggested
that the handling of the events leading to the Camelot
furor raised questions about the effectiveness of
SORO's management.  Therefore, the Army was asked to
look into that, too, although they were given liberty
to use SORO to assist in the preparation of new research plans.

   Although a lengthy press release was drafted, the
one finally issued said simply:

The Defense Department announced today that the Army's
Project CAMELOT has been reevaluated in the light of
preliminary planning conducted to date.  It has been
concluded that the project as currently designed will
not produce the desired information, and the project
is therefore being terminated.

While somewhat disingenuous in ignoring the current
furor, this was an accurate reflection of the facts.
But it was not used by the press--the image of lack of
credibility had been created.  The newspapers played
up the juxtaposition of the cancellation and Vallance's
testimony before the Fascell subcommittee, as though
it had been spitefully arranged.  The cancellation was
attributed to McNamara, or the President, or the State
Department's influence.  The DOD image and the overseas
social research program suffered some more.

   A few days later there was an exchange of phone
calls and letters between Secretaries McNamara and

Rusk, initiated by the latter (or, quite likely, by
someone of his staff). An American professor was questioning European government officials as part of a
study, under Navy auspices, of the "strategic thinking
of European elites," and Rusk was informing McNamara
that the governments were protesting. It turned out
that the project had begun under private foundation
sponsorship, but then had been picked up and expanded
by Project Michelson. The professor had not told his
interviewees of his government support--raising another
issue that was to reach its peak when the CIA scandals
broke in 1967. But the professor's connection was previously known to the State Department through routine
reporting and information exchange. It can generously
be concluded that the heightened sensitivities of the
period changed their view of it, and made any officials
involved less receptive in their attitude. It did not
seem to be noticed that the State Department officials
who knew of the project earlier, but raised no "red
flags," might be equally culpable. Secretary Rusk was
promised that, "In the future, Defense or Military Department support for studies involving the use of such
[interview] techniques abroad will be individually coordinated with your Department before implementation."

On July 12, a memorandum from the Secretary of Defense to all parts of the DOD stated that:

Hereafter all studies done in or for the Department of
Defense, the conduct of which may affect the relations
of the United States with foreign governments, are to

be cleared with the Office of the Assistant Secretary
of Defense (International Security Affairs) before
they are initiated.

This was welcomed by us in DDR&E as a useful step to
protect our efforts from what had by then begun to appear (to us) as a calculated effort by State to destroy
those efforts.  The period of negotiation with our
counterparts in ISA followed, intermixed with preparations to meet the Fascell subcommittee and intense negotiations with State that will be described later.

The Brown-Mann telephone call that had resulted in
agreement about leaks and "titles," had also elicited
the intelligence that the DOD's attempts to study problems of revolution and insurgency overseas were still
viewed with favor, at that level at least, and that,
in view of recent events, cooperation between the departments was all the more to be welcomed.  The "package" of memos and letters that had been prepared for
signature in June, asking the Army to establish a
joint office for social science research and inviting
the other agencies to participate, appeared particularly appropriate in view of all the accusations about
unilateral and uncoordinated DOD activity in the area,
and it was dispatched on July 16.  It was a forlorn
hope.  Friendly and encouraging answers were received
from all the other agencies, and the Services began to
designate people for the office.  But the appointment
of representatives from outside the DOD was delayed
for one reason or another.  Later congressional action

on the budget rendered the effort pointless anyway,
and it all came to naught.  Once again, however, the
DOD was on record as recognizing the sensitivities
and responsibilities associated with what it was trying
to do.  Once again, the record was private; it never
reached public attention and had no impact on later
events.

Shortly thereafter, on July 18, another guidance
paper was issued by DDR&E regarding the work in question.  The paper had, of course, been "coordinated"
with ISA and State, as well as with key members of the
social science community who were made aware of its
contents.  It dealt with the problem of sensitivity of
studies of foreign social systems related to counterinsurgency, and spelled out detailed guidelines for
the conduct of such work.  It pointed out, first, the
dangers that could arise from having the complete nature of research projects in counterinsurgency of
interest to the DOD widely known.  Since such work
could be injurious to United States foreign policy and
therefore to the national security, it properly came
within the definition of research that could be classified.  If any of the research were to be unclassified,
it would have to be divided into small, individually
innocent tasks.  The issue of whether the DOD--or other
agencies with action responsibilities--could under any
circumstances undertake studies of the kind in question
was not yet raised within the DOD; that was to come
much later.  Guidelines were established for clearance

of projects.  These were different for contract researchers and university scholars working under grants.
Unequivocally, contract research projects were required to be cleared by the military commander responsible for American DOD activities in the country where
the research was to be carried out; the latter responsibility included checking with the American Ambassador and the local government.  No travel was to be
undertaken without specific, separate clearance for
each trip.

It had been made known to us by several people in
the university community, largely those working with
ONR and AFOSR grants, that that community did not feel
it could tolerate such stringent constraints on its
activities.  We were still, at the time, sympathetic
and sensitive on the issue of academic freedom.  In
their case, therefore, although prior coordination of
projects was required, and the existence and details
of the projects had to be made known to overseas military commanders, ambassadors, and governments, the
freedom to travel and undertake the research, once a
project had been initiated, was left to the discretion
of the scholar.  He was, however, to notify his sponsor when such activities were undertaken.

These instructions were later to form the basis of
DOD continuation of its research in this area, even
though there were overlays of instructions from ISA
and the State Department.  The contract organizations
presented no particular problem--they accepted the work

with the conditions attached--and there was no attempt
to control substance, only procedures [we were to learn
later (Chapters 18 and 19) that the separation was not
easy or even possible to maintain, in most cases]. But
even with our nod to the sensibilities of the academic
community and their sponsors in the Services, both objected to the lesser degree of control with which they
were asked to abide. The academic community made the
point that once a study was agreed upon, they were the
best judges of how to go about it. Clearance of their
projects and control of their movements and contacts
would amount to control of their work. Despite the
mounting evidence to the contrary, they insisted that
their discretion was to be trusted, and that any regu-
lation at all amounted to interference with and control
of the academic process. We were sympathetic, but it
seemed obvious that some controls would have to be instituted if there were to be any research at all. The
guidance memorandum tried to reconcile the arguments
and establish special conditions for the academic researchers; but the problem did not go away.

At about this same time there was much discussion
of the titles and the public image of the work. The
problem seemed to be that in the sciences that were
more esoteric in the public view--for example, physics
or chemistry--the public accepted that there would be
a specialized language and didn't question it. "Social
science" was a different matter. The public expects
that studies involving people will be described in

plain English.  The fact that psychologists or sociologists or anthropologists may have developed their own
specialized languages--jargons--to go with the particular techniques of their research is much less recognized.  The problem this poses is, that if their work
is described in plain English, the public often doesn't
see what there is to study; examples will emerge later
of studies whose results appeared obvious after they
were obtained, although they were not always predicted
in advance.  And if a study is described in technical
language, it appears to some that jargon is being used
to cover up something that should be obvious.  Unfortunately, that is often true.  In the words of the
House Armed Forces Appropriations Subcommittee report
on the DOD R&D budget that year, some "studies appear
to be concerned with trivial matters on which intelligent people should not require studies in order to be
informed."[1]  The further problem, however, is that
there is often disagreement among reasonable people
about what is trivial or obvious.  The earlier DSB report had made a fairly solid case that there was very
much that was not known.  The problem was to convey
this message outside DOD.  DOD officialdom at a high
level was, of course, sympathetic to the public's problem, because the project descriptions were not couched
in their language, either.

Steps were initiated to have all descriptive material on social science projects, especially that which
might easily become public information, reviewed for

language, and to have at least the statements of the
projects' objectives, if not the descriptions of the
research techniques used, couched in plain English.
The connection between the research task and the DOD's
interest and mission was to be made clear. We even
toyed with the idea of making up a list of proscribed
words, apparently simple words that seemed always to
elicit a negative emotional response in some quarters--
examples might be, "cross-cultural," "motivation,"
"socio-political," "attitudinal stimuli," "cognitive
skills"--but common sense prevailed. This was an extraordinarily difficult instruction to put across to
those who were speaking in their accustomed, everyday
language, and the attempt to shield the social scientists from the outraged senator or the amused newsman
remained a struggle through the years.

A month after the latest McNamara and DDR&E instructions, on August 10, 1965, ISA issued its more detailed instructions for clearance procedures. In general, the control to be exercised was prudent but permissive. It was pointed out that "it is the manner in
which the proposed study is to be conducted, not subject matter per se, which is at issue." ISA would not
address subject matter unless there were some other
legitimate ISA interest, or duplication that might not
have been apparent to the initiators. The fact that
subject matter could be crucial if the fact of the
study were made public had still not penetrated; but
it would very shortly. The key point of the instruc-

tion was that it continued to leave to the judgment of
the sponsoring agency within DOD the decision as to
which studies required special attention and clearance.

This was to change again, within another month. At
that time Mr. Vance, the Deputy Secretary of Defense,
learned of a study planned by one of the Services to
explore public and congressional attitudes toward a
particular kind of weapon system, one that was at the
moment very controversial with respect to Vietnam, and
otherwise. The exploration was to use interview techniques. It was a small study, to be done wholly within
the United States, and hadn't even been brought to
DDR&E attention (it didn't have to be, then). The
next day, September 10, a memorandum from Mr. Vance
directed that each Military Department and OSD "designate a single representative who will review and approve all RFP's (requests for proposals) and contracts
or grants for research outside the physical sciences..."
This was broad and restrictive, indeed. The person
generally designated in each agency was the General
Counsel. He had been given no additional staff, and
was busy enough without this added duty. Strict implementation of this directive could be counted upon
to bring all social and behavioral science research to
a halt; and clearly, other studies, using operations
research or systems analysis, and having to do with
the effectiveness of military operations, weapons systems, and force structure, could also be included.

As Rains Wallace pointed out in a memorandum to

DDR&E on the subject of controls and clearances, a
"bureaucratic hydra" had been born:

For example, a contract with a university psychology
department to examine foreign research publications on
programmed learning would, in addition to the regular
review procedures required for any contract, and some
procedure for terminology review, be cleared by a
special representative in the particular Military Department, ISA, and possibly the State Department before the contract could be released for bid.  A contract to evaluate the effectiveness of a computerized
system for personnel assignment would receive the regular review, the terminology review, and the political
and public relations review.  Even assuming that the
various reviewing agencies would limit themselves to
the specific aspects assigned to them (which seems unlikely), it is apparent that the opportunities for
delay and infanticide are tremendous.

He also pointed out that the inclusion of behavioral
and social sciences together in all of the review instructions was penalizing the majority of work in
these areas (which was internal to the DOD, carried
out in the United States, and needed for things like
recruitment, human performance assessment, training,
and human factors engineering) for the difficulty
caused by a small fraction of the work.  He proposed
separating the categories into psychological sciences
and social sciences, and subjecting the latter, only,
to the required additional review.  This was not accepted.

But after many months of trial, the stringency of
the review requirements was relaxed somewhat in imple-

mentation.  The kinds of studies requiring review were
sorted out, and only certain studies required detailed
examination.  In the ARPA case (the one with which I
am most familiar), all such studies went to the OSD
General Counsel for review when in the planning stage,
before money was committed.  Delay rarely exceeded two
weeks, except in those cases where a real issue existed
and warranted the delay.  A response could be obtained
in a day or two, if needed.  After this, it did not
require further review at this level unless a substantive change was being considered.  Thus, while at first
the internal controls appeared onerous and unworkable,
they were applied sensibly, and did help the DOD exercise more positive control over the conduct of work
that remained controversial.

At the same time, steps were taken to help the DOD
sort out what it could and should try to do in the area
of social research, and to smooth its interaction with
the social science community.  Within a few days after
the first Pincus story, I was called by George Murdock,
an anthropologist from the University of Pittsburgh,
who also headed the Social Science Division of the
National Academy of Sciences/National Research Council.
I went to see him at the NAS/NRC offices in Washington,
and he put the problem straight and frankly:  something had to be done about DOD's social science research, since it seemed out of control and recent
events were endangering all social science research.
I accepted this as a legitimate expression of concern.

In retrospect, it probably foretold the attitude of
most of the anthropologists, who became the first, the
loudest, and the harshest against their colleagues undertaking work for government agencies having operational concerns overseas.  Out of the discussions with
Murdock arose the idea of establishing an NAS/NRC Committee on Social Sciences, to examine DOD's needs and
its role, and to see what might be done to improve
the situation.  The DDR&E accepted the idea, and in
fact felt it would be worthwhile enough that he initiated a request to the NAS to establish the committee.

The request pointed out the difficulties of work
overseas, its sensitivity, and asked the NAS to explore
how the DOD could accomplish the needed research without, at the same time, creating antagonisms and suspicion on the part of foreign governments.  It asked,
also, for advice on how the problems could be studied
in such a way that the communist press wouldn't pick
them up and, by adverse publicity and distortion,
create conditions under which the work would be impossible to do.  There was still no thought that the DOD
shouldn't do such work, or that it was improper.  In
fact, the discussions at high levels within DOD, with
the State Department (until Rusk's testimony before
Fascell), and with members of the social science community showed that there was still a general feeling
that the DOD's research program was necessary; the
point was made everywhere (and in Fascell's later report) that the problem with Camelot was not what was

intended to be learned, but how it was done.

A number of problems had to be resolved.  One was
the makeup of the committee.  Hostility toward the DOD
was becoming widespread in the social science community.  It was not necessary to establish a committee to
say that the DOD shouldn't do social research, since
there were by then many sources of that advice; one
was needed to deal with the problem of how such research should be done.  It was obvious from the comments of many social scientists, reported in the press,
that the DOD position would not at this time be generally understood or accepted.  Therefore, it was desired that at least some people on the committee be
familiar with how the DOD worked, and with the problems
it faced.  This is a problem in all bodies established
to review public programs--it appears, for example,
when the Atomic Energy Commission establishes a committee to review radiation standards.  There is a public
presumption of conflict of interest if the committee
members have worked with the agency; but not much help
can be expected if they don't understand intimately
how the agency works, and they are not likely to understand this if they haven't worked with the agency.
Therefore, a good deal of thought and discussion went
into the makeup of the nominees to the committee, and
the balance among their backgrounds.  Then, it had to
be decided whether the National Academy should deal
only with the DOD problem, and whether it was proper
to fund the committee from the DOD.  Obviously, other

agencies were concerned, and the committee should have
broader interests.  But it was pointed out that tradi-
tionally one agency can perceive a general need and
take the lead in asking the Academy for assistance,
with other agencies joining later in the sponsorship.

The letter requesting that the committee be established was sent on July 28, 1965, but it was November
before all the problems were resolved and the membership arranged; the first meeting was held on November
9.*  State was immediately invited to participate.
They were, of course, interested in the problem.  But
more to the point, they had by then been assigned review responsibility over all research having to do with
foreign areas, and the social science community was
deeply concerned about whether the State review procedures and controls might not be so restrictive as to

---

*The members finally appointed to the committee before
 the first meeting were Drs.:  Gabriel A. Almond, Stan-
 ford University, Political Science; Alex Bavelas,
 Stanford University, Psychology; Albert H. Garretson,
 New York University, Law; Allen R. Holmberg, Cornell
 University, Sociology and Anthropology; Morris Jano-
 witz, University of Chicago, Sociology; Lyle H.
 Lanier, University of Illinois, Psychology; Wilbert
 E. Moore, Russell Sage Foundation, Sociology; Karl J.
 Pelzer, Yale University, Geography; Ithiel de Sola
 Pool, M.I.T., Political Science; Herbert A. Simon,
 Carnegie Institute of Technology, Psychology; Thomas
 C. Schelling, Harvard University, Economics; Alexan-
 der Spoehr, University of Pittsburgh, Anthropology;
 George K. Tanham, The RAND Corporation, Political
 Science; and Donald R. Young, Rockefeller University,
 Anthropology (Chairman).  The membership varied some-
 what through the years, of course.

strangle all research overseas.  Thus, the DOD had
taken another step to try to put its house in order,
by asking for external review of its efforts by the
scientific community, and by starting to build a focal
point where the DOD, the State Department and the
social science community could converge and seek help
in an impartial arena.  It was hoped, also, that this
group might help reestablish the atmosphere of acceptance that had been created by the earlier committees
of social scientists who had advised the DOD (note
that there was some overlap in the membership), at the
same time that they helped the DOD fit into the new
world that had been created, in part by its own efforts.

The NAS/NRC Committee later broadened its efforts
to examine the more general problem of the sponsorship
and use of research in the social sciences by government.  Reports were issued in 1968[2] and 1971,[3] and
Lyons' book about social science and government, The
Uneasy Partnership,[4] grew out of his work with the
committee.  Although the committee was established
initially to give immediate advice to the DOD, its
pace, resulting from the time it took to explore the
issues in depth, was such that it didn't influence the
DOD's program.  In the next few years, as a sponsor of
DOD applied research using social scientists overseas,
I was asked to meet with the committee a few times.  I
was not offered, nor did I ask for, advice or guidance
from it.  Having been set up for one purpose, it then

took on a life and direction of its own.  We shall return to its reports in due course.

It was now obvious that unrestrained research in
the social sciences having to do with problems that
had important political implications was not going to
work.  The mechanism--which included American researchers, overseas military commanders, ambassadors, foreign
governments, foreign scholars, parts of the foreign
press, the American press, and growing parts of the
American scholarly community that were not directly
involved--was too delicately balanced, and offered too
many opportunities for something to go wrong, to hope
that overseas research on matters of substance and
sensitivity could be carried out without rather strict
controls.  Perhaps a hundred researchers could be dis-
creet, establish effective working relationships, and
carry out their work with delicacy and tact.  If the
hundred-and-first didn't, and this led to a blowup,
the work of the other hundred was immediately jeopardized.  Moreover, the idea was growing in the U.S.
press and in Congress that it was improper for the
DOD--and even other operating agencies of government--
to carry out studies of social systems.  The DOD was
therefore pulling in its horns, as well as trying to
find alternative means to undertake the work it did
wish to accomplish.  This would soon have an important
effect on its relationships with the university community (Chapter 17).

The State Department raised the issue of who would
control research on "foreign affairs." The questions
of what research was needed by the country, or how it
was to be performed, and if not by DOD then by whom,
were not raised until much later, and in a different
forum. By a series of maneuvers that left us in DOD
breathless and on the defensive, State gained the
sympathy of Congress and the public for its own position. The problem for supporters of the social research program in DOD, then, became that of trying to
reassert some reasonable limits on the power State had
gained. In this we were aided by the Budget Bureau
and, perhaps surprisingly, by some members of the
social science community.

After the June 27 meeting in Colonel Sullivan's
office on the Chile blowup, there was virtually no
further ODDR&E contact with members of the State Department until after the Fascell hearings, well into August.
The series of news stories about DOD research overseas,
fed by what seemed to be a carefully orchestrated sequence of leaks from State, led to the high-level telephone call described earlier. By then, other events
occurred to keep the program in the news. But the
earlier series of stories did manage to create an appropriate climate for State's later coup.

There was, in the interim, a lengthy private correspondence between Harold Brown and Ambassador Dungan in

Chile, who had known each other before.  In that correspondence, the positions of the two departments were
laid out clearly; it was unfortunate that the correspondence was never made public.  Dungan, although he
was not a career foreign service officer, reflected
perfectly what we in DOD took to be the State Department view of social research (perhaps he, too, had a
member of his staff, who was a foreign service officer,
prepare the initial drafts of the letters for him).
He expressed anger at what he considered to be the
bumbling and clumsy interference of the military in
affairs that were properly his concern; if DOD had
money to throw around, he said, he could hire two more
good political officers who would be worth more than
any number of research projects.  He questioned whether
the kind of research planned by the DOD was feasible
or useful at all, and he questioned the propriety of
DOD's funding research in foreign countries, regardless
of coordination with foreign governments and collaboration with foreign scholars.  The DOD position--that it
was deeply involved overseas and needed the information
that the research could provide, and that there seemed
no other agency with the concern and the budget to obtain it--did not sway him, despite apologies over the
occasional clumsiness of some of the researchers.  The
tone of his letters seemed to offer no room for doubt
that the diplomatic staff made no mistakes, while the
DOD's representatives almost invariably did, in deal-
ings with foreign governments.  Of course, the conflict

between military and civilian was strong in Latin America, and American military assistance, with its uses and abuses, was always very much an issue, so that one could hardly have expected him to take a calm or dispassionate view.

On Saturday, July 31, I had gone to the office to try to dispose of some of the backlog of other work that had piled up during the initial stages of the Camelot battle. On opening my safe, I found there—apparently delivered to and deposited by my secretary while I was at a meeting the day before—a letter from Secretary Rusk to Secretary McNamara, which had come to me for preparation of the reply.* The reply was due on the following Monday, August 2. The "Dear Bob" letter indicated that he (Rusk) was due to testify before Dante Fascell's subcommittee shortly, and before he did he would like McNamara's concurrence with a proposed letter, draft attached, for the signature of the President. The proposed letter, at first glance, gave the Secretary of State ironclad control over "government-sponsored social science research in the area of foreign policy." These words were to become the centerpiece of later arguments and maneuvers.

Thus I learned of the bureaucratic ploy which,

---

*It has been said of Washington officialdom, that no one in a responsible position ever writes a letter he signs, or signs a letter he writes. While this may be somewhat apocryphal, the incident to be described would not destroy the legend.

being forewarned and therefore forearmed, I was able
to resist in the future. This consisted of joining an
issue needing extensive consideration and discussion
without leaving time for such consideration and discussion, in the hope that the issue would be resolved
in haste and in State's favor. Fortunately, on that
Saturday those who had to agree to any proposed reply
before it could go to the Secretary for signature,
especially Harold Brown and John McNaughton, the
Assistant Secretary (ISA), were both in the Pentagon,
and available.

The reply did not explicitly request that the proposed letter not be sent to the President for signature.
Instead, it reviewed briefly the problems of and the
need for the research, and pointed out that five key
agencies were involved: State, AID, DOD, USIA, and
CIA. It proposed that a research council be established, at the level of Assistant Secretary, to review
economic, social, and political research needs for
all the agencies and decide among themselves what
should be done, and which departments or agencies
should undertake particular tasks. The decisions of
this group would be binding, or, in case of argument,
sent to the cabinet level for resolution. Thus was
escalated an idea that had germinated during the
earlier discussions among the research directors of
the agencies concerned. It would persist and reappear
in various forms for many years.

The letter of reply, addressed "Dear Dean," was

signed "Bob" on Monday, and sent, with the anticipation
that it would discourage the Secretary of State from
having his proposed letter signed by the President.
Great was our surprise, therefore, when on Wednesday,
August 4, Secretary Rusk, in his testimony before the
Fascell subcommittee, revealed that the President had
just sent him the following letter, dated August 2:[1]

Many agencies of the government are sponsoring social
science research which focuses on foreign areas and
peoples and thus relates to the foreign policy of the
United States.  Some of it involves residence and
travel in foreign countries and communication with
foreign nations.  As we have recently learned, it can
raise problems affecting the conduct of our foreign
policy.

For that reason I am determined that no government
sponsorship of foreign area research should be undertaken which in the judgment of the Secretary of State
would adversely affect United States foreign relations.
Therefore I am asking you to establish effective procedures which will enable you to assure the propriety
of government-sponsored social science research in the
area of foreign policy.  I suggest that you consult
with the director of the Bureau of the Budget to determine the proper procedures for the clearance of
foreign affairs research projects on a government-wide
basis.

  Along with his publication of the President's
letter, Secretary Rusk sent a letter to all agency and
department heads in government, informing them of the
President's instructions, and saying that to implement
it he had established a "Foreign Affairs Research
Council."  This was to be chaired by the director of
the Bureau of Intelligence and Research, and include

representatives of other offices in State such as the
regional bureaus, the Office of Politico-Military Affairs, and the Policy Planning Council. Supported by
a staff (which came to include the very people we had
been dealing with before Camelot, and who had expressed
the desire to control DOD's research program), they
would "formulate policy for departmental action with
respect to Government-sponsored research bearing on
foreign affairs....determine Department needs for
foreign area research...(and)...also examine Government-
sponsored research projects in terms of the foreign
policy risks....and means for reducing such risks."[2]
Over the same period of time, during which DOD was
trying to exercise control over its own program, and
on into the fall of 1965 (and beyond), the discussions
and conflicts with State were to revolve around the
last of these assigned responsibilities.

   The first argument about State's responsibility to
review and exercise control over DOD's (and other
agencies') research arose within DOD itself. This was
over how to deal with State. Those of us in ODDR&E
who had been involved from the start were firmly convinced from the discussions we had had with State
before the Camelot affair, and from what we had observed
of and read into their behavior since, that it was
pressing hard to gain a stranglehold on the DOD research program. ISA took the position that the President's letter was a reasonable expression of policy,
and that a means had to be found to implement it. ISA

therefore wanted to cooperate from the start, to help
State organize to review overseas reserach; whereas in
ODDR&E we wanted to hold back, to see precisely what
State had in mind before offering anything. The resolution of the argument was brought about primarily by
State itself. Before State published its proposed review procedures, ISA had sent to it for review a project description for a policy planning study, to be
performed by Henry Kissinger (then at Harvard), regarding a problem of national security originating
overseas. It was a project that John McNaughton,
personally, felt was important and should be undertaken. State reviewed the project and refused to
clear it, arguing that it was too sensitive; where-
upon the intra-DOD positions converged, focusing on
the issue that State was extending itself to judging
the substance, and deciding on approval, of DOD's work
rather than (as Rusk's letter had stated) limiting
itself to finding means for, and advising on, reducing
the risks that might have been involved.

In this, DOD was supported at the many discussions
with State by the Budget Bureau, whose policy remained
that one department of government should not exercise
ultimate control over work done by another using money
appropriated for that work by Congress. Enforcement
.of this policy position was doubtless aided by the
fact that one or two key Budget Bureau positions were
occupied by people who had formerly been with the
Defense Department.

The issues involved were several, all interacting.
First, State was planning to establish a staff to review the work that would be larger than the total DOD
staff in ISA, ODDR&E, and the Services responsible for
planning, contracting for, and overseeing it.  This
appeared to be Parkinsonism, with a vengeance; it was
obvious to us in the DOD that the work of review was
less than the work of planning and implementation, but
(we assumed) would be extended "to fill the time available," delaying or stopping virtually all work.  Secondly, and more fundamentally, the question arose as to
whether a group of people who had never performed or
managed research could sensibly review it. (We assumed
that State would appoint such people to its council.)
How, for example, could they understand what research
techniques were "sensitive," if they had never employed
them?  How could they appreciate the interaction among
problem definition, methodology, and results, if they
had never been through the process themselves?

This issue so troubled a number of the social scientists who were aware of or involved in the DOD programs,
and many others who had performed research under other
government agency sponsorship (including the National
Science Foundation), that they took it up directly
with State and also with the newly formed National
Academy of Sciences committee.  It led directly to the
invitation to State to attend the first meeting of
that committee.  Even those social scientists who were
not sympathetic to the DOD efforts feared the poten-

tially stultifying effect of review of social science
research by those who had never performed any, and who
had purely bureaucratic motives.  Thus, in this time
of shifting alliances, DOD found strong support where
in the absence of the threat none would have existed.

The argument then shifted to definition of the
scope of the work that State would have to review.  At
first, the staff of the Foreign Affairs Research Council proposed that they should review all work with
foreign policy implications.  They stated that in their
interpretation any American presence overseas had such
implications, so that this would include virtually all
R&D performed overseas.  We in DOD pointed out that
overseas programs had many facets.  The Services were
supporting work in basic physics and chemistry at
foreign universities.  There were weapons and equipment
being tested in Southeast Asia related to the war
there.  ARPA and the Army had research programs overseas to measure the parameters of the physical environment affecting, for example, how off-road vehicles
could move through jungle and rice paddies, or how
radio waves propagated through the jungle, for use in
designing communications equipment.  There were also
operations research studies, in Vietnam, Europe, and
elsewhere, of military operations and their effectiveness; and there were studies in detail of the motivations, organization, and operations of guerrillas in
Vietnam and Thailand.  None of these appeared to us
to fall within the definition of "social science re-

search in the area of foreign policy."

With Budget Bureau support, we insisted that the scope of State's review process be limited to a literal interpretation of those words: that is, work performed by social scientists to help determine what foreign policy should be, or the implications of alternative foreign policies.* Very little of the DOD program, or of the research called out in the DSB report, fell in the area of this definition, it seemed to us. The State people made the point that even hardware research could cause foreign policy problems if done improperly. But we noted that no such work was ever undertaken without the approval and general supervision of U.S. military authorities responsible for the DOD presence in a country, and of the government of the country itself. We noted, also, that if State wanted to include everything, amounting to hundreds of millions of dollars per year of research and development overseas, their staffing problem, both in numbers and disciplines, was hopeless. Nor did we see how they could undertake

---

*As with so many documents drafted for interagency or international purposes, the words in the President's letter, which caused so much argument, probably reflected the originating culture. State's and others' insistence that all work overseas was "foreign policy research" or something akin to it probably arose, not from deliberate distortion, but from the inability of those without technical training to focus precisely on definitions of technical matters that had no meaning for them. Conversely, DOD was likely to see the technical differentiations in detail, but to miss the nuances of policy implication with which it was unfamiliar.

such an effort without getting into the substance of
the work, which was, except for research that fell
within our literal interpretation of the words in the
President's letter, far beyond their competence and
responsibility.

Another key question was whether classified research
performed wholly within the United States should come
within the scope of State's review procedures. By definition, analytical and study work was classified if
its public disclosure could jeopardize the foreign
policy and the national security of the United States.
If it was classified, and therefore not disclosed, and
not performed overseas, we didn't see how it could
"adversely affect United States foreign relations,"
and therefore we didn't see why the Secretary of State
should have to exercise his judgment over it.  State's
position, as with the ISA study they had blocked, was
that "if word of the study gets out..."   But even at
that juncture DOD's record in such matters was not
bad; most often, word got out when others in government, outside the DOD, chose to publicize a study if
they learned of it.*

We pointed out again the impossibility of the task
of reviewing for foreign policy implications all
classified research performed within the United States.
For example, the RAND Corporation alone might have

---

*There was a certain amount of self-discipline within
 the DOD community, in these years before the celebrated exception of the Pentagon Papers.

some dozens of study projects underway in any one- or
two-year period, and since in some way almost all of
them dealt with the defense and national security of
the United States, and therefore with the strategy or
tactics of military operations that could take place
overseas, would State, in addition to the Air Force
and OSD, insist on reviewing all of RAND's program
each year and approving or disapproving all or parts
of it?  And, suppose that in the free-working atmosphere of that organization one of the researchers decided to undertake a brief study to analyze a recent
speech of Ho Chi Minh or De Gaulle (an analysis which
no one in State or DOD might know about until the results were published)--would State insist that their
permission would now have to be obtained in advance?

There were also procedural problems.  In the draft
of proposed clearance procedures that State "floated"
for comment on August 27, 1965, it was proposed that
State "must be informed of a proposed project before
a request for bid is made...or a contract is concluded,"
in addition to "names of researchers and indication of
the time of proposed field work..."  In our interpretation, this meant having to go to State with each
project at least three times--before proposals were
solicited; before the contract was signed; and before
work could begin--and maybe more if contract renewals
or repeated trips abroad were involved.  In addition,
it separated procedures for State, Defense, CIA, AID,
USIA, and the Arms Control Agency from those for any

other agencies.  In the case of the first group, State
"approval" would mean, the draft said, that "State
believes that on balance the value of the project out-
weighs risks of possible adverse effects on foreign
relations."  It also stated that "the timing of consultations with or notifications to missions [i.e., U.S.
embassies in the countries in question, without whose
agreement the research could not be undertaken even by
DOD rules], will depend on the nature of the project."
For the other agencies, a project "will be presumed
cleared unless other State action is communicated to
the agency within fifteen days..." of notification
about the project to State.  Thus, State was at the
same time proposing to exercise judgment over substance
by judging the value of the research to sponsoring
agencies whose missions were different from its own,
and setting the stage for indefinite delay of projects
to be undertaken by a few agencies over whose work
State would thereby have established domination.  But
while it was seeking such authority it was also denying
its own responsibility for the work in case something
should go wrong again, since they also stated that
"clearance is not necessarily an endorsement of the
need, method or value of the project."

    None of this sat very well with any of the agencies
involved, including ISA and the Budget Bureau; and the
social science community also raised a storm.  Arguments over all of these issues continued until State
published its instructions in final form on November

18, 1965.  By then, compromises had been worked out
which met State's minimum requirements, but still resolved all the key issues in a tolerable way for the
DOD.  The instructions began with a definition of
"Government-sponsored foreign affairs research," as
including:

...research programs in the social and behavioral
sciences dealing with international relations, or
with foreign areas and peoples, whether conducted in
the United States or abroad, which are supported by
grants or contracts awarded by agencies of the United
States.  In-house research is not included.

Projects involving foreign travel or contacts with
foreign nationals, sponsored by DOD, USIA, ACDA, AID,
or CIA, were required to be submitted for clearance
(not "approval").  There was a list of exceptions
wherein the need for notification was left to the discretion of the departments or agencies themselves.
The exceptions included projects sponsored by any
other agencies; projects involving foreign travel in
which contacts abroad were to be made with American
officials only; unclassified projects not involving
foreign travel or contact with foreign nationals; and
projects which initially would not require such travel
or contacts, which were excepted until these were required.  Ambassadors were to be kept informed of all
overseas work and travel by the sponsoring agency or
by State, as might be decided for each case.  Classified projects planned to be conducted wholly in the

United States, with no foreign contacts, were completely excluded from clearance requirements. A project
would be cleared once; routine contract administrative
actions, renewals, repeated trips abroad on a cleared
project, and the like, did not have to be submitted
for clearance again. All projects were presumed
cleared if State did not respond to a submission in
fifteen days.

It was stated explicitly that "Research projects
will be reviewed only for the purpose of avoiding adverse effects upon United States foreign relations."
Possibly as reassurance to the social science community,
State added a preamble quoting Secretary Rusk to the
effect that

...The Department has reaped some benefits from the
research of others and, in general, has welcomed the
interest of other departments in social and political
research on foreign affairs.

In addition, ARPA made an informal agreement with
State regarding the work of its field units in Southeast Asia--Vietnam and Thailand. Since ARPA's program
directors were in continual contact with CINCPAC and
the local U.S. military commands, embassies, and
foreign governments, in carefully worked out relationships, all work done by them was closely controlled
without the need for State's intervention. Therefore,
the ambassadors' approval was presumed to be substitu-
ted for that of the State Department, since they would

have to ask the ambassadors in any case. Projects
started by ARPA field units did not have to go through
the State clearance procedures in Washington, but it
was agreed that State would be kept informed of such
projects. Although ARPA tried several times to have
this agreement confirmed in writing, the Bureau of
Intelligence and Research refused, in effect holding
over ARPA's head the threat of accusation of lack of
coordination with State if something went wrong. But
nothing ever did.

By the time State's final instructions were issued,
tempers had cooled; many of those deeply involved had
departed, or were about to depart, from the government
(including myself, temporarily, and Nagle); and "the
system" settled down into a new routine.

ARPA projects, at least (those were the ones with
whose fortunes I remained familiar), went through the
steps of R&D program review, clearance by the OSD
General Counsel, clearance by ISA, and, if necessary,
by State, in addition to the various military, embassy,
and other overseas clearances required by DOD and ARPA
internal procedures. The entire process took several
months--for some projects perhaps a year. But the two
steps that had initially been the most feared--review
by the General Counsel for propriety and germaneness
to the DOD mission, and review by State--seldom, if
ever, added more than a month to the process. In later
years there even came to be some cooperative work between DOD and State.

By the time this routine had been established,
however, Congress and the social science community were
giving ever-closer critical scrutiny to the social science research program and its ramifications.  These
are two other threads of the chronicle that must be
picked up in July of 1965 and followed into succeeding
months and years.

As we have seen, the international furor over Camelot
in Chile, and the news stories about State-DOD infighting over matters that had a strong foreign policy
flavor, stimulated the interest of several members of
the House and Senate.  As far as it appeared in public,
DOD was inserting itself into matters that were State
responsibility.  The events in Chile showed that we
were not doing a very good job of it.  All of the news
stories were sympathetic to State.  This state of affairs, not unnaturally, bore further investigation.

Senator McCarthy, who was then coming into the lead
among those opposing the Vietnam war, had been the
first with a query to the Secretary of Defense after
Walter Pincus' first article, and had hinted that he
would initiate a formal Senate inquiry into the matter.
He later deferred to Congressman Fascell, whose committee held hearings over the period from July 8 to
August 4, 1965.  In the words of the committee's
report:[1]

For the past 3 years, the Subcommittee on International
Organizations and Movements has been conducting a continuing investigation of ideological operations in
foreign policy.  From the beginning of that study,
the role of the behavioral sciences--what they tell us
about human attitudes and motivations, and how this
knowledge can be applied to governmental undertakings
designed to carry out the foreign policy of the United
States--has been of keen interest to our subcommittee.
Reporting on this subject almost 2 years ago...the

subcommittee acknowledged the contribution that the
behavioral sciences can make to the achievement of our
national objectives on the international scene, noted
that the bulk of foreign affairs research in this field
was being performed by or for our Military Establishment, and warned that the heavy concentration of effort in this particular area may lead to over-militari-
zation of our foreign policy.

The DOD was to be treated more gently by this group
than by any other in its entire history of dealing
with Congress on problems of social research related
to its overseas programs.  But the key issues, as far
as Congress was concerned, were raised here.  They
were elaborated later, by the Senate, and the congressional view of the DOD image and motives then took an
even less sympathetic turn.  The issues were:  the
propriety of the work DOD undertook; coordination of
such work within the executive branch; and the responsibility of the State Department and other agencies
for studies related to foreign policy.  Other questions
were raised about such research, and it was fascinating
to see how the military, in responding to them, could
be its own worst enemy in this regard.

In its report, the subcommittee took the position
that the knowledge the research sought was of importance to the DOD:[2]

To sum up, the U.S. Military Establishment, in carrying out its assigned missions, continually comes into
contact with individuals and institutions in foreign
countries.  Our own military personnel abroad--some
1 million today--must draw upon knowledge obtained

through behavioral sciences research to avoid situations and activities which can cause friction, anta-
gonize local foreign populations, and create other
difficulties.  At the same time, 'wars of national
liberation' with which the free world is confronted,
are unlike conventional wars and new instruments are
needed to fight them.  There are no fixed frontlines
in those conflicts.  The problem here involves the
behavioral patterns of the insurgents, as well as of
the people of the nation where the war is being fought.
To do their job in assisting the nations defending
themselves against Communist subversion, U.S. military
personnel--and the people who are being aided--must
understand the motivations of the enemy, its weak
points and its strengths.  Behavioral sciences research
helps to provide this basic information.  It consti-
tutes one of the vital tools in the arsenal of the
free societies.

But then it moved on to the basic problem as it had

emerged:

Nevertheless, as the recent experience with Project
Camelot has demonstrated, some U.S. research efforts
can provoke extremely unfavorable reactions abroad not
only from the Communists and their sympathizers but
also from academic and political groups that are generally friendly to the United States.  There exists in
every country a sensitivity to foreigners probing into
delicate social and political matters.  Also, the
level of sensitivity varies according to who does the
research and its subject matter.  Careful attention to
these factors is certainly indicated in the allocation
of responsibilities for research on subjects related
to our foreign policy, in the preparation of research
designs, and in the selection of foreign areas for on-
the-spot field investigations.

Further problems arise when the military become involved in foreign affairs research, and when the scope
of such undertakings appears to exceed the bounds of
the legitimate interests of a particular research pro-

ject's sponsors.  In both instances, the motives of
the sponsors often are suspect....It is not entirely
surprising, therefore, that the U.S. Army's sponsorship of Project Camelot aroused some concern.  What is
more to the point, however, is that others who have
more central responsibility for the conduct of our
foreign affairs and who are directly involved in the
task of promoting economic and social progress in the
developing countries, had not initiated this type of
research themselves.

The issue was posed more graphically by Congressman
Donald Fraser of Minnesota during Dr. Vallance's testimony:[3]

The fact that this kind of basic research is being
undertaken on behalf of the military I don't find to
be a discredit to the military.  I find it to be an
indication of a lack on the part of our Government of
someone else who should have more central responsibility for this kind of research.

Our military assistance programs are primarily in the
hardware field, although we also finance some of these
civic action programs.  Should this be considered an
opening wedge to the study of the processes of development, the cultural changes and breakdowns and so on?
Should this be the entering wedge for this kind of
basic research?  This suggests to me there is something
wrong.  Not on your part because you are doing a job,
but in terms of the assignment or allocation of responsibilities within our Government.

Basically it seems to me that what we do in this field
has to be placed in some context.  If it is true that
the Army or the military or Defense requires certain
intelligence information so that they can better predict and project their own planning, that is one thing.
But ultimately our goal for these nations is the development of mature economic systems predicated on
their own sovereignty.  When we are working with these
nations to help them, it seems to me it ought not to

be the military that is providing the main thrust for
this, and the research that is involved ought not to
be flowing from the military.

I make the statement so that you can comment on it,
but it should be taken in no way as a criticism of
your work because I think your work is important and
valuable.

I only wish there was an agency of our Government that
was not military which was sponsoring this research
because I think the problem of development of these
countries is very crucial, that Defense ought to be
playing a very secondary role in this concern.

At this point, then, the DOD was not being blamed for
what it had undertaken.  Rather, its involvement was
considered unfortunate and inappropriate, and the State
Department was being questioned for not carrying out
the logical responsibilities it should have assumed in
the area.

   Along with this fundamental question went the subsidiary one of how such work was coordinated across
government.  Again, the facts of the case had been
brought out but did not appear to the subcommittee to
provide enough substance.  Its report stated:[4]

Second, there is no single focal point within this
growing Government-wide effort for a sustained and
fruitful collaboration with private scholars and the
academic community.  The Department of Defense, it is
true, receives counsel from the Defense Science Board
which, at least on occasion, includes representation
of the behavioral sciences.  The relationship here,
however, is limited by the Military Establishment's
primary concern with military matters.  The Arms Control and Disarmament Agency has its own Social Sciences
Advisory Board which focuses upon subjects of interest

to that Agency. The Department of State, through the
External Research Staff and other offices in the
Bureau of Intelligence and Research, compiles information about private research pertaining to foreign affairs and, as necessary, seeks the advice of individual
specialists on particular problems that the Department
may encounter in the field of behavioral sciences research. These and related arrangements are in themselves specialized and fragmentary.

To help correct these deficiencies, the subcommittee
recommends that there be established an Office of the
Behavioral Sciences Adviser to the President. Such
office could provide the direction essential to an effective Government-wide effort in the field of behavioral sciences, develop mutually beneficial long-
term relationships between the Government and the
academic community, strengthen both the formulation
and the implementation of foreign policy, and assure
orderly development of the Government's programs in
this field.

This recommendation was not different in spirit from
the recommendation that had been made in the McNamara-
Rusk correspondence. Another variant with significant-
ly different implications was to be made later by
Senator Harris of Oklahoma, when he initiated hearings
on the subject of a National Social Science Foundation.
But the issue being raised was, in a sense, a response
from a different quarter to the question asked in the
1963 Smithsonian Report: "Is it polite to study
friends?" The response here was, first, that it depended on who did the studying, and, second, that such
study was so sensitive politically that a responsible
focus in government at the highest level must be provided to pass on it. It appeared that the subcommittee,

whose report was published well after the President's
letter to the Secretary of State was written and signed,
did not believe that State would, or could, carry out
this responsibility successfully, and felt it should
be centered in the White House.  That was unlikely to
happen, of course, because the prevailing view did not
rate its importance as high as the committee did.  And,
as always, it would be easier for the President to pass
it on to the Secretary of State than to try to grapple
with it when the value of such work did not appear obvious to him or his subordinates in the White House.

The question of the value of this social research
and whether it should be done at all ran as an under-
current through the hearings, alongside the issue of
its role in affairs of state.  Questions in this area
were raised explicitly by Congressman H.R. Gross of
Iowa.  He made no secret of his feelings about researchers hired by the government who, he said, purpor-
ted to tell the military how to do their business:[5]

Mr. Gross.  Who does let those negotiated contracts
    with the universities to provide the brainpower
    to run the military departments?

Mr. Deitchman.  Contracts with universities are let
    by the military departments and ARPA.

Mr. Gross.  Are you mixed up in this business of war
    gaming in Vietnam?

Mr. Deitchman.  No, sir.

Mr. Gross.  Do you have anything to do with that?

Mr. Deitchman.  No, sir.

Mr. Gross.  Do you know about it?

Mr. Deitchman.  Yes, sir.

Mr. Gross.  Tell the committee a little bit about it.
     I don't think they know about this war gaming in
     Vietnam....

Mr. Gross.  All right.  I guess we all know what war
     gaming is, what fighting a war is, but what I
     am talking about is why the Pentagon hired a
     private contractor with some so-called civilian
     smart boys to go over and tell the military how
     to fight the war in Vietnam.  This is what I am
     talking about, the war gaming I am talking
     about.

     If you know anything about this, tell the com-
     mittee, please.

Mr. Deitchman.  When civilians are hired to help with
     a war game, they know about data gathering and
     analysis of data.  War games are done with mili-
     tary people.  The military people work with
     them.  They use the civilian firm to assist with
     the mathematical aspects--

Mr. Gross.  I am glad to know the military people work
     with them.  Apparently they don't work with the
     military.

Mr. Deitchman.  They work together.  When the military
     wishes to study a war gaming situation, it ob-
     tains the assistance of a firm that can help
     with the statistical analysis of what has hap-
     pened in the war game, and they study any mili-
     tary situation this way, as a matter of learning
     about how such situations may work.

Mr. Gross.  Tactics, strategy, it is all wrapped up in
     the same bundle, isn't it?  That is what we were
     told yesterday.

Mr. Deitchman.  The only war games I know about that
     are done with contractors are games that look
     to tactics.  Games that look to strategy are

> done by the military, by the Joint Chiefs of
> Staff.

Mr. Gross.  What qualifies this civilian contracting
firm to have an understanding of military tactics
and strategy in Vietnam?

Mr. Deitchman.  Their long experience in working with
military people on such problems.

Mr. Gross.  How long have they worked with them?

Mr. Deitchman.  I am not sure what firm you are talking
about.  Among the firms that I know the military
use, there has been experience since World War II
and even prior days in working with the military.

Mr. Gross.  You mean they have military personnel in
these contracting firms?

Mr. Deitchman.  Yes, sir.

Mr. Gross.  Why doesn't the Pentagon avail itself on
an in-house operation of this military personnel?

Mr. Deitchman.  Many times it does.  There is a division of labor.

Mr. Gross.  I have taken more than my share of time.

Mr. Fascell.  Mr. Rosenthal?

Mr. Gross.  And gotten nowhere, incidentally.

Congressman Gross opened an area of questioning
that led others on the subcommittee to come to share
his view.  The issue was not Camelot, but the study of
the Viet Cong, based on prisoner-of-war interrogations,
that had been undertaken by the RAND Corporation.  It
had been mentioned in our prepared testimony, and after the above exchange with Gross, Congressman Rosenthal of New York asked about it.  It was described by
Major General John W. Vogt, then chief of ISA's Policy

Planning Staff. The transformation from what the
scientists who had initiated the project understood it
to be, to what the committee was told, was appalling
to me, and the researchers shared the responsibility
for the transformation.

The study was called "VC Motivation and Morale."
The original intent was to learn something about the
nature of the Viet Cong revolutionary movement, including answers to such questions as what strata of society
its adherents came from; why they were adherents; how
group cohesiveness was built into their ranks; and how
they interacted with the populace. While much is now
known on the subject, almost nothing was known when
the work was conceived and begun. This was to be a
study of a social system, and the people who did it had
to know, a priori, something about the particular social system--about Vietnamese society, culture, and
history, and about events there since World War II.
Preferably, at least some of them would know the language, and would be known to some important Vietnamese
officials, easing the problems of access to and interaction with the prisoners. There weren't many people
with such qualifications in the entire United States.
If there were a few in the military or intelligence
communities, they were likely to be heavily occupied
with immediate operational problems associated with
the war, and would not have had the time to spend
several months on these detailed questions--important
as they were. The military and the DOD could be

faulted if they ignored the questions (which, in my
view, they did for much too long), but they didn't ignore them indefinitely.  They found the appropriate
experts, and as a matter of convenience they gave a
contract to the RAND Corporation, an instrument of the
military system, to perform the study.  This all appears, even now, eminently reasonable, and it might
even have struck most of the members of the subcommittee that way.  But this was not the story they heard.

After the first part of the study, dealing with the
questions outlined above, had been completed and the
researchers had come home to prepare their report,
another member of the RAND organization had gone to
Vietnam to continue the study.  With the concurrence
of the U.S. military command in Vietnam, he had begun
to probe into current VC operations--how they organized;
how they operated in the field; their methods of recruiting and military training; and their reactions
to the increasing American air and ground combat operations.  This approached much more closely to straight
military intelligence.  Nevertheless, it was welcomed
by the U.S. military community because in the hurried
buildup of the MACV organization the military intelligence part of that organization had remained rudimentary (although ultimately it carried on this aspect
of such work itself).

In late 1964 and early 1965, the first translated
interviews from this new direction of the RAND study
were just coming in, and they were very exciting to

the military in Washington, whose contact with events
in Vietnam, however frequent, must perforce be limited
and fragmentary. It was these results, not the earlier
ones, that the committee heard about. This happened
largely as a bureaucratic accident, since it had been
agreed in advance that General Vogt, who was responsible for overseeing this study, rather than the OSD civilians, would tell the committee about it if the
question were asked.

The reaction was predictable:[6]

Mr. Frelinghuysen. I don't mean to sound skeptical of
     what I have heard of this study of the Vietcong.
     However, it should be a natural responsibility
     of the military to interrogate prisoners and
     come up with some intelligent conclusions about
     the nature of the opposition, and the fact that
     the opposition is changing as they draft people
     and so on.

     I wouldn't think it would take a wizard to know,
     whether you are talking about aborigines or
     sophisticates in Washington, that people have
     meals in the evening; anyone could draw whatever
     military conclusions he wants from the fact that
     they have evening meals. There may be something
     of more substance that couldn't have been ob-
     tained through conventional channels. On the
     face of it, it would seem to me that you might
     come up with the idea that such a survey wasn't
     getting us anywhere except to increase our under-
     standing that it is not easy to beat the Viet-
     cong.

     I can't help feeling some sympathy with Mr. Ros-
     enthal's position. We haven't spelled out
     exactly what it is that all this massive effort
     is accomplishing. It really is a massive effort,
     as there are not so many behavioral scientists

around and we are trying to concentrate a good
many of them in particular areas.  What is this
contributing to our understanding and the effective use of our force, whether it is military or
otherwise?...

General Vogt.  Let me give you an example.

The military man is interested of course in finding out what is difficult for the other fellow
in fighting his war, what is it that really makes
it difficult, what kind of an operation on our
part would impose extra-heavy burdens on this
fellow.

We have discovered through this study that I
have described here that one of the things that
they find most difficult is the business of
having to move a camp from point A to B repeated-
ly.  We have discovered quite a few things about
it.

When we talk to the fellows who are actually
involved in this fighting, we find that they have
been fighting all day and we have forced them
out of their encampment area, they have to find
another place, locate sources of water, provide
means of getting that water up to the main part
of the camp, dig trenches, put up warning posts.

They have to go through a very elaborate business
of re-establishing a new location and encampment.
This wears them out when they have to do it periodically.  Just physical digging of the trench
and working all night so their position is secure
before they can go to sleep is a back-breaking
proposition to them.  This changed our feeling
about how they lived.

Mr. Gross.  Did you have to hire a consulting firm to
tell you about this?  The more you gentlemen
from the Pentagon talk, uniformed and civilian,
the more you indict your own establishment for
lack of in-house capability to do the things for
which you are supposedly trained and for which
we are spending one helluva lot of money.

That is implicit in what you are saying.  You go
out and hire people to tell you how to run the
establishment known as the Pentagon and pay a
fee to these so-called nonprofit institutions to
tell you how--excellent salaries to those boys
at the top levels in these outfits, I may say
parenthetically.  The more I hear you talk, the
more I am impressed with your admission that you
just don't have the capability to run the establishment over there, that you have to go out and
hire these people to do it.

How did the consultants that have been sent over
to Vietnam find out what time the Vietcong eat
supper?  Are they up at the front where the
mortar shells are falling and machineguns are
going, to find out when they eat supper, the
Vietcong?  Or did the first increment of American
soldiers sent in there, or marines, or whatever
they were, did they find out when they eat and
provide this information at some rear area?

You know the answer to this.  You know that we
already knew all about what time the Vietcong
usually eat supper.  We didn't have to send consultants over there to find that out.

Some years ago, Walter Reed Hospital put out
handbooks, if you may call them that, on the
habits of the Vietcong and South Vietnamese.
They are available and have been for several
years.  Go get them.  They are enlightening.
You didn't have to send consultants over there,
I hope, to tell the military how to fight the
war...

Mr. Frelinghuysen.  Your illustration disturbs me.  The
fact that research has uncovered the fact that
it is an effort, in a jungle, to move from one
place to another seems to me a conclusion that
could have been drawn by a child.  Surely it
could be drawn by anyone who has had the experience of being in a jungle, anyone having to move
from one place to another, as the Vietcong makes
our own side move.  As an illustration that is

> a good illustration of where we should not have
> to depend on something outside the establishment.
>
> I don't mean to sound critical when I say this.
> What disturbs me is the fact that we are going
> to spend 3 man-years to come up with a conclusion
> that in a jungle it is hard for people to move.
> It is hard for people to move in a military sense
> under any condition, and of course in a jungle
> it is harder.

Here, then, was another illustration of how the
subtle understandings of the social scientists could
be distorted when they were accepted and retranslated
by those with operational responsibility, and without
the training of the social scientists to look at problems their way.  The study, which had been intended to
elicit the basic workings of a revolutionary movement
and the motivation of its adherents, had been made to
seem like a routine examination of minor enemy tactical
operations.  While it might be possible to make a case
for civilian assistance in the former area, the latter
should have been derived from straight military intelligence.  But of course social scientists had abetted
these oversimplifications and distortions by the way
they themselves changed the direction of the study.
Discussions such as this must have led to the remark
of the Appropriations Committee regarding some of the
work not needing study by intelligent people.

There were other bases for the congressional attitude, as well.  During the summer of 1965, after the
Camelot fiasco and while the committees were still do-

liberating about the DOD budget, Rains Wallace and I
went to visit one of the committee staffs to discuss
the social science program. The members of the staff
were interested in the reasons for DOD's efforts.
There was a lengthy discussion of the background to
the DOD's social science research efforts, and the
need that had led to its expansion in the current directions. The conversation turned to research in villages in Vietnam--of how anthropologists and other
social scientists go about gathering and interpreting
data; of the time and effort they expend learning the
language and culture; of the substance of what had been
learned about the intricate paths of Vietnamese political factionalism, and the complex roles of their diverse and strange (to us) ethnic and religious groups,
such as the Hoa Hao and the Cao Dai; and of the importance of learning about and understanding these things
if American military personnel were to work successfully with their Vietnamese counterparts.

One of the committee staff remarked, after this
discussion was over, that all this notwithstanding,
his congressman believed that if he wanted to know
what a Vietnamese villager thinks, he would go and
talk with one for a while, and he would know. He saw
no need for expensive research projects to learn what
any politician can find out, and does find out, in two
or three days. It was cold comfort to reflect afterwards that some congressmen evidently don't find out,
because they fail to get elected, even where they speak

the language and know, and are part of, the local culture.  Nor, at that time, did many politicians, even
Vietnamese, talk to Vietnamese peasants even for a
few hours.  In any case, interviewing was not enough.
Knowing what to ask for (in the Vietnamese language)
and arranging not to appear as an important politician
(so that people would talk frankly) and making sure to
talk to a representative sample are all required in
order to find out what is really going on.  Nevertheless, the difference in outlook between research-
oriented R&D managers and politically oriented congressional staff was highlighted, unmistakeably.

The Appropriations Subcommittee, later supported by
the full House and the Senate, reduced the DOD social
science budgets by almost precisely the amounts of the
planned increase for FY 1966.  Ironically quoting Dr.
Robert Sproull, a physicist and Director of ARPA, who
said during his testimony:[7]

I might add that this is a very difficult field in
which to be sure one is sponsoring only high quality
work....It is a field in which it is very difficult
indeed to tell the articulate linguist from the really
promising scientist*

---

*Some social scientists of my acquaintance were later
to express their indignation about this statement,
pointing out that the difficulty existed primarily in
Dr. Sproull's mind, and that the distinctions could
be made by trained social scientists whom Dr. Sproull
had only to consult to be instructed on the subject.
Of course, in view of the performance Dr. Sproull had
just observed on the part of some trained social scien-

the committee reduced the ARPA, Air Force, and Navy
budgets for behavioral sciences by $500,000 each, and
took two bites out of the Army budget--$500,000 from
the "behavioral and social sciences" part of the
"military sciences" "line item," and $1 million from
the "human factors research" "line item," from which
SORO was funded. The program was thus set back to
where it had been when the DSB panel undertook its
study. Some parts of the DOD had been stimulated to
look into a new class of problems, and this was to continue later. But the entire concept of research contained in the DDR&E directives and the DSB report had
been nullified.

The congressional actions thus far had been rather
benign in comparison with what was to follow. On
September 15, 1965, Senator Fulbright made a speech on
the floor of the Senate,[8] in which he reviewed the
recent events in the Dominican Republic in great detail. His main point was that the United States had
to face and support the prospect of social revolution
in Latin America, but that the opportunity to side with
the forces of freedom and social advancement had been
missed in the Dominican Republic when we acted to support a military regime he viewed as corrupt, out of
what he considered to be unreasoning fear of communist
elements that had sided with the rebels. Almost in

tists who had participated in Camelot, he might be for-
given for being uncertain about whom to consult.

passing he remarked:

> ...one notes a general tendency on the part of our
> policymakers not to look beyond Latin American poli-
> ticians' anti-communism.  One also notes in certain
> Government agencies, particularly in the Department of
> Defense, a preoccupation with counterinsurgency, which
> is to say, with the prospect of revolutions and means
> of suppressing them.  This preoccupation is manifested
> in dubious and costly research projects, such as the
> recently discredited Camelot; these studies claim to
> be scientific but beneath their almost unbelievably
> opaque language lies an unmistakeable military and re-
> actionary bias.

So much for Dr. Vallance's "stable society with domestic tranquility and peace and justice for all."

In a now virtually ancient work entitled How To
Think Straight, Robert H. Thouless remarks that "words
which carry more or less strong suggestions of emotional attitudes are very common and are ordinarily
used in the discussion of such controversial questions
as those of politics, morals, and religion."[9]  In the
brief passage of his speech, Senator Fulbright expressed the new attitudes that had grown toward the
American military and the DOD as a result of the Vietnam war, and the attitudes that were being espoused by
diverse members of the American public and the majority
of the social science community in the universities
about America's participation (the more emotional words
in the universities being "intervention," or even
"imperialism") overseas.  The death of DOD's Camelot
bespoke the death of Kennedy's Camelot which had helped

spawn it.

This was the beginning of Senator Fulbright's effort, which was later joined by Senator Mansfield, to
reduce the DOD's influence on foreign policy.  In part,
he attacked DOD research on problems overseas as a
manifestation of that influence.  He made periodic
speeches about DOD's "research on foreign policy,"
often inserting lists of projects into the record,
whose titles illustrated the whole range of DOD's
interest in foreign countries and overseas conflicts.[10]
We shall see some of their impact, shortly.

The articles of Walter Pincus had told of DOD's
"$20 million for social science research."  Our testi-
mony before the Fascell subcommittee had broken this
down[11] (it was actually $27 million in FY 1965), show-
ing that about $5 million of this had to do with
"studies of foreign countries, counterinsurgency, and
unconventional warfare," and military assistance, with
about an additional million for "foreign areas information"; and the point was made that of this sum only
about one-and-a-half million was actually spent in
overseas research, and the related work that had been
described in our formal statement to the Fascell subcommittee.  But in his later testimony before that
subcommittee, Secretary Rusk said that "the foreign
affairs research community spends at least $30 million
per year in support of contract studies that relate to
foreign policy (emphasis added)....$30 million spent
in the behavioral and social sciences can have a far-

reaching impact upon foreign affairs. These studies
are contracted out by...the Defense Department, by AID
and ACDA...less than 1% of this amount is spent by the
State Department." Later, in his June 1966 hearings
on a National Social Science Foundation bill, Senator
Harris noted that "The Federal Government spent approximately $35 million last year for social and behavioral
science research _in_ foreign countries" (emphasis added).[12] Thomas Hughes, head of State's INR, later
guessed that the DOD share of this might be "roughly
12½ million" of social science contract research relating to foreign areas and foreign affairs.[13] This was
later contrasted by Senator Harris with State's
"measly $200,000."[14] From all this the impression
conveyed was that DOD's "social science research on
foreign policy" was large--much larger than it actually
was in terms of people working on the problems. This,
of course, made it look much more threatening than it
actually might have been. State's approximately $4½
million and 300 people devoted to the same problems
in-house[15] were disregarded in the public debate,
apparently (and perhaps in fact) being considered irrelevant.

Senator Fulbright, of course, was concerned about
the fact of the work and its orientation. Much other
work, unrelated to foreign policy, was swept up in his
net, as the lists of projects in the record show. He
followed the subject closely; whenever a news article
appeared that referred to it, or a request for bid or

pertinent contract information was announced in the
forum of the Commerce Business Daily, whether the subject was a contract or a DSB study or a column about
a research project in Thailand, a letter from Senator
Fulbright to the Secretary of Defense followed, asking
for particulars.  Most of the time the carefully written responses to his letters were followed by silence,
leading us to hope that the particular question had
been satisfactorily answered.  But of course, that was
a vain hope.

In 1968, amid the tensions of the peak of the American buildup and employment of combat forces in Vietnam,
Senators Fulbright and Mansfield made a major attack
on Defense Department "social science research."[16]
Among the study titles that were cited as examples of
the military establishment's interest in matters far
beyond their sphere were a study of the economy of
India and a report entitled "Witchcraft in the Congo."
The first study had been justified, after the Chinese
attack on India in 1965, as necessary to plan the
military assistance program then being undertaken to
assist in the strengthening of India's armed forces.
It was designed to help formulate a policy of loans,
grants, and assistance in building an arms manufactur-
ing industry, the justification being that for the
last item, at least, something had to be known about
the Indian economy's flexibility and capacity for expansion.

The Congo "study" was not a study at all, but repre-

sented a summary paper written in answer to an Army
question put to the Counterinsurgency Information and
Analysis Center at SORO (see p. 139 ); the latter was
now reorganized and renamed the Center for Research on
Social Systems--CRESS--and separated from its contractual relationship with American University.  This was
the time when the United States was providing a small
amount of assistance to the government of the Republic
of the Congo against a group of rebellions that
threatened to tear it apart.  American policy was that
stability in central Africa depended on the Congo remaining a viable nation.  While there was no very
vocal quarrel with this policy on the part of Congress,
the sensitivity to the possibility of American involvement in wars in developing nations was such that a
storm was raised over four transport aircraft sent to
transport Congo government troops from one part of
that huge, underdeveloped country to another.[17]  The
Congo rebels called themselves "simbas" (lions) and
were reported to have convinced themselves by diverse
magical ceremonies that they were invulnerable to
bullets.  Mindful that the British had had some success
in Kenya with a "de-oathing" ceremony to undermine the
psychological effect of the Mau-Mau blood oaths, the
Army asked CINFAC what qualities there might be in the
beliefs of the Congo rebels that would offer similar
opportunities.  The paper on "Witchcraft in the Congo,"
the product of a few days' work by the center, was
the response to the question.  While this was explained,

such studies and reports remained symbols of the DOD's
interest in studying foreign peoples, which Senator
Fulbright believed was an improper activity for the
DOD to undertake.

It appeared obviously necessary to the DOD to try
to counter the effects of this furor. Dr. Donald Mac-
Arthur, Deputy DDR&E for Science and Technology (i.e.,
responsible for overseeing all of DOD's scientific
research program), his assistant Rodney Nichols, and
I visited the staffs of the House and Senate Armed
Services committees and Armed Services Appropriations
subcommittees. We explained the nature of the projects in question, showed the context and the large
scope of the work in which they were embedded, and
tried at length to justify such studies as were done.
We also explicitly made clear DOD's attempts to assure
that all such research was relevant to the DOD mission.
We agreed that some fraction of the work might be subject to argument in this respect, and that the DOD was
willing to make adjustments to meet the will of Congress in these areas; but we expressed the feeling that
it seemed highly unfair to have one or two studies--
and minor ones, at that--singled out as the basis for
an attack on the entire DOD research program.

The conversations ranged over the philosophical
problem of performing specifically oriented basic research. Basic research could always be shown to have
ultimate relevance to DOD problems. For example, research in the sciences of materials led to improved

engines and armor; research in basic physics led to
new forms of detection systems (some of which would
also be applied, later, to the prevention of airplane
highjacking); research in lasers led to communications
and range finding systems. But the research itself
did not always have the application in view, and one
couldn't always expect a researcher working on the
frontiers of knowledge to understand immediately what
the ultimate application would be. (This, in fact,
became the key argument of those in the universities
who wanted to reject all DOD-supported research as
evil.)[18] In the social and analytical sciences, the
DOD, since Camelot, was making much more of an effort
to assure the direct and obvious relationship between
research subjects and applications that appeared necessary to justify such work.

One of the Senate staff members at this point asked
about RAND's "VC Motivation and Morale" studies. I
pointed out that these had developed most of the information and deep understanding (beyond the "order-of-
battle" analyses of primary concern to the military
intelligence community) that had become available in
the past three years about the National Liberation
Front, its adherents, its ways of relating to the population, and its means for keeping its own members
under tight organizational control. Much of this knowledge was reflected in Douglas Pike's book on the Viet
Cong.[19] Moreover, the methodology for such study,
primarily the means for gathering and analyzing rele-

vant data in an alien culture, had been integrated into
the work of the intelligence community. The work was
obviously directly relevant to the military's problems.

None of this persuaded any of the staff members of
any of the four committees. While as individuals they
might accept and understand our explanation of the
studies and analyses, they pointed out that Congress
was becoming extraordinarily sensitive about DOD research. Ordinarily, DOD research in the physical
sciences was viewed quite permissively; but with the
rising antiwar sentiment, and with the university
community disengaging from and making attacks on
classified DOD-supported research on campus, and, in
some cases, on all DOD-supported research on campus,
all DOD-supported basic research was coming into question. The controversial studies and analyses DOD insisted on supporting, representing less than 1 percent
of all the DOD's $300-plus million worth of basic re-
search, was jeopardizing all the rest, and they didn't
think they could defend any of it unless DOD backed
down on the 1 percent.

If we needed confirmation that the staff people
were accurately reflecting the attitudes of their
principals, we could pay heed to Senator Stennis's
remarks on the floor, during one of the discussions
on the subject initiated by Senator Fulbright:[20]

I consider that [social and behavioral sciences] to be
the softest spot in all the [DOD] research and development program, although I did not have intimate, perso-

nal knowledge about it.

Thus was another nail driven into the coffin.

Senators Fulbright and Mansfield delivered the coup
de grace the following year. But we have already
moved far ahead of the other parts of the story. It
is time again to backtrack and see what was happening
elsewhere. Before we do, however, let us pause for a
moment's reflection.

We spent many hours, in DOD, trying to devise ways
to placate Senator Fulbright with respect to this particular problem. It seemed to us that he was at the
same time castigating the DOD for being a blundering,
ignorant, trigger-happy giant; and yet objecting when
the DOD tried to learn enough to act in a more educated
and enlightened way. Surely, some of us thought, if
we could meet and reason with him we could convince
him of the logic and the need for most, if not all, of
the research and studies DOD felt it had to undertake
to play its role properly. But we finally concluded
that this would serve no useful purpose. We assumed,
ultimately, that from his point of view, if the DOD
were studying foreign areas, this must inevitably appear to be undertaken against the contingency that the
DOD would have to operate in those areas. And if DOD
expected to do that, it had enough power and influence
in the government to make the planning a self-fulfilling
prophecy. Senator Fulbright made clear his belief, as
in the September 15, 1965, speech, that the DOD exerted

too strong an influence on foreign policy in any case, and that this influence was, in his own word, "reactionary." Whether this was so or not, it appeared logical to us, as a next step, that if the DOD could be prevented from studying foreign areas, this would at least symbolically reduce its appearance of influence; if this acted over the long run to reduce its influence in fact, all to the good.

This interpretation of the senator's views did seem to fit with what he said on the Senate floor. For example, in 1968:[21]

...I would like to see if we could not begin to get this matter under control...Not only does it not produce anything of value, but it is also affirmatively bad to go around messing in a foreign university and studying the civilian life of foreigners and what motivates them and so on, and especially under the auspices of the Defense Department.

It gives the impression that our country has become 100 percent militaristic, which I know is not so. I do not want it to become so [emphasis added], and nobody else here wants that to happen, either...

And, again, in 1969:[22]

I suppose that in some areas psychological understanding is necessary and helpful. If we had had any understanding of the psychology of the Vietnamese, I do not think we would have gotten into that war. There was a complete lack of understanding of what the Vietnamese people were like. I cannot say it would not have been helpful.

I do not think that particular one has any relation to the military responsibility [emphasis added]. I doubt

that the military is the proper one to handle it,
simply because they are not familiar with that type
activity.

In addition, the senator said often, in many ways, that
the Camelot project was misguided and stupid; and each
time he allied with it the thought of DOD's improper
role.  If his outlook was as we surmised, it became
clear to us, then we were involved, purely and simply,
in a clash of convictions and beliefs in the political
arena.  No amount of explanation would help.  So we
kept answering the senator's letters as reasonably as
we could, hoping to assuage his wrath each time, but
inexorably losing in the broader conflict.

The reaction to Camelot by the news media caused annoy-
ance and some resentment in the DOD; but the media had
reacted to DOD doings of greater magnitude in the past,
and this new reaction was no surprise.  That many members of Congress should see impropriety in DOD's social
science research was also readily comprehensible, if
regrettable.  State had telegraphed its attitudes and
moves well in advance.  The clamping down of controls
by the chiefs of the DOD was taken as a natural consequence for a program that had caused embarrassment
while it lacked intrinsic support.  But it is fair to
say that the depth of the anti-DOD reaction, the emotional soul-searching, and the virulent condemnation of
their esteemed colleagues by members of the social
science community was very much unanticipated by all
of those social scientists, and others, who had had a
hand in trying to build the program of social research
related to the problem of revolutionary warfare.

The fundamental issue was presented as an ethical
one, although, as we shall see later, it carried overtones of political conflicts among social scientists.
It was voiced in many forms, but basically it came to
the question of whether, by working on applied problems
to help government achieve its purposes, social scientists were not violating their academic freedom and
professional ethics.  Implicit was the view that study
of social processes from the viewpoint of avoiding vio-

lent rebellion was reactionary, and that revolution, violent or not, should be studied and supported as a beneficial and necessary instrument of social change. It wasn't expressed explicitly, but in a large segment of the social science community that had been deeply disturbed by the Vietnam war, the value system had changed.

The violence of the reaction was a shock in part because the documents supporting and encouraging the DOD's efforts to enlist social scientists in these endeavors were in the public record, and presumably known, at least within the social science community. And, as the Harris hearings later showed, it was also well known that ONR and AFOSR supported research by social scientists in foreign areas and about problems of foreign policy; some of the academic community had found this support welcome and respectable. Through all the years past, there had been no complaints of the sort that were now being raised. Whence the change? It was complex and multifaceted, and, one must add in fairness, it was far from universal in the community.

The case against the DOD and its adherents was staked out, as it were, in two articles published soon after Camelot "broke." Most later writings and discussion represented elaborations on the theme. The articles were by Irving Louis Horowitz, Professor of Sociology at Washington University,[1] who later testified before the Harris committee[2] and edited a book,

The Rise and Fall of Project Camelot;[3] and Kalman H.
Silvert,[4] a political scientist specializing in Latin
America, who was with the American Universities Field
Staff, who also testified,[5] and whose revised article
appeared in the Horowitz book.  The Silvert article
appeared in July, and that of Horowitz in November.
They punctuated a cacophony of letters and articles in
diverse journals, especially from Latin American scholars; and they elevated to "scholarly" debate the barrage of news articles, congressional statements, and
investigations already described.

It had already become clear that the Camelot news
had reinforced an atmosphere of suspicion in Latin
America that was affecting all American researchers
there, including those supported by university or
private foundation funds.  Silvert pointed out that
American research on Latin America was not well supported, had few adherents, and few students who understood the sensitivity of Latin American scholars to
domination from the north.  He remarked that "The
extremely noisy debacle...cannot be explained in the
narrow terms of a few bumbling individuals or even of
misguided policy; the ground for today's disgrace was
well prepared by the ethical incomprehension, cavalier
attitudes, and tolerance of ignorance manifested by
American universities and scholars for many years."
He questioned whether scholars could preserve their
"academic" freedom and still work for the government
on policy problems;  "...how does a scholar under con-

tract know that he is adopting one hypothesis instead
of another for truly scientific reasons, rather than
because of a particular applied interest or even political prejudice?....do these scholars think themselves
beyond the lures of money, prestige, and personal political passion?"   The statement, one might add, would
seem to apply to many another scholarly activity as
well.

These relatively gentle statements of parts of the
problems were elaborated further and from a different
point of view at a meeting of the Social Science Research Council, held in September of 1965, in which I
was invited to participate.  The council is a nonprofit
organization formed in 1923, representing the various
social science disciplines.  It is privately supported
to "articulate and advance the research interests of
imaginative and highly competent social scientists
wherever they may be."  Its board is designated by the
professional associations in the individual disciplines.[6]  Thus, in some sense it represents the entire
professional community.  The subject of this particular meeting was the problem of "access" in foreign area
research.  I was asked to join a panel discussing the
problems of government-supported research overseas;
and at the heart of the discussions was a searching
for the lessons of Camelot.

Two points that were made in the course of the
panel discussions, and in later conversations I had
with members of the council, stood out.  The first,

which led me to realize that Camelot was not so much
the cause of the furor as the trigger for a bomb that
had long been ticking, had to do with the problems
created in Latin America by privately supported American researchers.  This was the question, alluded to by
Silvert, of their attitude toward the local scholars--
a certain arrogance; a feeling that the Americans were
coming to put the local people under the microscope,
rather than to work with them on their problems.  This
had been manifested by such incidents as American professors taking their data "home" for use in their own
publications rather than analyzing them abroad together
with their foreign colleagues.  And there were a large
enough number of researchers in the various countries
of Latin America to irritate the people they inter-
viewed--sometimes the same people were interviewed on
similar problems by two or more completely independent
researchers.  Of course, all research in Latin America
was not like this; but there was enough like this to
be remembered, and to create the near-hostile climate
into which Camelot intruded.  These sensitivities, and
sensitivity to official American activity, were obviously mutually reinforcing.

The second major point was whether, if such research
results as DOD desired were really needed, they couldn't
be obtained by some independent, "objective" agency,
such as the National Science Foundation.  This was a
complex issue indeed, even more so when viewed in retrospect.  The immediately obvious problem was whether

an agency needing <u>applied</u> research results--specific
answers to specific questions such as those raised in
the Defense Science Board report--could seek the necessary research and information through an agency designed for basic research, one that depended on scholars to originate proposals on subjects that interested
them, for work to be performed according to their own
schedules.  It didn't seem likely, and the Fascell subcommittee was to recognize this, saying in its report:
"Research activities should always be related to each
department's or agency's specific operational responsibilities."[7]  In any case, the basic research questions
and the applied questions were likely to be only remotely related to each other, necessitating <u>some</u> work
by the operational agency to translate one into the
other.  Therefore, the problems of getting the applied
work done couldn't entirely be evaded by fobbing them
off on a foundation organized for basic research.

A more fundamental difficulty was the shifting into
a new context of the ethical problem facing individuals,
of hiding their sources of support if these happened
to be the DOD or CIA.  The implication of the suggestion to shift support of the work to a government
foundation was that, if the operating agencies couldn't
undertake to support overseas research directly, perhaps another agency, innocuous in image, could do so
by providing a "cover" when the scholar himself wasn't
supposed to.  But then the innocuous agency would have
to take the money covertly from the one desiring the

work, a process later forbidden to the CIA and the DOD; or it would have to ask Congress for the money publicly, and that would "blow the cover." It was evidently not yet recognized that it was the combination of the nature of the question and the fact that the U.S. government was asking it that raised hackles overseas, not the subsidiary issue of what instrument that government selected to obtain the answers. The increased frustration attending this realization was to embitter many in the social science community even more against the United States Government, and came later to be reflected in the harshness of the "New Left's" attacks on those who worked with government support.

Earlier, Horowitz expanded on this problem and on the related ones. Regarding the support of the research by the Army and its meaning, he said:

In deference to intelligent researchers, in recognition of them as scholars, they should have been invited by Camelot to air their misgivings and qualms about government (and especially Army sponsored) research--to declare their moral conscience. Instead, they were mistakenly approached as skilful, useful potential employees of a higher body, subject to an authority higher than their scientific calling.

What is central is not the political motives of the sponsor. For social scientists were not being enlisted in an intelligence system for 'spying' purposes. But given their professional standing, their great sense of intellectual honor and pride, they could not be "employed" without proper deference for their stature. Professional authority should have prevailed from beginning to end with complete command of the right to thrash out the moral and political dilemmas as re-

searchers saw them.  The Army, however respectful and
protective of free expression, was "hiring help" and
not openly and honestly submitting a problem to the
higher professional and scientific authority of social
science.

But of course, that last had been done in 1958-1963,
and the Army was following the advice proffered at that
time.

   After attacking the project as scientifically unworkable (because it was not designed to take a morally
"objective" view), Horowitz went on to say:

In one Camelot document there is a general critique of
social science for failing to deal with social conflict
and social control.  While this in itself is admirable,
the tenor and context of Camelot's documents make it
plain that a "stable society" is considered the norm
no less than the desired outcome.  The "breakdown of
social order" is spoken of accusatively.  Stabilizing
agencies in developing areas are presumed to be absent.
There is no critique of U.S. Army policy in developing
areas because the Army is presumed to be a stabilizing
agency.  The research formulations always assume the
legitimacy of Army tasks--if the U.S. Army is to perform effectively its parts in the U.S. mission of
counter-insurgency it must recognize that insurgency
represents "a breakdown of social order..." But such
a proposition has never been doubted--by Army officials
or anyone else.  The issue is whether such breakdowns
are in the nature of the existing system or a product
of conspiratorial movements. . .

It never seemed to occur to its personnel to inquire
into the desirability for successful revolution.  This
is just as solid a line of inquiry as the one stressed
--the conditions under which revolutionary movements
will be able to overthrow a government.  Furthermore,
they seem not to have thought about inquiring into the

role of the United States in these countries. This
points up the lack of symmetry. The problem should
have been phrased to include the study of "us" as well
as "them." It is not possible to make a decent analysis of a situation unless one takes into account the
role of all the different people and groups involved
in it; and there was no room in the design for such
contingency analysis.

In discussing the policy impact on a social science
research project, we should not overlook the difference
between "contract" work and "grants." Project Camelot
commenced with the U.S. Army; that is to say, it was
initiated for a practical purpose determined by the
client. This differs markedly from the typical academic grant in that its sponsorship had "built-in"
ends. The scholar usually seeks a grant; in this case
the donor, the Army, promoted its own aims. In some
measure, the hostility for Project Camelot may be an
unconscious reflection of this distinction--a dim feeling that there was something "non-academic," and
certainly not disinterested, about Project Camelot,
irrespective of the quality of the scholars associated
with it.

He also indirectly accused the social science community
of remaining silent about the project because it didn't
want to jeopardize its sources of support in the DOD.[8]
Thus was the motif of corruption of the scientists
joined with that of imperialism of the sponsor.

At the same time, Horowitz castigated the State
Department for taking part in "a supreme act of censorship,"[9] and for missing the moral issues--all the executive branch (at least that part having to do with
foreign affairs) became part of the immoral system.
R.A. Nisbet was to write later, in apparent contradic-
tion,[10] that whether behavioral scientists make the

contribution of research results to the military directly or through foundations or universities is a
matter of operational significance, but not an ethical
matter.  But then he rejoined Horowitz, pointing out
that the unethical aspect of their behavior was the
failure of the social scientists to tell the Army that
the project was professionally and scientifically unwise.  To others' accusation of moral failure on the
part of the social scientists, he added the failure of
purely professional ethics.  He went on to stress
Congressman Royball's question at the Fascell hearings:
"Wouldn't the fact that the Army was heading the Project itself create a problem in many countries?"
This, Nisbet felt, the scientists should have pointed
out.  That is, instead of taking the Army's money to
do the job the Army wanted done, they should have de-
murred and pointed out to the Army that it was improper
for it to spend its money that way.

Thus far had we come from the judgments, values,
attitudes, and recommendations of the 1963 Smithsonian
report.  And, as Silvert, after asking "How many scholars who knew of this widely publicized project actually wrote to SORO questioning the wisdom and ethics of
the matter?" pointed out in a footnote, "...The writer
was requested to join in Project Camelot last year.
He declined, but raised no troubling questions."  In
other words, the realization of the problems now being
identified came after, not before, the hue and cry a-
bout Camelot was raised.

It appears that what was at least partly involved can only be labeled as professional rivalry--a fear on the part of some members of the community that their sources of overseas research data--their professional life's blood, one might say--was being jeopardized by other parts of the community. Gabriel Almond, who was at the SSRC meeting described above and was, at the time, the incoming president of the American Political Science Association, was reported in a newspaper article by Walter Pincus[11] to have said, at a luncheon session of the Association's convention where Camelot's consequences were being discussed, that the great expansion of social science activity by American scholars abroad had, in addition to resulting in some cases of poor preparation and understanding, made "legitimate" foreign research difficult for all U.S. scholars. That is, he seemed to be suggesting that the field was getting too crowded and this made things difficult for those already there. Others at the meeting were reported to have spoken against support of research by the DOD, describing such events as an academic (not DOD-supported) survey of Latin American diplomats (presumably "legitimate") running into trouble when the diplomats feared the researcher represented the CIA or another U.S. government agency. Thus, it was implied, the field was not only becoming overcrowded, the new entries were sowing distrust of everyone.

One is also tempted to speculate about whether the emotionalism of the reaction to Camelot did not bespeak

a certain feeling of guilt on the part of some of the
social scientists who decried Camelot the loudest. All
the elements were there. Many of them had been taking
DOD money to support their work, or their colleagues
were taking DOD money. This had been combined with
other money for general support, a procedure that had
not been thought unethical at the time. Many of them
knew of Camelot--they did not speak out against it until their Latin American colleagues pointed the accusing finger. The outcry reminded them that their own
behavior had not been impeccable; some of them, too,
had displayed signs of the arrogance of their particular power--in this case, ample money to go abroad and
undertake research of more interest to themselves than
to their foreign colleagues. And, underlying it all,
a deep and growing dissatisfaction with their country
and its part in what was becoming a dirty and unwinna-
ble war. There was much sensitivity abroad on this
subject, as I was told at the time by a number of
scientists who were in contact with their foreign counterparts, especially in Latin America. All of this,
it is now clear, was simmering in the background.
Camelot acted like a mirror in a room when the light
was turned on suddenly; in an instant many social
scientists saw themselves as they believed they were
viewed from outside. They were unhappy with the image,
and they turned violently on their colleagues, and
their colleagues' mentor, who were responsible for
turning on the light, and whom they could accuse of

having caused the trouble. And they undertook their
own share of soul-searching and self-accusation.

Thus, the history of the war and the DOD's experiment in social research remained intertwined. From
the time the United States entered the war in Vietnam
in an expanding role and the research experiment was
conceived, until the time the experiment saw the light
of day in a glare of accusatory publicity while the
United States found itself deep in the war with no
resolution in sight, the value system had changed in
an important part of the American intellectual commu-
nity--including key members of Congress, many social
scientists, and important representatives of the press.
Almost every one of the original premises, given in
Chapter 3, was overturned for this group:

- Communism in Vietnam, or anywhere, was not a
  threat to the United States; nor was communism in
  small countries necessarily in sympathy with the
  sources of communism--the USSR and China--who were
  no longer a monolith.

- America's relations with the developing nations
  should recognize the urges of their people toward
  greater freedom; if those urges led to violent
  revolution the United States should support it
  instead of supporting reactionary and suppressive
  "status quo" regimes.

- "Counterinsurgency" was the means by which these
  legitimate urges toward freedom, possibly expressed

in revolutionary action, were suppressed; it
opposed revolution and represented intervention
by the United States in the affairs of the developing nations to aid and abet such suppression by
their dictatorial governments.  It was not a morally acceptable strategy for the United States.

• The DOD (along with the CIA) was the American
instrument of counterinsurgency; its support for
studies of foreign peoples was therefore unaccep-
table because its motives were sinister.

• Social scientists who worked for the DOD and other
"mission-oriented" agencies were giving up their
academic and intellectual freedom.

One doesn't have to agree with or accept all or part
of either set of premises to recognize that a change
had taken place.  Perhaps it was not a change in values;
perhaps, one could speculate, the two sets of values
existed side by side in American life.  One was in the
ascendancy for a time, until events led to the resur-
gence of the other.  Sometimes the shift took place
within individuals; at other times different individuals
gained the public attention.  Whatever the explanation,
the new premises gained ever wider acceptance.  They
evolved, over time, into a new sort of catechism,
which is illustrated in the extreme by the following
passages from Michael Klare's article in The Nation:[12]

Every imperium has been faced with the task of finding

enough troops to maintain hegemony over colonial territories without straining the financial and manpower resources of the mother country. The occupation army of
an imperial power is always outnumbered by the indigenous population of a colony; when a liberation movement
has secured the active support of sufficient numbers of
people in a country to offset the technological advantage of the occupier, the colonial reign is doomed.

Like all imperial powers of the past, the United States
has been obliged to employ mercenaries in order to
maintain a favorable balance of power in its colonial
territories. In fact, a primary objective of our Asian
policy is to install client regimes in each country
that can be compelled to supply native troops for
America's counterinsurgency....Since even when in control of the governmental apparatus the ruling junta is
dependent upon U.S. aid to finance development projects
and meet military payrolls, Washington can insist that
such regimes provide troops for combat against insurgents in their own or neighboring countries.

In Southeast Asia, the Department of Defense (DOD)
found that the use of indigenous troops in counterin-
surgent operations creates problems that do not arise
in actions against an external enemy. Since such
troops are sent against their own countrymen--and often
against members of their own village, or even their
own family--serious questions of motivation and morale
arise....To develop a research and development (R&D)
program for our mercenary armies, similar to the extensive R&D program for the American Army, Defense
Secretary McNamara in 1961 established an on-going
program of counterinsurgency research known as Project
AGILE.

....In the area of behavioral research, AGILE has
sponsored research on ethnic minorities thought to be
potential sources of mercenaries (e.g., the Montagnards
of South Vietnam), and on the development of strategic
doctrine for the armies of client governments.

The anthropologists, in particular, felt that they had been "used"--a feeling reinforced by the revelations of CIA support for scholarly and university research and institutions. Shortly after the Camelot news broke, the American Anthropological Association met (November 18-21, 1965) and a violent argument ensued over whether the members of the association should be permitted to perform research for action-oriented agencies of the government. A resolution to explore the ethics of sponsored research was introduced,[13] and referred to the Committee on Research Problems and Ethics, headed by Professor Ralph Beals of UCLA, then the president of the association. At a meeting a year later (November 19, 1966), the association argued about the report of its committee, and referred it back to them for further work. A "Statement on... Research and Ethics" was finally approved by the membership in April of 1967.[14] It was lengthy, and established many guidelines for anthropologists' professional behavior. Among its statements were the following:

I. Freedom of Research
   1. The Fellows of the American Anthropological Association reaffirm their resolution of 1948 on freedom of publication and protection of the interests of the persons and groups studied:

   Be it resolved:
   (1) that the American Anthropological Association strongly urge all sponsoring institutions to guarantee their research scientists complete freedom to interpret and publish their findings without censorship or interference;

provided that
(2) the interests of the persons and communities
or other groups studied are protected; and
that
(3) in the event that the sponsoring institution
does not wish to publish the results nor be
identified with the publication, it permit
publication of the results, without use of
its name as sponsoring agency, through other
channels.-- American Anthropologist 51:370
(1949).

To extend and strengthen this resolution, the
Fellows of the American Anthropological Association endorse the following:

2. Except in the event of a declaration of war by
the Congress, academic institutions should not
undertake activities or accept contracts in
anthropology that are not related to their normal functions of teaching, research, and public
service. They should not lend themselves to
clandestine activities. We deplore unnecessary
restrictive classifications of research reports
prepared under contract for the Government, and
excessive security regulations imposed on participating academic personnel.

3. The best interests of scientific research are
not served by the imposition of external res-
trictions. The review procedures instituted
for foreign area research contracts by the
Foreign Affairs Research Council of the Department of State (following a Presidential directive of July, 1965) offer a dangerous potential
for censorship of research. Additional demands
by some United States agencies for clearance,
and for excessively detailed itineraries and
field plans from responsible scholars whose
research has been approved by their professional
peers or academic institutions, are contrary to
assurances given by Mr. Thomas L. Hughes, Director of the Bureau of Intelligence and Research,
Department of State, to the President of the
American Anthropological Association on November
9, 1965, and are incompatible with effective

anthropological research.
4. Anthropologists employed or supported by the Government should be given the greatest possible opportunities to participate in planning research projects, to carry them out, and to publish their findings.

The resolution, which was approved by a 12-to-1 mail vote,[15] effectively prevented most anthropologists from participating in work for the DOD, since they could not easily suffer the antagonism of their peers and continue as part of their professional community. A minority opposed the constraints implied by the resolution, but the general orientation of the group included attitudes toward applied research completely antithetical to any usage of the results of their work by government for its purposes, except, as noted, in case "Congress declares war." The definition of "public service" in the sense of the resolution is subtle, indeed, under these circumstances. What was really meant, one presumes, was that they could engage in that form of public service which met with general favor in their professional community at any particular time. Moreover, some of the anthropologists later showed that they could be rather hard on their fellows who did not wish to march to the same drummer.

With the condemnation of research on problems applied to ends these social scientists disapproved of came a new view of their role. In addition to avoiding what they viewed as unethical involvement with government, they came to view it as their responsibili-

ty to change the policies with which they disagreed.
Showing some cleavage even in these ranks (since the
view did not square with the lofty detachment advocated
by Horowitz) it was determined that research was no
longer to be the sole objective.  Political activism
was to follow the knowledge gained through the research.
This was reflected in the various resolutions against
the Vietnam war, or against specific operations in
Vietnam, such as defoliation or the use of napalm,
passed by many professional organizations.  While this
might appear as a new attitude, it is clear that the
social scientists were acting in the "tradition" of
the physical scientists who had developed nuclear weapons during and after World War II, when the latter resolved that scientists must assume a share of social
and political responsibility for the uses to which the
results of their work are put.  Camelot appeared to be
the social "atomic bomb" that led the social scientists
to share the physicists' view.  Typifying the attitude
was a "draft declaration of Latin American specialists
on professional responsibility," circulated for signature in October, 1965.  It said, in part:

We consider it our individual and collective personal
and professional duty to promote improved conditions
of human life, political and economic independence,
political and social democratization and economic
development in all countries of the hemisphere.  We
pledge ourselves in our work and in our private activity always to promote and never to hinder the achievement of these goals.  Whenever U.S. Government policies
conflict with these goals, we consider it our duty to

promote alternative policies [emphasis added].

While these words are high-minded, idealistic, and in
keeping with American values, they appear subtly different from the general concern for the survival of
mankind expressed years earlier by the physical scientists. There are narrower, more culturally-oriented
implicit value judgments here, which suggest that the
framers and signers of the resolution would decide,
themselves (presumably agreeing among themselves on
what policies would and would not meet the goals), what
policies were suitable and desirable for "all countries
of the hemisphere." But the pattern was set, even if
the community bent over so far backwards that they
tainted themselves with the sins for which they castigated the government. The politicization of the
sciences had begun, and was to continue apace as a
subject for debate and conflict in the scientific community.[16]    Of course it could be argued that all
client-oriented research is political if the client is
political. The scientist can then choose, if he wishes,
the political orientation of the client he works with.
We will examine this question in detail in the last
chapter of this book.

In all that has preceded in this chapter, we have
referred to the "social science community." It must
be clear, however, that this "community" was not monolithic. I have already alluded to a certain amount of
what appeared to be professional rivalry underlying

the strength of the reaction to the Camelot revelations.  There had been, in fact, what might be termed
a "DOD social science establishment"--the group, and
many others like it, that had participated in the
Smithsonian studies and whose members, with many colleagues, worked with the government and with the DOD.
These men were some of the key people in the development of a strong association of social scientists to
which the government could turn.  Their role and position are ably suggested by Thackray:[17]

In 1962 W.H. Auden could say, "When I find myself in
the company of scientists, I feel like a shabby curate
who has strayed by mistake into a drawing room full of
dukes."

...The demand for apparatus beyond the purse of any one
society or institution and the continually increasing
need for federal support have also contributed to
changes in the social system of pure science.  Perhaps
the most obvious of those changes is the emergence of
the new breed of dominant dukes.  Unlike either the
elegant amateurs or poor professionals, these men draw
their fame, their monetary, intellectual, and social
rewards, and their power in society directly from their
enormous scientific ability.

There were, it might be noted, a number of such
"establishments."  Another included many leaders of
the professional associations (e.g., some of those
serving on the NAS/NRC committee, or as leaders of the
SSRC), who had become vocal against DOD-supported work
but who, nevertheless, were not willing to go as far
as the more radical members of their groups in condem-

nation of government and any relationship with the
government by social scientists.  Both these "elite"
groups were represented on the newly formed National
Academy of Sciences committee, and in that forum their
differences were muted.  But the group that had been
working closely with the DOD was attacked by the other
indirectly, in the press and in the professional societies; the attackers came to assemble many more supporters than the group sympathetic to the DOD.  The
latter tried in a number of ways to defend themselves,
but the DOD, as most bureaucracies a rather impersonal
and ungrateful master, made the job harder by refusing
to enter the fray in the media, where much of the battle was being fought; and by refusing to agree that
those who had been associated with Camelot could enter
the fray officially on the DOD's behalf.

These social scientists could, of course, have discussed their work without violating any trust.  The
problem was that the government itself did not wish to
speak up regarding its need for Camelot or something
like it, or about its need for the support of the
social scientists who had been helping it.  Without
this kind of support, the latter could only appear to
be a small, beleaguered group who had been caught out
and were now trying to explain their malfeasance.
Many of these social scientists simply "dropped out."
They went back to their own work quietly, and with
great fortitude in view of the damage that was being
done to them professionally.  They did not switch sides

or join the attacks on the government or on their colleagues. A few maintained their ties with government,
and undertook a more active defense.

In an editorial in the American Behavioral Scientist,
"A. de G." asked:[18]

1. Is it not true that since 1940, the Army, Navy, and
   Air Force have contributed incomparably more to the
   development of the pure and applied human sciences
   than the Department of State?

2. Is it not true that the State Department might on
   dozens of occasions have sought much more extensive
   research and intelligence facilities than it has
   actually sought or employed?

3. Is it not reasonable that the Armed Forces' mission
   in respect to insurgency should include research on
   areas where revolution might occur?

4. Are Cuba and Santo Domingo, Lebanon and Vietnam,
   and other cases too, going to stand as historical
   proof that the Army can send men in to be killed
   but cannot help anyone go in to forestall by pre-
   ventive understanding the occasions of killing?

5. Is "clearance" so vital to an Ambassador that a
   large, important activity should be destroyed for
   want of it?

6. Is it wise for any agency to seek to get a few more
   research funds by invidious comparisons with the
   worthy research efforts of another department of
   government?

7. Are leaks, false assertions, quotations from Anti-
   American sources, and other tactics to be condoned
   in treating with problems of scientific research?

8. Should the Social Science Research Council, the
   American Political Science Association, the American
   Psychological Association, the American Association
   of University Professors, the American Sociological
   Association, the American Historical Association

and the American Anthropological Association, in
conjunction with various international counterparts,
have acted promptly to investigate the situation,
inquiring, among other matters, whether issues of
freedom of inquiry were not present?  And, while
they are at it, might they not investigate the ugly
and distorted articles carried in the Washington
Press, particularly the Washington Star, against
Project Camelot and social science research?

9. Should Senator McCarthy and Ambassador Dungan be re-
proved by agencies of opinion for acting hastily,
crudely, and quite possibly wrongly in the Camelot
incident?

He then commented:

There is absolutely nothing an American can do in any
country of the world to avoid all criticism from all
quarters of the country.  Should American companies
surrender a billion dollars of French investments because General de Gaulle makes menacing noises toward
them?  Why then should American professors surrender?
The task of the American ambassador is to defend American rights, not to surrender them, and certainly not
to surrender them out of pique.

Project Camelot was an open project, conducted by the
American University, with Army funds, to solve problems of pressing and universal interest in the present
day.  It was skillfully manned, well-planned, and supported by some of the best foreign scholars in Latin
America.  Certain State Department officials have
little to be proud of in the incident.  They may have
harmed the national defense effort and impeded social
science.*

---

*This and the preceding quote are from Alfred de
Grazia, "Government and Science:  An Editorial,"
American Behavioral Scientist, Vol. IX, No. 1 (Sept.
1965), p. 40.  Reprinted by permission of the pub-
lisher, Sage Publications, Inc.

But most of the defenses were private.  This was unfortunate, because it allowed continuation of the one-
sided public view of the controversy (although it is
doubtful, even now, whether the press would in general
have presented the other side fairly, if it had been
argued in public).  Dr. Joseph E. Barmack, Chairman of
the Psychology Department at the City University of New
York, who had been a consultant to the DOD, wrote to
the dean of his College with respect to the Silvert
article:

Silvert's article on first reading appears to be a
dispassionate objective assessment of the state of
American social science research in Latin America.
However, on closer examination he had seriously distorted the analysis and I am afraid his article may do
more harm than good.  He has transformed the problem
of getting more social science information about Latin
America and other areas into a problem of ethics, a
problem of academic status, and unwittingly, into an
overestimation of academic versus real world values.
The available facts do not support his analyses.

He goes on to question...whether social scientists who
are consultants to the Department of Defense should
have a haven in a university.  He believes that any
such consultantship compromises objectivity.  This is
a gratuitous inference.  Problems of involvement with
a client are common to all applied fields; in medicine,
in industrial psychology, in clinical psychology
among many others.  However, ways have been developed
for dealing with clients objectively and ethically.
Political science is not a science but a technology.
It is an applied field too.

There is a serious risk in his proposal of discouraging
academically based people working on problems of the
government.  The risk is that the academician will iso-

late himself from the problems of the real world and
preoccupy himself with trivia or pseudo-problems.
There is also a risk in restricting research on government problems to people in government.  They are far
more vulnerable to the biases of the power structure
than are the university people.

Ithiel de Sola Pool, who had participated in the DOD's
efforts from the start and was to remain active in them
afterwards, wrote privately to Senator McCarthy:

The press reporting of the relationship between the
Defense Department and the State Department in regard
to social science research on foreign areas has been
misleading.  There has been no lack of effort on the
part of the Defense Department to keep the State Department continuously informed about its social
science research activities.  The problem is indeed
the contrary one.  The research people in the Defense
Department recognize that the kind of information they
need about places like Viet Nam, the Dominican Republic or other countries in which they have future responsibilities, are often also kinds of information
that the State Department should want.  They have
urged the State Department to conduct serious social
science research on foreign areas too, but to no avail.
The research that the Defense Department has supported
in the social sciences is in general absolutely appropriate to its mission but that does not exclude it
being also useful to the State Department.  Ideally
one would expect close liaison and cooperation in
securing studies of such topics as the organization of
guerrilla forces and the conditions under which the
populace will support them or resist them.  In fact the
support of serious research has been left by default
to the Defense Department which has taken its responsibility seriously while continuously informing the State
Department and involving it as much as possible.

The absence of an effective State Department role in
research may be attributed to two factors:  expectation

of Congressional nonsupport and prejudice on the part of some persons within the State Department against social science research as such.

The social sciences are but one way of viewing what goes on in the world. The national policy maker should have available to him several sorts of information coming through different channels and collected by different methods. He has the information collected by foreign correspondents and reported in the press, he has the reports of experienced foreign service officers, he has intelligence reports. In addition to these three channels, he should also have studies by social science foreign area specialists. Each of these channels has its advantages and its defects. The press, the F.S. O.'s reports and intelligence reports are far more topical than anything an anthropologist or political scientist or area specialist might provide. On the other hand recent events in the Dominican Republic have demonstrated once more how fallible the ordinary channels can be. The social scientist tends to spend months or years in one place interviewing systematically chosen samples of hundreds of respondents and uses a variety of other devices for providing extreme depth to his observations. Had there been some good anthropological or sociological studies of the Dominican Republic going forward, American and OAS policy makers would be in a much better position now to interpret intelligently the realities and needs of the situation.

...The question has been raised, however, whether the Ambassador should not have a veto on governmentally supported research activities. In many cases the answer is, of course, "yes." The answer however, turns out to be fairly complex. Clearly the kind of thing that it was erroneously alleged Project Camelot was doing, namely conducting a Defense Department sponsored survey in a country, should only be done with the knowledge and approval of the Ambassador. (What I understand happened in that case was that a university researcher unauthorizedly used the Camelot name.) On the other hand, a great deal of scientific research these days is partly or indirectly government supported.

Clearly a university scholar carrying on his work overseas should not feel that because some government research money has gone into his funding, he should
either be authorized to say his is a government activity or be required to check out his research plans with
the local mission.  The major universities in this
country that are engaged in archeological, anthropological and sociological studies abroad, will not accept the constraint that their studies will have to be
politically cleared just because they have received
some NSF or NIH or ARPA or ONR money.  The scientist
continues to think of himself as a private university
researcher and should be encouraged to do so.  That is
why the issue is complex.

But such representations made little difference in the

general drift of events.  For one thing, the drift of

opinion in the entire intellectual community favored

those who were attacking the existing order.  The

other "establishment"--the one including the leaders

of opinion in the social science professional associa-

tions--were being given their day in court.  Almost ex-

clusively, they were the ones called upon to testify

before the Harris committee.  The testimony was diverse,

subtle, and sensitive.  These men were not radicals by

any means, and criticism of their colleagues was muted.

They were trying to learn the lessons of the immediate

past, and to see ahead to what should be done about

them.  But almost universally, the testimony tended to

reinforce the new value system that was emerging.  The

idea of a separate National Social Science Foundation

received strong support, and was reflected in a bill

Senator Harris introduced in 1969 to establish such a

foundation (a bill which was not enacted by Congress).[19]

One of the few premises of the old system that was
not overturned or attacked in the testimony before
Senator Harris, or in any of the other forums where
the issues were being argued, was the idea that social-
ly oriented research was "good"; was important; could
help solve social problems; and should be undertaken.
Not surprisingly, all the social scientists who attacked the DOD, and those who testified before Senator
Harris, continued to support this view.  And the DOD
itself--or those in it who still cared, and there were
many--continued to hold to this premise and to act
upon it.  The subsequent events and consequences were
many, important, and instructive.  They are the subject
of the next chapters of this book.  But first, two
more observations are in order.  These are personal
observations, but they do bear on the later evaluation
of the meaning of these events.

It was interesting to note, first, that the social
science community--that part of it which attacked the
DOD and the researchers who had been working with the
government--became very unscientific even as it made
its attacks on the supposed distortion of science
which Camelot represented.  It must be granted that
many of the arguments against DOD research on foreign
social systems, and those pointing out the implicit
biases of the military sponsors of such research and
the risk that participating social scientists would
share those biases, have some validity.  But, as in
any deep and serious public controversy, the arguments

that had been initially made in favor of the work did
not immediately lose their validity.  There remained
two sides to the question, especially since the social
scientists involved, and many of the military and civilian officials at the upper levels of DOD who supported them, believed that the country was on a path essential to the maintenance of its position on the international scene, and should be helped to follow that
path as wisely as possible--not to establish and maintain an overseas "empire," but to maintain a position
protecting itself against many forms of indirect attack
by others avowedly trying to destroy it.  The sometimes
conflicting desires of assuring assistance to social
development overseas in consonance with basic American
democratic values, and preventing deterioration in
American foreign relations while carrying out a foreign policy in the American interest, motivated all of
them.

One would expect the news media and the general
public to move from one view of foreign policy to
another through advocacy of a new set of arguments
replacing an older set.  This is in the tradition of
American politics.  But one would not expect this from
those who called themselves "scientists," and for whom
"objectivity" was supposed to be the most fundamental
precept of their intellectual lives.  Those who attacked their colleagues for not having paid attention to
both sides of the social and political issues then proceeded to be just as biased on the other side.  None of

the writings, testimony, speeches, or resolutions by
social scientists examined both sides of the issues
fairly, trying to draw a balanced assessment that could
enlighten and uplift the public debate. For example,
Horowitz, in the preface to his book, states that he
did his best to interview all parties involved in
Camelot--critics as well as supporters of the project.
But to my knowledge he did not interview any of those
in OSD, civilian or military, who had created the conditions that made Camelot possible, about their motives
for doing so. While many of these people were not officially available to the press, they would have been
available to Horowitz. One must conclude that the exclusion reflects an unconscious bias for the positions
he was already taking. Nor did Horowitz (or any other
of this group), after accusing the DOD of ignoring the
possibility of beneficent revolution, explore concurrently the possibility that all revolutions might not
be in the best interests of the societies where they
took place.

In Horowitz' writings, and also in virtually all
that others in the social science community wrote
about Camelot, the many errors of fact that had originally been perpetrated in the press stories were picked
up and repeated uncritically. None of the social
scientists who entered the fray as the issue became
more intense took the trouble to investigate sufficiently to get the facts straight, much less to understand
and describe the background of events that had led to

Camelot in the first place. If the earlier group who
had worked with the encouragement of the DOD could be
accused of looking at only one side of the questions
they were dealing with, those who accused them were
doing the same. Both groups based their writings on
the values and premises they held, and did not look at
the implications of the possibility that opposite values and premises might exist concurrently.

Another aspect of this question involves the very
questions of morality and ethics that the DOD's opponents raised. The "anti" chorus was very strong, and
the condemnation of their colleagues was loud and frequent. In the morality that was growing in opposition
to the Vietnam war, "dissent" became the watchword.
If you were in dissent, you were "concerned"; if you
felt "concern," you had to take an activist role, and
become "involved"--against. "Constancy"--a fundamental
property of what earlier generations knew as "character"--did not receive attention, or was rejected. If
you felt the government was wrong, you should not try
to help it change; you must oppose it. If a commitment
had been made to help it, and government didn't instantly follow your advice, the commitment should instantly
be rejected.

One wonders, when thinking about the social scientists who desired to continue to help, and who suffered
ever more virulent attacks for their trouble, what is
more virtuous: to remain steadfast in one's convictions against all opposition, or to sense the winds of

change and allow one's self to be wafted whichever way
they blow? Truly, Camelot and the reaction to it both
raised and reflected one of the great moral issues of
our time. The analogy has been drawn, by some on one
side of this issue, between the United States at this
time in its history, and Hitler's Germany. One who had
adult awareness at that earlier period instinctively
rejects the comparison. But it will be left to the
more dispassionate historians of a later generation--
those who were not "involved"--to judge, if ever a
final judgment can be made.

# IV  DOD KEEPS TRYING

Prefatory Note:  A Personal Interlude, 2

At the end of January, 1966, as the immediate furor
over Camelot came to an end and many of the other research and development efforts I had tried to stimulate
seemed (unlike the social research program) successfully launched, I left the Pentagon and returned to the
Institute for Defense Analyses.  In the relative peace
and quiet of an atmosphere removed from the daily crises
of the government bureaucracy, I had a chance to sort
out my thoughts about the stimulating two years just
past.  There was enough to do of immediate interest,
and I lost track of the DOD's efforts to apply the social sciences to counterinsurgency problems.  I knew
that ARPA was continuing its attempts, and I was aware
that SORO was sinking back into its original pattern
of library studies after changing its name and many of
its research personnel.  I had no contact at all with
the Air Force and the Navy programs, but assumed they
had returned to the earlier pattern as well.  If I
thought about it, I was certain that they would try to
carry on but would have a harder time of it; and this
was confirmed by the few items of news that came my
way.

The return to IDA turned out to be just an interlude.  In August of 1966, Dr. Charles M. Herzfeld, who
had been Sproull's deputy in ARPA and had then replaced
him as Director, asked me to join ARPA as Director of
Project Agile.  During my earlier tour, Herzfeld and I

had worked together closely. We shared many accomplishments in stimulating research and development efforts in the physical sciences and engineering related to the ongoing conflicts in the world. In addition, he strongly believed in the importance of applying the social sciences to the DOD's problems overseas; he often risked the displeasure of his superiors in the DOD to make the point and support this part of his program. As Director of Agile, I would be in a position to initiate and supervise directly some of the important efforts that, from ODDR&E, I could only try to persuade the Services or ARPA to undertake. And so, in November of 1966, I once again entered the bureaucratic maze.

Although the social research effort was but a small part of the Agile program—running at a total of about $2½ million per year, which it never exceeded—I still believed in its importance. I felt that I had learned a few things about how to undertake such a program. I was well aware of its sensitivity and the many obstacles to its success; and I had no illusions about the permissiveness of Congress or the upper levels of the DOD. Forewarned by earlier events and presumably forearmed, I set about building a program in the social sciences that I hoped would be useful and important, and trying to establish it in such a way that it could be protected from the worst ravages of the outside world until it had had a chance to prove its value. The demands and impact of that world were, nevertheless,

to pose continuing problems and crises; constant adjustments in subject matter, choices of talent, and ways of
doing business were necessary.

The first steps in reshaping ARPA's program of social research on insurgency problems were designed to give that program as broad and solid a base of executive branch support as possible, and to reduce its vulnerability to attack.  In taking these steps, we adhered to the principle that the work must be useful to the DOD, and therefore that it must be clearly and demonstrably related to the DOD mission and operations.  In this, we did not go as far as Senator Fulbright would have wanted, since we still focused attention on the overseas operations of the DOD and the allies of the United States.  But each project was defined in such a way that it dealt with a problem that could be described in terms of international military and military-related operations then taking place—for example, the Military Assistance Program, if not actual warfare, as in Vietnam—that rendered the subject of the research of direct concern to the DOD.

Every effort was made to select problems for research support about whose importance, both in fact and in appearance, there would be little doubt.  This was sometimes difficult when we had to respond to specific requests of foreign governments to the U.S. government, or to requests overseas commands or embassies made of the DOD.  But in such cases there was, at least, the fact of the request to help establish the legitimacy of the work.  We were most careful never to undertake

work on our own initiative--that is, we never initiated
a project simply because ARPA or the researcher happened to feel it was interesting. Wherever a project
proposal started--and it could begin with a researcher,
or with ARPA (presumably, as a research organization
that had been delving in depth into these problems for
some years, ARPA should have some institutional knowledge of what the important long-term problems were),
or with an American military command or embassy (which
had short-term problems and often sought help in solving them), or a foreign government connected with the
United States through a military assistance agreement
--we insisted that the project couldn't start until it
went through the entire approval chain, within the DOD
and outside it.

It was recognized that this might often preclude
what might appear to be interesting and useful work;
but that which was undertaken would, we believed, be
far better protected by several branches and layers of
the government bureaucracy, in case questions were
raised about why it was being done. Moreover, it would
also be firmly connected with the "user" community, so
that the results would have a "home" for implementation. In effect, this approach was intended to assure
that the research and the DOD organization that undertook it were instruments of policy and not makers of
policy. If the work were attacked, all those who had
requested and approved it would have to be attacked as
well. This approach had its obverse aspect also.

We found that <u>most</u> of the time, if a project were
worthwhile, the case for it could be made, while on
occasion, if a member of outside officialdom pressed
us too hard to undertake a task that seemed too risky,
or too sensitive, or useless, we could maintain friendly relationships while relying on other parts of "the
system" to help exert better sense and judgment.

Steps were taken to reduce the visibility of the
work. This may seem inconsistent with the efforts to
assure a broad base of support. But it's all in the
point of view. The innovator--and there have been a
number--who creates a new element of technology or
makes a new scientific discovery against all opposition,
often "bootlegging" funds, is admired and frequently
rewarded. But if he fails he is prepared to receive,
and often does receive, the censure of his peers and
other elements of society. This seemed a risk that
would have to be taken. If the research provided obviously useful results that affected national policy
in ways that were viewed as beneficial, it would be
accepted. If it did not, it would soon wither in any
case. But it needed some protection while undergoing
the test, or there would never be a chance to find out.
This, in itself, turned out to be an interesting experimental research question, of which there was sufficient awareness even at the time.

At any rate, there wasn't very much that could be
done to reduce visibility. The program was kept relatively small. It supported, at various times, between

15 and 25 professional researchers and a number of foreign research assistants overseas in all the activities.
An identifying label for the research program--"Social
Science Research"--was eliminated. All the Agile programs were problem-oriented and identified by the subject of the research. We were studying real problems,
and some of them required social scientists, just as
others required physicists or engineers. Therefore
the program was identified, and projects were distributed, according to the problem areas with which they
were concerned--village defense, or troop training, or
civic action, and the like. And finally, since in most
cases the projects dealt with on-going operations of
both the American and foreign governments, much of it
was classified. The intent was both to minimize the
possibility of embarrassment to the United States and
host governments where the work was underway, and,
since the results were generally expected to bear on
policy and operations, to prevent knowledge of such
results from telegraphing the moves of the United
States and its allies to others who might use the knowledge for unfriendly purposes. The classification also
had the effect of making it harder for--but certainly
not stopping--the press from continuing its barrage of
hostile or amusedly tolerant articles regarding "DOD
social science research." All this may seem now to
have been rendered somehow sinister by the affair of
the Pentagon Papers; again, it's all in the point of
view, and there appears no need at this point to do

other than relate the facts as they existed.

I had also determined, early during my ARPA tour,
to try to orient this part of the Agile program as much
toward quantitative measurement and analysis as possible. There were several reasons for this. One was a
continuing interest, which I shared and believed in,
in furthering the intent of the Defense Science Board's
recommendations about "hardening the soft sciences."
It seemed, on reflection and after extensive discussions I had with Rains Wallace during the period we
worked together, that if social science were to be
dignified by the name "science," it ought to be able
to do well the first step of science, that of measuring
the phenomena with which it tried to deal. In the
words of Lord Kelvin:

I often say that when you can measure what you are
speaking about, and express it in numbers, you know
something about it; but when you cannot measure it,
when you cannot express it in numbers, your knowledge
is of a meager and unsatisfactory kind; it may be the
beginning of knowledge, but you have scarcely, in your
thoughts, advanced to the stage of science, whatever
the matter may be.

This was, in fact, the approach that helped make the
work of the behavioral sciences for the DOD in the selection, training, troop performance, and human factors
engineering areas so successful.

But there were many reasons why this aim was especially difficult to attain in the counterinsurgency area,
which we shall discuss later. Nevertheless, in addi-

tion to its desirability from a purely scientific point
of view, the approach would help focus the research on
matters where there was some chance of obtaining some
data to support what would otherwise be arguable opinions, helping thereby to reduce the speculative elements of any study where so much more political sensitivity and controversy were likely to exist.  It would,
in particular, help to avoid pitting the judgment of
the researcher against the judgment of the political
operator, in an area where the latter ruled.  In this
program orientation the research would have to be
based on attempts to gather and analyze data, thereby
dealing with real events, places, and people, and only
with those phenomena where data could be expected to
exist.  It would, by this means, have to deal with
evaluation of situations, actions, and programs, rather
than with predictions about them.  It would thereby
concentrate on providing verifiable information for
policymakers and operational program directors to use
in their own planning and decision making, rather than
trying to forecast, in competition with the judgment
of these responsible officials, what would be likely
to happen.  This seemed a proper role for science.

Thus the new pattern was set.  It was restrictive,
and not exactly the type of program the social scientists who had authored the Smithsonian reports had had
in mind.  But it seemed nevertheless that if the social
sciences had anything to contribute, this should give
them a reasonable chance of doing so.  Now let us see

what happened.

Although the issues that emerged and conditioned the results were many and complex, they can be grouped into four problem areas within which there were many subtle variations: who could undertake the work, and how they could interact with the bureaucratic system; the problems of planning and performing research under the diverse constraints that were imposed; technical problems of the research and of performing it in the field; and, how the results were used, if they were used at all. We will explore each of these in turn, and then see how the outside world was responding while all this was going on.

It was clear from the start that the field of available
people for the research would be restricted. Many
social scientists had made apparent their antipathy to
the DOD and what it was trying to do, and the university community would obviously have to be approached very
gingerly. On the other hand, there was some strong
feeling, not without justification, that at least some
of the researchers in the non-university community
lacked the expertise, the political awareness and sensitivity, and, shall we say, the wisdom to undertake
the research that was required. Thus, throughout the
entire process there was a search for appropriate and
willing sources of expertise, and as experience grew
the field was narrowed to the point where very few such
sources remained.

The problem with the more hostile university scholars
was brought home rapidly--again by the anthropologists.
Within a few days of my entering ARPA, the entire social
science program that ARPA had continued, since Camelot,
threatened to explode the way Camelot did. The first
event had to do with a proposal that had been submitted
to ARPA in preliminary form by a university-connected
research group in the Washington area, regarding the
possibility of studying some tribal societies in the
Congo. The leader of this group, without having had
any indication about whether the research proposal
would be accepted, had set about arranging his team for

listing in the proposal.  In the process, we later
gathered, he approached an anthropologist experienced
in that area, giving him to understand that he, the
research director, firmly anticipated receiving an ARPA
contract for tribal research in the Congo.  The anthropologist immediately raised a storm, writing to the
American Anthropological Association and the press
that an attempt was being made to enlist him in intelligence activities for the suppression of Congo tribes
in the conflict that was then in its final stages
there.  Only a firm denial by ARPA that a contract existed or was contemplated allowed the matter to come
to rest.

At about the same time, I received a letter, signed
by Charles Keyes of the University of Washington for
a group that also included the anthropologists Lauristan
Sharpe, Michael Moerman, and Herbert Phillips, all of
them experts on Southeast Asia and Thailand, saying
that they had learned that ARPA was about to undertake
a massive social research program in Thailand which
sounded much like Camelot.  They wanted an explanation,
and if they didn't get one, or weren't satisfied with
the one they did get, they would go to Congress and
the press.  The program they were referring to, which
came to be known as the Rural Security Systems Program,
was just getting underway.  In the words used to describe it initially to Congress, the purpose of the
program was[1]

(to) gather and collate critical information on the
local geography, the way of life of the local people,
and on their attitudes toward the Government; ...set
up and help maintain current files on insurgent incidents and operations, and on the many Government programs and activities undertaken for counterinsurgency
purposes in the northeast; and....provide assistance
in analyzing the effectiveness of various counterinsurgency programs, as well as helping, through analytical techniques to plan further CI programs.

As part of the initial planning, ARPA (before my
arrival) had let a small contract with a social
scientist who had just left his association with an
industrial organization to establish his own company,
to conduct a survey of the possibility for and interest
in social science research in Thailand.  He had written
a form letter to some 300 diverse social scientists (I
seem to recall that high number, but could be wrong at
this late date), describing the nature of the research
contemplated, and implicitly conveying the impression
that many social scientists with their families would
converge on Northeast Thailand to perform research in
connection with the gradually appearing insurgency
there.  It was through this means that the anthropologists who wrote to me had acquired the information that
led them to write; and I came face to face with the
problem virtually on my first day back in the government.

   After some internal efforts to assure that no such
plan would be seriously considered by ARPA, I invited
Keyes and the others who had written to visit me and

talk about the program.  They were reassured that no
serious thought was being given to an effort of the
kind described.  But it was also pointed out that a
program was being initiated to help the Royal Thai
Government, with full approval and agreement by that
government, the American Ambassador (Graham Martin),
and the State Department, to resolve the problems of
insurgency in its northeast provinces, and to help it
ascertain in the process how it might go about developing this Appalachia of its country to make insurgency
there less likely.  This was the very problem that
troubled the anthropologists, since they felt that by
providing this assistance the United States was increasing the pressure for rapid change and modernization
beyond the capability of Thai civilization to accept
it.  This professed uneasiness manifested itself in a
number of ways.  One was the suggestion that the rapid
social change was destroying a culture that had yet to
be observed and understood.

This argument appeared in a more explicit form
shortly after this meeting, when we were informed that
Peter Kunstadter, an anthropologist working with tribal
groups in Thailand, had expressed his concern to a
fellow anthropologist who was visiting him that if the
DOD saturated the area with social scientists studying
the local people for "applied" reasons, he would not
be able to continue his research on the culture in its
existing state.  Our interpretation was that, in effect, he was concerned that we would be spoiling his

museum.

After the discussion with Keyes and the others, they agreed that modernization was rapidly coming to all the peoples of Thailand, both through the offices of their own government and from the inexorable drift arising from prolonged contact with the West, and that if the DOD were supporting research on how the changes affected people and on how to ease the inevitable burdens of their cultural evolution, this was an objective which they would not condemn. Having reached this happy conclusion to a delicate confrontation, I then asked whether, since they were among the recognized American experts on Thai culture and history, they would be willing to help us do a better job by helping in the research. The responses varied. One said that if the work were later to be criticized, he would not want to be associated with it but would rather be free to join the critics (although he later sent us a copy, which was very helpful, of his yet-to-be-published Ph.D. thesis on life in Thai village society). Others promised benevolent neutrality.

But one of the group decided that it was time to "put my money where my mouth is," and to help us if he agreed with our objectives. This was Dr. Herbert Phillips of the University of California (Berkeley), who became an ARPA consultant and who in the course of the next two years was to provide much useful understanding of the background to the problems with which ARPA was involved in Thailand. He was to be attacked, later, for this particular interpretation of ethical behavior; and Michael Moerman was also to suffer, although his connection with the DOD was much more tenuous.  Other anthropologists' view of their efforts differed from theirs; an article that appeared later in the <u>New York Review of Books</u>, describing the government's association with social scientists, suggested that behind a request for pure research, a research grant, or a consultant's fee would be a government that could use the knowledge gained to <u>damage</u> the subjects of the very same research.[2]

The occasion for assessing this judgment was a "summer study" held by the Institute for Defense Analyses' Jason group,* in 1967.  One of the members of Jason, Murray Gell-Mann (who was later to win a Nobel Prize in Physics), was interested in Thailand; was concerned over U.S. policy there; and convened a group of government officials and social scientists knowledgeable about Thailand to explore the policy questions.  The

---

*Jason is a group of eminent university scientists, primarily in the field of physics, who devote a significant portion of their time to organized study of defense problems.  Meeting at IDA periodically to learn about those problems during the academic year, they then met together in another location for several weeks during each summer, to perform substantive analyses of a number of those problems. Their reports have been valued at and have been advisory to the highest levels of the DOD.  In 1973, their affiliation was transferred for administrative reasons from IDA to the Stanford Research Institute.

group included Phillips and Moerman. The objective
was to learn what was known to Americans about Thai
society, and to assess the impact of American aid and
policy on that society. If useful information could
be synthesized, it could become a report to the government on the subject.

For three weeks the visiting officials and social
scientists spoke freely, frankly, and not always comp-
limentarily, about Thai society, Thai government, and
American activities there. As it turned out, the
picture that emerged was mixed; the group found some
things it liked and some it disliked about both the
Thai government's actions and American policy in supporting them. There was no special report, but detailed minutes of the discussions were kept by the
participants. Through what was later reported to me
privately as an act of theft by a student activist
working in his office, the copy of the minutes held by
one of the attending social scientists was made public
in 1969. Not unexpectedly, the intent of the meeting
was lost, and an outcry ensued about the anthropologists who were helping the U.S. government's "counterinsurgency." Phillips and Moerman were attacked by
members of the American Anthropological Association.[3]
The view now strongly held (in 1969, when this news
emerged) was that anthropologists must keep themselves
"pure," and must be willing to champion the oppressed
peoples of the world, including those whom anthropologists would define as "primitives" or "peasants."[4]

The arrogation to self of superior attitudes toward
other peoples by "defining" them was apparently lost
on the authors of such words and the community that
agreed with them.  But it was clear that any research
to gain knowledge that could be used, for any purpose,
had become anathema to them.  It was not clear, however,
whether it would be acceptable to use the knowledge
for purposes these anthropologists could agree with--
for example, revolutionary protest--and was unaccepta-
ble only if they didn't agree.  Or, were they honestly
interested in science that could be called "pure," if
such were definable?  If the latter, would they, as
their colleague in Thailand appeared to, require the
peoples they wished to define and study not to change
while the "pure" scientists studied them?  The positions of various social scientists on these points are
not clear even yet.

In this case, the American Anthropological Association set up a board of inquiry under the highly respected Margaret Mead, to ascertain whether there had
been any wrongdoing.  In its report, while the kind of
research at issue was condemned, and some rules of
ethics were recommended for anthropologists to protect
the subjects of their research from government interest,
the specific individuals were absolved of sinister
motives and malfeasance.  But the association refused
to accept this verdict, and in effect sent the committee back to find against the accused.[5]

Phillips and Moerman were not the only university

scholars attacked for association with the DOD.  A
scientist at a midwestern university, who was an
expert on Thai institutions and governmental systems,
undertook an ARPA contract to explore the institutional
problems of change in Thailand and, incidentally, how
these affected and were affected by the various conflicts in different areas of the country.  He finished
the preliminary, exploratory part of his work, and we
were negotiating with him for a contract to continue
while clearance for the project was being sought.  He
was well known to Thai social scientists and to Thai
government officials; the prospects were hopeful.  He
planned several years of his future career on the basis
of the anticipated ARPA support, and he counted on his
relationships with Thai government officials to assist
in obtaining the data needed for his research.  When
his past and planned work became known, I was told, he
was attacked by fellow faculty members and student
activists, who demanded that he give up the work or
resign his position.  Sadly, the contract was not
worked out after all, for a variety of reasons having
to do primarily with the American Embassy's view of
the research; and so he suffered for naught.

Still another case involved Gerald Hickey, the anthropologist who had devoted ten years to study of the
mountain tribes of Vietnam.  His anthropologist colleagues granted that he was sympathetic to the Montagnard, had preserved his intellectual freedom, and had
probably saved the Montagnard from extinction during

the ravages of the war by interceding on their behalf
with the American and Vietnamese governments. Nevertheless, he was denied even an office to work on a book
at his alma mater, the University of Chicago--the issue
was not whether an office was due him, or available,
but that he had committed the unpardonable sin of
accepting DOD money, through the RAND Corporation, to
support his work in Vietnam.[6]

These incidents make clear that many of those who
expressed their concern for academic freedom meant only
a very special kind, and were not ready to grant true
academic freedom to their own colleagues.

The impact of the general outlook of the activists
on university faculties and in student bodies was felt
keenly in indirect ways as well. At least three not-
for-profit research organizations were working for ARPA
in Thailand on a variety of problems in counterinsurgency, only some of which involved the social sciences.
These were the Stanford Research Institute, the Cornell
Aeronautical Laboratory, and the University of Michigan
Institute of Science and Technology. All three organizations were independent, but connected with their
parent universities in various ways--through Boards of
Trustees, sharing of research funds in some cases, use
of faculty as consultants, and use of full-time institute staff as part-time faculty.

In 1967 and 1968, as the Vietnam war was building
to the peak of American involvement, these organizations
came under attack by members of the associated univer-

sity faculties and activist students for contributing
to "war research," and for being part of the military-
industrial complex. The work they were doing in Thailand for ARPA figured strongly in these attacks, for
many reasons. In the Students for a Democratic Society
(SDS) publications, Project Agile assumed an image much
like that of the CIA, as an object of condemnation for
events in Southeast Asia. The faculties felt that the
government was corrupting their universities with classified research, and especially with counterinsurgency
research. In the case of the Cornell Aeronautical
Laboratory, scholars of Latin American affairs at
Cornell University played a strong role in the attack,
because they reasoned that if CAL (which was actually
a separate organization in another city) were performing counterinsurgency research using the name of Cornell, this would jeopardize their own ability to do
research in Latin America, à la Camelot. Thus, lengthy
conflicts began which, in the case of SRI and CAL, led
to breaking the organizations' connections with the
associated universities. This was particularly painful in the CAL case, because the separation was accompanied by a long court fight over whether the university could sell the not-for-profit laboratory to a profit-
making financial combine, leading to serious erosion
of the organizational integrity and key staff of the
laboratory. At the University of Michigan the Institute of Science and Technology did not separate until
many years later, but it gave up much of the work that

it ordinarily performed under DOD sponsorship.

All these events, most of which occurred over the two-year period 1967 and 1968, led to a gradual separation between the universities and ARPA in this area of research. This was reinforced by problems within ARPA's basic behavioral research program, which was distinct from Agile's program. Those problems were typified by a study program in which ARPA had funded a number of independent scholars to perform research in the Himalayan region. There was no immediate, applied objective; as part of the intention to build capability for overseas social research, ARPA had undertaken to support a number of scholars, through university grants, in studies of their own choices regarding the peoples of that region. Of course, it could be argued, and would undoubtedly have been true, that the DOD had ulterior motives; that if at some time, for example, the United States became involved in a further India-China conflict, the knowledge would have applied value. But anyone's published work could be put to such use.

The fact that the program existed came to public attention when one of the scholars learned that his support came to his university from the DOD, and spurned the support. Senator Fulbright noted the incident on the Senate floor.[7] The Indian Government disavowed the program, and ARPA felt impelled to do so also.

The ultimate consequence of all these problems, however, was the growth of the view in ARPA, as articulated by Dr. Eberhardt Rechtin, who succeeded Herzfeld

as Director in 1967, that research at universities on
applied matters, which was classified, and supported
by the DOD, simply represented an incompatible set.
There were, in addition, problems of another kind, arising largely from university researchers' bent for seeking DOD funds to perform research of interest to themselves, but only incidentally of interest to the government. For example, as late as 1968 one anthropologist,
who had earlier been concerned that he not come under
attack by his colleagues for undertaking counterinsurgency research, nevertheless indicated his willingness
to accept ARPA support for an overseas linguistic study
he had in mind. Therefore, the decision was made, in
mid-1968, that no further work of this kind would be
supported by ARPA at universities.

All of this took some time, however, and while it
was happening other experiments with institutions for
research were also under way. One, in particular,
showed early promise of becoming a model mechanism
for university scholars to undertake research of this
kind if they wished to, independently of the institutional conflicts that were emerging in DOD-university
contractual relationships. Its genesis was some years
before all these events. An independent research organization, the Simulmatics Corporation, had been
formed that served as an "applied research outlet" for
a number of university professors and students. It had
been active in social research of the kind (but not in
the places) sought by the DOD. As far as we in ARPA

were concerned, a group like this had impeccable credentials and helped avoid many problems.  Those who
were members of the organization, such as Dr. Ithiel de
Sola Pool, who had long been associated with the DOD's
social research efforts, could easily attract other
well-known scholars; among them were many who were experts on Vietnam, had been there before, spoke the
language, and knew many of the key Vietnamese figures
who could grant "access" for research.  The contracting
mechanism would be with a private organization, not a
university; and the researchers would join it as individuals, to study a particular problem.

In 1967, it wasn't difficult to see the trend of
the university-DOD relationship, and the Simulmatics
alternative appeared to be a mechanism through which
such problems could be avoided while we could still
have the benefit of university scholars' expertise.
Therefore a substantial contract covering several research tasks in Vietnam was let, and we hoped that by
this means we could build an institution that could
carry on the DOD's work in the social sciences overseas.  It didn't work out this way, but for a set of
reasons wholly different from those that might have
been anticipated.  These originated in the institutional constraints that will be examined in detail in
the next chapter.

The first problem arose from the administration of
the company and its general management of the work.
Its expenditures overseas were, in the DOD's view,

loosely controlled, in a pattern that was completely
at odds with the stringent reporting requirements of
Defense contracting agencies. Many expenditures were
questioned by those agencies, such as the house or
"villa" Simulmatics rented in Saigon for living and
office space. (The villa itself was not an unusual
thing--researchers had to have someplace to work and
to live. In this case it was the "style" and the cost
that upset the government auditors.) Then, after agreements to spend certain amounts of money on each task in
the contract, the expenditures varied widely, apparently in keeping with the researchers' varying research
priorities and opportunities, so that it was hard to
keep up with what was being done on which topic, and
it was clear that large "overruns" would be in the
offing on at least some of the tasks. None of this is
to say that the company's management was dishonest, or
excessively careless. It was, rather, a result of an
ethical system and outlook that differed markedly from
that of its sponsors. The differences cropped up in
many ways, in addition to the one associated with financial management. One of the others occurred in
matters of family.

In general, researchers in Vietnam agreed to go
under the same conditions as obtained for the U.S.
military, which, after 1965, meant that no families
were sent. All systems of ethics have their contradictions, and this one was no exception. While the
military could look with equanimity on wives coming

over on Vietnamese government visitor's permits and
working for civilian contractors in Saigon (for example, Standard Oil or BRJ-RMK, the large construction
contractor), they felt strongly that it was wrong for
wives to be employed by the company that their husbands
worked for. Yet a number of attempts were made by the
younger members of this company to make such an arrange-
ment. In another case, a university professor who
joined Simulmatics to perform what became an excellent
study on an important subject, made his wife a member
of his research team and wanted his son to join them
as a research assistant. His wife was, in fact, a
qualified psychologist, and the son was a social science
student in college, well qualified to perform the research assistant's task. The professor saw nothing
wrong with this, since both could contribute to the
research and, in his son's case, he would do as well
as any other research assistant while the experience
would be useful for his career. But, again, the DOD
auditors presumed it to be a "boondoggle," and the
matter had to be sent all the way to Dr. Foster, the
DDR&E, for approval. The wife was approved, but the
son was not; and it was clear that we wouldn't routinely
go through "one more like that."

Other problems related to those of ethics, and with
other overtones of substance, arose from the very eminence of the scholars who agreed to do the research.
They were very busy people, accustomed to taking on
several jobs at once and using graduate students and

research assistants to gather data and perform analyses under supervision. This worked well in the United States, where they could keep close watch on what was happening; but some of the procedure carried over into the work in Vietnam, causing a stir on several levels. First, it was not easy, administratively, for them to travel between the United States and Vietnam, since a "theatre clearance" was needed for each trip, and sometimes events such as the Tet offensive in 1968 could stop civilian travel to South Vietnam for some time. Second, the DOD believed it was contracting for some months of the professors' time, thinking the time would be consecutive, and was distressed to learn that in many cases the principal investigator had planned several short trips to oversee much less senior, less expert researchers who would do most of the field work. Among other things, this meant that the data gathering --the contact with foreign officials and population-- would not be done primarily by the one who had been asked to do it because of his expertise, sensitivity, and "connections," but by a junior researcher, unknown to us, in whom there was much less confidence.

The most serious of these problems arose in the area of "academic freedom," from a wholly unexpected (to us) direction. The scholars felt they had undertaken a contract in which they were the experts who would specify what should be done, when, where, and how. At least in part, any task was not simply a service the experts had agreed to perform, but was of professional interest that coincided with their own research and career plans. (For this reason, I believed, the researchers felt free to rearrange the funding associated with specific tasks.) When they arrived in Vietnam, they wanted to get on with the job, with complete freedom of movement and freedom to see whomever it was necessary to see to get the work done. All they wanted from the government was logistic support--assistance in arranging meetings if necessary, communications, and transportation.

The view held by the military members of MACV and the military representatives of ARPA in Saigon was different. They felt, first, that they were responsible for the safety of the visitors. "Getting around" in a war-torn country involved the provision of military aircraft and ground transportation at some cost to the government, and adherence to some rough schedule that depended on aircraft availability. To assure the researchers' safety it might be necessary in some cases to provide a military escort. Therefore, the military wanted some advanced planning about who was to be visited by whom, when, and where. This led to a demand for a certain rigidity in the research schedule that many of the social scientists from universities were not willing to countenance, since each research contact could lead in a direction that might not have been anticipated in advance.

In addition, visits with Vietnamese officials could be sensitive politically (or, at least, the official

American community felt that they were), and individuals among the American military and civil authorities were not always willing to give of their time freely to the many researchers in the area unless they felt they had some stake in the study, which was rare for most of them. Thus, the military people responsible for monitoring the work wanted advance notice of such visits for the additional reason that they could help with the arrangements, clearing administrative roadblocks and assuring themselves and those to be visited that the visits were necessary to the studies. The social scientists viewed this as an infringement on their freedom to perform the research for which they had contracted. While the military sponsors denied any intention to control the direction of study, it couldn't be denied that they exercised a measure of judgment with respect to the answers to the question, "Why do you have to see so-and-so?" "He might be a useful source of information," which would be justification enough for the researcher, was not always so for the military contract monitor. Not only did this inevitably mean that the military were in some degree imposing their views on how the research was to be done, it reflected also a measure of concern about the view of the research that their superiors in MACV would express. Like all good bureaucrats, the military man viewed a study that had been "approved" as an obligation which he had to protect, even against the danger he perceived that the one who may originally have pro-

posed it might destroy it by his own lack of circumspection.  And so the judgments about whom to see included bureaucratic as well as scientific influences
that the social scientists interpreted with some justification as interference with their work.

   There was no clear-cut right or wrong in all these
differences; they were, rather, the clashes that could
be expected between two cultures who saw the world
through different eyes.  All these differences led,
through several research tasks, to an increasingly
strained atmosphere between the Simulmatics Corporation
and ARPA.  This was exacerbated by the freedom with
which some of the researchers talked to reporters (who
pursued stories aggressively in Saigon), leading to
periodic press stories; in one of them a social scientist working for one organization expressed doubt about
the validity of the work of the others (neither were
identified in the story;  but we had a good idea of
who they were, from the context).  These articles
heightened the feeling of sensitivity about the work
at the upper levels of the DOD, and stimulated interest
in the General Accounting Office which was starting, on
congressional request, to investigate some of Agile's
overseas work.

   Finally, it became necessary to make a judgment as
to whether the problems being created by this contract
and the risks it increasingly posed to other parts of
the ARPA program were worth any results that might e-
merge.  The tensions obviously reduced the potential

of the results to be useful. There had been one or
two reports of unquestioned substance and value, while
the remainder were controversial in terms of their
scientific validity or adherence to the desired work
program; or they were as yet incomplete while the al-
loted funds had been spent; or were being challenged
by officials who disclaimed their utility. Reluctantly,
we decided to terminate the contract. Thus, this experimental approach to enlisting university social
scientists in the research for the DOD failed, largely
for bureaucratic reasons, despite all the promise it
had shown at the beginning.

There is a certain irony in this. When this particular program was beginning I had met with many of the
group of social scientists who were going to Vietnam,
in anticipation of some of the very problems of working
in the wartime military environment that they later encountered. I had tried to impress upon them that as
social scientists they would have to learn about, and
how to work with, a strange (to them) social system of
whose existence they might not be fully conscious--the
U.S. military in Vietnam--in order to perform research
with respect to the social system in which they were
most directly interested--the Vietnamese, on both sides
of the war. Clearly, this lesson hadn't been learned
by any but one or two of this group of social scientists.

Thus it came about that the DOD was inexorably separated from the university social science community--

even from those whose commitment to the U.S. government's purposes hadn't been changed by the Camelot
events--and often through no obvious fault on either
side.  This left private research institutions as
almost the only source of talent for the research the
DOD desired.  This was not an unmitigatedly good source,
either.  Private industry on occasion hired psychologists or sociologists to work with the hardware teams;
but basically people from these disciplines were alien
to the culture of this part of the "military-industrial
complex," their ideas never took on the force that
would have come with "critical mass," and their contributions were minimal.  Most of the not-for-profit firms
had trouble attracting the high-quality social science
staff needed for the research, in a time of problems,
such as those described earlier, that some of them
were having with the universities.  We were left, therefore, with very few sources of first-rate talent--the
RAND Corporation, which had a social science department
of long standing and excellent reputation, and one or
two private firms, such as the American Institutes for
Research, specializing in social science research of
the quantitative character we were looking for.

   RAND's social science group at that time was composed largely of political scientists, with a sprink-
ling of other disciplines, including anthropology.
Many of the men in this group were "lone wolves" who
preferred to pursue their own interests and ends, and
it was a constant struggle to assure that the different

parts of their work remained related to each other and
relevant to our needs.  But some interesting and useful research, which will be examined in another context,
was performed when the circumstances could be arranged
that their interests coincided with those of the DOD;
this occurred mostly during the 1964-1967 period, when
the group that had undertaken to study the Viet Cong
through prisoner and defector interviews was at its
full swing.  Given the disciplinary orientation of the
researchers, however, much of their work had a particular methodological orientation whose validity was
later criticized by others in the social science community, for reasons that will be discussed in Chapter 19.
This lent an uncertainty to some of their results that
was most troublesome in a number of contexts.

The second kind of organization generally undertook
measurement-oriented research, as had been visualized
in the DSB report's recommendations and in the planning
for the ARPA program.  This, then, seemed the last,
best hope--and it was steadily eroded by the problems
of field constraints on subject matter and methodology
that we shall examine in the following chapters.  We
tried, also, to hire social scientists as part of the
ARPA staff for overseas research.  Qualified people
could be found who were willing to join the government
for a period of time for this purpose.  But the bureaucratic system raised a host of problems connected with
salary, "job description," personnel ceilings, and the
like, and it was found virtually impossible to arrange

that an available social scientist, who probably would
have to arrange leave from a university, and a desired
task would meet at the same time.  Therefore we gave up
that approach as well.

It is appropriate to mention, in the context of the
narrowing field of talent available to the DOD, the
continual appearance of serious people who made themselves heard, but whom I came in my impatience to view
as a sort of "lunatic fringe," who made the job harder
by interrupting the always difficult task of trying to
make sense of a research area that appeared to defy
logical management endeavors.  In one case, a proposal
was made to establish a computerized system of extensive personal data on all of the population of Vietnam.
It was thus hoped that the government would better be
able to do such things as collect taxes and, in particular, to keep more effective information on the movements of the Vietnamese population, thereby helping to
identify and subsequently isolate the Viet Cong from
the neutral or friendly population.  We had to point
out, first, that this would put the United States in
the position of imposing a system, à la 1984, on the
Vietnamese which we were unwilling, on moral and ethical grounds, to see imposed on our own population.  In
addition to this moral question were a number of practical ones.  One was the anticipated difficulty the
Vietnamese might have in mastering the highly sophisticated technology that would be required.  Another was
the difficulty of access to all the population in a

war-torn country, and subsequent injustice to many who
might miss being entered into the system.  Finally,
there were the many opportunities for graft and corruption, of which the South Vietnamese were displaying
enough at that time, that would be opened by the creation of a data system subject to manipulation by those
with appropriate motives and access.

   In a related context, we were approached by a psychologist who expounded the theory that one of the
reasons the United States was having such trouble in
the war in Vietnam was that we could not get the Vietnamese government and population to behave as we wanted
them to.  She proposed that the methods of operant
conditioning, including punishments and rewards for
particular behavioral manifestations or desiderata, be
applied, so that eventually we could make the entire
population of Vietnam and its government behave in a
way that the United States decided it should.  She
professed to be able to induce the famous behavioral
psychologist, B.F. Skinner, to go to Vietnam to direct
such an effort.  Again, the question was raised as to
the morality of such an approach, which we certainly
would not tolerate in our own country.  I pointed out,
also, that there would be far from unanimity within
the United States as to what behaviors were desired.
Moreover, it was not clear that if pigeons, or even
individual humans, could be thus conditioned in the
laboratory, this technique could be extended to an
enormously diverse population of some 14 million people,

of a culture alien to ours, and under wartime pressures
and field conditions.

The trouble with these and other spuriously clever
ideas from this group was that they were also occasionally visible to others at the upper levels of the DOD.
This added to the appearance of disorder and illogic
in the view they held of social research, and made the
program we were interested in that much harder to justify.

There was, of course, no choice but to work within the
rigid system of approvals that had been established for
all work overseas, including, especially, research on
social problems.  Otherwise, nothing would have been
done.  But acceptance of these procedures narrowed the
scope and content of work that could be undertaken very
considerably, and had a profound adverse impact on its
real value.  In effect, by allotting to various external power centers the authority to say what work could
be done--or, more particularly, what work could not be
done--the DOD gave those centers rather than its central R&D planning offices or its experts on research
and social systems (in-house or contracted for) the
final word in shaping the program and trying to make
it useful.

The constraints on the work were never applied directly to achieve desired answers.  As in the interaction between the university scholars and the military
described previously, there was, to all outward appear-
ances, no deliberate and conscious attempt to restrict
intellectual freedom or to mold research results to
preconceived notions.  Rather, the influences derived
from much more subtle interactions between the interests
and policy premises of those who passed on the work,
on the one hand, and their view of the propriety and
sensitivity of the work, on the other.

As soon as an ambassador, or a commanding general,

was given the opportunity and responsibility to judge
a research proposal, he must necessarily ask himself a
number of practical questions. It was well known by
this time that some subjects of research could cause a
stir. It would first have to be asked, how great was
the risk of this happening? It would then have to be
asked, whether the subject was important enough to take
the risk--whether the potential utility of the results
that could be obtained justified the trouble that might
be caused. Inevitably, and because we are all human,
a subject that fell within the ambassador's or general's
or admiral's interest, with hypotheses that fit his
conceptions of the problem and the likely solutions,
was likely to be weighed as more important and worth
more risk than a research problem that threatened to
challenge those hypotheses, even though in the long
run the latter might prove much more important to him.
The definition of "sensitive" was thus elastic.

In addition, as far as these responsible leaders
were concerned, a study was a study--ideas of scientific methodology in study of the social systems they
dealt with on a practical basis every day were not within their training. If a sensitive question could be
approached through an internal "staff study," this was
equivalent to a scientific research project as far as
they were concerned, and often preferable. The difference could be explained, but the going was uphill.

The same forces acted on the side of the host country, whose officials had their own ideas of problems

and hypotheses that were interesting and important--
often different from those of the Americans, and sometimes more liberal or permissive in outlook, but always
oriented to their own preconceptions. And, of course,
the American ambassadors and military commanders did
not pass on these matters entirely by themselves,
although they frequently gave them their personal attention. They were at least in part responsive to the
opinions and judgments of directors of the subordinate
agencies of the American mission, or subordinate military staffs and commands. Therefore, the agency heads
and staffs imposed their own ideas as well--sometimes
advocating a piece of work and sometimes opposing it--
all on different subjects, at different times, and for
different reasons.

Any research proposal therefore had to fit a series
of differently shaped templates, and only a few came
through the tests successfully and with a significant
problem left to study. Thus the "approval" process
acted also as a selection process that molded the subjects of study in safe and sympathetic directions, as
far as those in the hierarchy of power and operational
responsibility were concerned.

A number of interesting results emerged from this
process. The "system" would obviously be more permissive about research subjects farther from its nerve
centers. Approvals, therefore, were more forthcoming
for work of lesser significance or importance--with
the proviso that there was a lower bound, where if the

work were insufficiently important it would be ruled
out as a waste of resources.  This forced the research
community, which was always pitting its own knowledge
and expertise on the country and subject against that,
gained by different means, of the operating community,
to tread a fine line between narrow bounds in defining
and proposing its research subjects.  They could be
neither very sensitive and therefore, probably, of
vital importance, nor of purely academic interest.
Further, since all those involved in the approval process had different ideas and desires, the researchers
would approach one and then another, seeking paths of
support and indifference; trying to avoid or soothe
opposition; and trying to gain advocates who could
influence the ultimate decision.  Thus the definition
of research programs departed from objectivity, science,
and analysis, and became in large measure a political
negotiating process whose outcome was as uncertain as
the outcomes of all other such activities.  It was impossible under these circumstances to define and carry
through a coherent and logical research program, all
of whose parts were interconnected and mutually supporting.  The program was somewhat more orderly than
random, but it was far from the logically planned sequence of studies in specific, interrelated subject
areas that would satisfy the scientific mind.

Another consequence of giving the power of life and
death over all research to operational authorities resulted from the fact that individual research projects

often did produce interesting results.  The research
resources overseas were in effect the resources of the
authorities to manipulate, and they knew it.  Therefore,
particular research projects in areas of interest to
ambassadors, or agency heads, or military staffs and
commanders, would be requested by them.  Knowing where
the real power was, we usually agreed to undertake projects requested this way.  The subjects of the requests
were likely to be reasonably important in most cases.
An applied social research program in an area of conflict should be useful; and it would always be helpful
to be able to tell Congress or the GAO that a project
was undertaken at an ambassador's or CINC's request
rather than on the researchers' initiative.*  But this
put more pressure on the fragile and relatively scarce
resources, fragmented the program still further, stimulated a certain process of "horsetrading" which politi-
cized the research planning even more, and consequently
created underlying tensions that arose to haunt us at
inconvenient times.

This continual negotiation for research approvals
and resources forced the individuals in the research
community to involve themselves in numerous alliances
with American and local government officials.  As a
result, projects came to depend on the interests of
those officials.  Given the frequent turnover in over-

---

*We used to keep a "Gabriel" file of such requests and
 of post-research thanks and commendations, to flash
 at appropriate times.

seas posts--changes of ambassadors, changes of military
commanders, the annual rotation of officers in Vietnam
--many a project found itself in midstream, partly
completed, with the new officials wondering why that
particular effort had been undertaken in the first
place. Some significant fraction of projects was terminated prematurely and incomplete, and the utility of
those that were completed was left very much in question. And all of the negotiations took time. As the
situation became more complex, and more and more actors
came on the scene, the time between initial proposal
and final approval to proceed stretched out, until it
was a year and sometimes more. In the rapidly moving
events of Southeast Asia, the answer to a question that
might take six months or a year to obtain through research was often desired and needed when the question
was put. By the time the resulting research project
was approved (except for those explicitly requested by
the ambassador or commander himself), the question
might well be passé--and even more so by the time the
research was finished. No wonder the new men on the
scene questioned its existence and had low tolerance
for its continuation.

These, then, were the research planning and administration problems that accompanied the determination and
necessity to "go by the book." Let me illustrate a
few cases.

Two areas of effort that had been singled out for
attention in the earlier advisory reports encompassed

the problems of military advisors--in effect, the im-
plementers of policies determined elsewhere; and military civic action--the attempt to use a nation's armed
forces in nation building rather than war.  Two years
after Camelot, these still seemed to be key problems,
and ARPA decided to try to undertake coherent, long-
term research programs in each area through a cooperative effort with the Army.

On the advisor question, it seemed impossible to
hope that thousands of men could be found each year
who would perform like Lawrence of Arabia.  The evidence from many overseas areas was that only relatively
few men really succeeded in establishing the relationships that allowed them to be effective in "advising,"
training, and furthering American policy.  A few earlier
studies had hinted at the circumstances of success; but
it seemed still to be a matter of accident that the
right man was found in the right place at the right
time.  To a great extent, it seemed to be a matter of
personality more than training.  What kind of person,
we asked ourselves, was able to fit into a strange environment and establish an effective relationship with
a counterpart from another culture?  What were the
criteria according to which a man could be predicted
to achieve success in the job; and once he was selected,
how could he best be trained for the job?  And by what
criteria would it be known that he succeeded?  Because
he was well-regarded by his counterparts?  But suppose
they didn't learn well?  What if he made enemies, but

his counterparts learned well what he had been assigned
to teach?

A proposed research program was built around such
questions as these, and we set about obtaining the approval of the authorities. Part of the data obtained
would have to include job performance ratings of many
advisors, to be correlated with personality profiles,
background, and training data. At this point the military commanders overseas balked. They would not allow
probing into efficiency reports or interviews with
their advisory staffs, despite any amount of explanation about the research design or preservation of
anonymity in the results. One MAAG chief expressed
the opinion that he could pick a potentially successful
advisor in one interview. Maybe he could; but we knew
some of his staff. However, the attitude was typical.
The program was never undertaken.

One small project in this area was initiated, however, in Thailand, where the chief of the Military
Assistance Advisory Group was interested in improving
relations between his men and their counterparts. The
research design required comparative interviews with
the American advisors and with the Thai military whom
they were advising. Therefore, the Thai military establishment was brought into the discussions. As the
result was expressed by one of their generals, "We
think it's fine if you study what's wrong with your
people, but we know what we think of our relations with
you so there's no need to talk with our people." And

permission for that part of the project was denied. The project was carried out by interviewing Americans only, and it was changed to a one-sided effort in support of American training for community relations. The original objective had been lost.

The civic action effort failed for a different reason. The philosophy of civic action was that if the military forces of a government have contributed to local development, this will create a benevolent image which will, in turn, be transferred to the government and established authority as a whole. The act of development assistance would, further, help make the government more benevolent, and the local rural people would be less inclined to succumb to the blandishments of insurgents and revolutionaries. Finally, the civic action would help develop the backward areas of the country, a good result per se. While all this was "doctrine" to the American military assistance advisory corps, it seemed to the research community to be more in the nature of hypotheses to be tested and proven or disproven by research. Some previous, isolated projects (Project Colony, described in Chapter 11, was one), and informal discussions with many advisors overseas, had suggested that the desired transfer of affections only sometimes took place--that it often depended on particular circumstances, culture, history, and on how the development projects were carried out; whereas to the American military the important matter was what was done--build a road, or a well, or a school--not who

wanted it and who used it. There were many anecdotes
of civic action "demonstration" projects that led to
raised, and later disappointed, expectations; of projects undertaken because they made sense in one culture
but were ignored or counterproductive in another; and
of claims for success that went far beyond what a
searching study of the facts would warrant.

A program of research was planned to find out whether the whole idea of civic action made sense, and if
so, under what circumstances it would, and when it
wouldn't. To do this, it was necessary to gather data
systematically on many projects, and to ask some searching questions. But then the premises and "doctrines"
of the U.S. military advisory staffs would be open to
question. We learned, early, that statistics on civic
action projects that were much touted were rudimentary
or non-existent. I was once told by a MAAG officer in
Iran about an "enormously successful" road-building
program by a local army unit. How many miles of road
had been built, I wanted to know, and where, and what
were the roads used for? There were no answers. Moreover, we found, local governments were not always anxious to learn that populations who were recipients of
what the government believed to be largesse might, in
fact, be more dissatisfied than they had been before
the largesse was distributed. So this research, too,
was not undertaken. An understanding of one of the
fundamental premises of American counterinsurgency
theory, and of the conditions causing many apparent

successes and failures of military civic action in developing countries, had to be left to a few isolated,
tantalizing studies, and to many anecdotal, incidental,
unverifiable reports.

Another instance of the effect of sensitivity to the
subject and possible findings of social research occurred in an attempt to learn something about the impact
of the presence of American bases on local attitudes
and cultural change in Thailand. With the lesson of
Vietnam that such a presence could have devastating
effects, including inflation, destruction of traditional cultural life, and disruption of local government
authority over its citizens, the problem appeared a
serious one. It was discussed with Ambassador Graham
Martin, with the idea that a serious study using social
research techniques might elicit enough about the nature of the dynamic interactions between and within the
respective communities--American, and the local popula-
tion--to point the way to solutions that would minimize
the deleterious effects of the interactions, and the
inter- as well as intra-cultural tensions. Ambassador
Martin's response was that he knew perfectly well what
would have to be done to minimize the effects of the
American presence. Any such study might simply serve
to critique or interfere with his approach, and possibly heighten Thai sensitivity to the problem, none of
which he was interested in having happen. Ambassador
Martin then went to a new assignment, and his succes-
sor, Ambassador Leonard Unger, agreed that this was

one of the most important problems he faced.  But he,
too, pointed out its sensitivity.  He would agree to a
study if one could be defined that would not stir up
local government resentments and would not obviously
interfere with the outward tranquility of either community.

While we set about eliciting a research plan and
proposal from a contract research organization, an unsolicited proposal in the same area, for research to
be undertaken in the same country, came to us by coincidence from a university source.  This resulted from
the initiation of Project Themis, a program to improve
the research capability of the smaller universities,
for which President Johnson, with congressional urging,
had instructed several departments of government, including the DOD, to allocate funds.  A system of reviewing Themis proposals had been established by DDR&E,
and one dealing with the impact of a large American
presence on a traditional, developing society, submitted by Felix Moos, a well-known social scientist
knowledgeable about both the country and the appropriate research techniques, had come to our attention.
It appeared interesting, and some tentative inquiries
were made of the ambassador.  It became immediately
clear that the subject was considered too sensitive to
risk the possible consequences of the kind of free
access and movement that university researchers would
demand, and the idea was dropped.

In the meantime, the contract research organization

had taken some time to develop a plan for the research.
When this was finally discussed with the ambassador,
we learned that after our initial conversations he had
asked one of his political officers to study the question and make recommendations; the subject was now
closed to inquiry by the research community.  Doubtless
the political officer's analysis (which I didn't see)
was anecdotal and terribly unscientific.  But it may
well have been perceptive and perspicacious.  Certainly
it satisfied the ambassador's need for discretion and
unobtrusive inquiry.  In the long run, the impact of
the American presence was far less disturbing in this
country than in Vietnam, even though it was not totally
unobtrusive.  Clearly, this time, the tradeoff between
the desire to minimize risk and the need or desire for
detailed information was resolved in favor of the former, and, from the evidence, with reasonable success
anyway.

It had been found that many of the studies undertaken in Vietnam had produced highly interesting results.  Studies of Viet Cong origins, organization,
and patterns of behavior in the villages; of the ori-
gin and problems of refugees from the war; of the effectiveness of the paramilitary Regional and Popular
Forces; and of problems faced by American advisors,
had given the American military and civil authorities
in Saigon information and understanding they didn't
have and were glad to obtain.  For a time, in late
1966 and early to mid-1967, such studies reached a peak

of acceptance and popularity with those authorities.
Two consequences of this success were that the military
command more frequently requested studies of particular
interest to them, and that the research community felt
emboldened to propose studies that, it turned out,
transcended the bounds of political acceptability.
The effect in both cases was disastrous, and social research in Vietnam rapidly passed the heyday of its
support by the operational community.*

   In one case we were asked to undertake a study of
psychological warfare in Vietnam, with specific attention to three questions:  the potential vulnerabilities
of the Viet Cong to psychological warfare; what programs to undertake to exploit these vulnerabilities;
and how it would be known that they were effective.
The query came from General Westmoreland, directly,
and a rapid but careful response was in order.  Rather
than go through lengthy contracting procedures, we
assembled a group of the country's best-known experts
on psychological warfare and counterinsurgency, added
the support of military "psywar" specialists, and asked
the group to accomplish the study in a short time.

   This group (including the military members, who
were easily convinced) felt that if the questions were
interpreted narrowly they would be too restrictive,

---

*Economic research is not included here; such research
 was initiated during this period and continued
 to be useful and important to the American and Vietnamese planning efforts, until the collapse.

and that the study would have little value. To provide
satisfactory answers to specific questions about psychological warfare, they felt, they had to explore the
entire area of the impact of military operations by
both sides on each other and on the Vietnamese population. The group pointed out, for example, that it did
little good to paint a stark picture, on leaflets, of
the Viet Cong as vicious monsters (a common practice),
when the recipients of the leaflets knew many of the
Viet Cong as their relatives and friends, and knew
that the issues were not clearly black or white, but
gray and complex. And they indicated that any attempts
of the Saigon government to say that it acted in the
best interests of the population would be negated if
the conduct of the war, with such activities as bombing
of villages in response to Viet Cong groundfire (even
though there might be a deliberate effort to draw fire),
were destructive of the population and its possessions.
Therefore the specific questions were answered within
this broader context, and a number of suggestions, both
specific and general, were made for improving psychological operations and for affecting the enemy's and
the neutral population's attitudes by changing the
conduct of the war.

The report ran into a multiple buzzsaw. The broad
approach had been approved by General Westmoreland
when it was discussed with him, but general supervision
of the study had been delegated to lower staff levels.
Many of those who had stimulated the questions and en-

couraged the approach that was taken, such as Barry
Zorthian, the head of the Joint U.S. Public Affairs
Office (JUSPAO), were gone, and there were new men in
their places. Not only did the report deal with some
subjects on which the collective military command did
not want the opinions of civilian experts, but its
specific recommendations, which included proposals for
organizational changes that appeared essential if the
psychological warfare effort were to be made more effective, cut across existing rivalries between the
military (MACV) and the civilian (JUSPAO) psychological
warfare practitioners. The analysis and recommendations
highlighted shortcomings in the operations of both, and
in their interaction and coordination. Neither group
would consider them seriously. In fact, the new arri-
vals on the scene, who had already started to make
changes according to their own ideas, viewed these new
inputs which reached them, apparently, "from the blue,"
as gratuitous and inappropriate. It was said in the
letter General Westmoreland signed on the subject, as
it often is in such situations, that the report was
not really responsive to the request; but, anyway, it
was overtaken by events and "we're already doing what
it recommends." And that was the end of it, except
for a marked increase in resistance to the idea of
further research.

But the subject of the circumstances of the use of
artillery and aerial bombing within Vietnam remained
a troublesome one. Virtually all of the social scien-

tists who were in contact with the population had come
to the conclusion, not based on study but rather on
scattered conversations with villagers and with some
American advisors, that more was being lost, in terms
of loyalty and respect of the population for the Saigon
government and the Americans, than was being gained in
hurting the Viet Cong, by bombing and shelling of vil-
lages--even where it was known that they were Viet Cong
strongholds, or where Viet Cong attacks against allied
forces were deliberately based in and mounted from the
villages.  Ithiel de Sola Pool, who had long worked
with and had excellent standing with the military community both in Washington and Saigon, broached the subject of performing an extensive field study, using interview techniques, of the "rules of engagement."  This
would try to determine, first, the impact of operations
--air and ground--on the population and on the Viet
Cong.  Then it would try to make an objective assessment of what was being accomplished militarily against
the Viet Cong under the rules as they were.  Finally,
changes would be recommended for consideration that,
based on the data, would be expected to reduce the
negative impact on the general population but still
maintain, or perhaps increase, the effectiveness of
operations against the military forces of the Viet
Cong.

     This was a technically ambitious scheme, perhaps
impossible to implement.  But it dealt with one of the
key issues in the prosecution of the war, and for that

reason alone it might have been worth serious attention and possibly a pilot study to test feasibility,
if only to make certain that the question was explicitly considered. General Westmoreland, himself, however,
made it clear when the proposed project was discussed
with him that the subject was not for study, and the
matter was dropped.

The kinds of studies that were undertaken successfully in Vietnam generally fit the pattern of operations and philosophy for prosecution of the war that
were common among the military and civilian authorities,
in both Washington and Saigon, at the time. Some of
these, such as the "VC Motivation and Morale" studies,
have already been mentioned. Others included support
of the anthropologist Gerald Hickey in gathering information about the tribal groups of the Central Highlands,
which was used to assist in trying to effect a reconciliation of the ancient enmity between those groups
and the ethnic Vietnamese; assistance in designing and
implementing the Hamlet Evaluation System; establishment of computerized systems for storing and comparing
troop performance data taken at different times; logistic analyses; and the like. All this work presented
problems in scientific research methodology, which
those who reflected on it came to feel was generally
inadequate and was leading to uncertain and possibly
misleading results. These problems will be examined
in more detail in the next chapter. The point to be
made here is that a theatre of war offered little op-

portunity for careful adaptation and testing of research methods suited to the situation and the local
cultures. Such things take time, and results were
wanted quickly.

Those who approved the research programs assumed
that methods existed to carry them out. Satisfactory
outcomes could not be promised from new and experimental methodological departures; and the researchers,
themselves, until they gained some experience, tended
to assume that the methodology they knew would be readily applicable. But, in fact, each study was in effect
an experiment with methodology. While some few social
scientists appreciated this early and sometimes adapted
successfully, we began to realize that a more orderly
and deliberate attempt to improve the scientific basis
of the research was in order. The war environment was
a poor place for such an effort--in terms of access to
subjects, control of comparative situations, stability
of situations, or any other desiderata for careful
scientific work. Therefore, at the same time that
work directly relevant to the war was undertaken in
Vietnam an attempt was made to pursue the longer term
and "iffy" experimentation with methodology elsewhere.

But the "offical" climate "elsewhere" was scarcely
more conducive to such undertakings. In one case, we
attempted to apply a new method of eliciting the basic
values and socio-cultural attitudes of a population in
a situation of low-level insurgency in Thailand, where
it appeared that if village culture and the changes

affecting it were better understood the government
could be more effective in improving the lot of its
people.  It would seem on the face of it that such
values and attitudes would be obvious, at least to the
countrymen of the villagers.  But deeper reflection
shows that most groups don't easily articulate their
values and cultural orientations, and that their attitudes often appear only in actions bespeaking tensions
between groups and antagonism toward those in authority.
One of the causes of violence in social change appears
to arise precisely from such divergences between those
in authority and the groups they are supposed to govern,
since the two are likely to have divergent cultural and
social backgrounds.  There could, for example, be as
much cultural distance between a wealthy, Western-
educated Vietnamese, or Thai, or Indian, and the peasant villager in his country as there is between that
member of the elite and his Western counterpart.

A standard approach to eliciting social patterns,
norms, and values is through the work of anthropologists, who live with the respective groups and come to
understand them intimately over periods of years.  Obviously, if information were desired much sooner, other
methods would have to be tried.  One could, of course,
ask the information of anthropologists who had been
working in the area for a long time previously, and
this was done.  But in periods of rapid change of culture, attitude, and values, in multiple interacting
communities, even an anthropologist might not have

been at all the places where such changes had taken place, and where it was important to know about them and about their subtle variations.

Thus it would be valuable to have a method for assessing values and attitudes in a new area, without reliance on the happy coincidence of prior anthropological study, or the need to wait years for new study. A novel method for studying the values and attitudes of groups or subpopulations had been devised in another context by the experimental social psychologist, Alex Bavelas.* A contract research firm proposed, at ARPA's urging, to adapt the method to basic attitudinal studies in Thailand. Known as Echo, the technique called for obtaining a sample, from the population of interest, of answers to such questions as "List ten good things that can happen to you"; or "....that you could do"; and "list ten bad things"; etc. A group from the same culture then placed the answers in like categories (for example, "getting an education is a good thing" might appear in several forms easily recognized by one who shared the view), and ranked them according to frequency of appearance. From these data,

_____

*Dr. Bavelas, who was, at the time of these events, a professor of psychology at Stanford University's Graduate School of Business, had specialized in group psychology for his degree. During his career he explored, among other things, patterns of communication in task-oriented groups, and had devised a number of extraordinarily ingenious experiments in group psychology to trace paths and patterns of communication under various conditions.

it would be possible to construct a picture of the
values of the population, uncontaminated by the values
of the researcher--what, in general, they felt was good,
bad, or important.  Comparative tests of the method
with groups of a given population, asking them to express preference between the set of values obtained
from other members of their population by the Echo
technique and another set of values, obtained from
another population, confirmed that the set elicited
from the test population was more satisfying to the
population it described, permitting the inference that
these were the values of that population.

Much work was necessary if the techniques were to
be applied across language and cultural barriers, and
if it were to be extended to cover a broader range of
attitudinal data; it was not even certain that the
"target" population could accept and respond to the
Western conceptions of answering such questions and
grouping the answers in categories.  Much more difficult would be the problem of extending the technique
from simple elicitation of values to such detailed and
subtle questions as attitudes toward certain authorities, or responses toward specific actions of particular social groups or programs.  If it were successful,
however, the method might offer a rapid sampling technique more subtle and discriminating, and more accurate,
than the conventional opinion surveys which could well
be biased or misleading, but which the operational
community was always ready to accept.

Some preliminary work in developing and testing of
the technique was done in the United States, and a proposal was made to try to develop it for practical application in Thailand.  The proposal was greeted with
official skepticism, but the ambassador reluctantly
agreed that preliminary tests could be made with a
sample population of Thai nationals who worked for the
American community.  This was undertaken, and the initial results were encouraging.  However, several un-
toward circumstances began to converge.  More money
would have had to be added to continue the project at
the anticipated scale.  But the U.S. official community
clearly did not view it in a favorable light, and
there was serious question whether it would be allowed
to go further.  The principal investigator, violating
the rules he had agreed to abide by, undertook exploratory discussions with members of the Thai university
community in Bangkok; while they were interested,
their official community--the Ministry of Defense,
under whose cognizance all ARPA work in the country
fell--neither understood nor shared that interest.
Rather, it questioned whether a research project was
being undertaken without prior approval.  And the
growing congressional scrutiny was reaching the point
where the preliminary methodological work in the United
States, essentially basic research using university
students, would defy acceptable explanation.  Therefore, we decided not to pursue the effort further,
just at the point where some payoff might have been in

sight.

One of the key factors in this decision was our interest in another project, which to us appeared much
more important and for which it was decided that it
would be preferable to risk what little credit remained
for social research. We have already noted, in many
different contexts, the view that the social sciences
had not yet learned to measure accurately the social
behavior of groups of people. Most of the techniques
available require interaction between the researcher
and the subjects of the research. The fact of the
study, its subject, and the presence of the researchers
all affect the social system being studied, in ways
that are uncertain and difficult to assess. We had
already become concerned about the validity of some of
the prisoner interview results in Vietnam, where in at
least some of the cases there was reason to suspect
that the outcomes of interviews were in the direction
the interviewee believed the interviewer desired. Thus,
it seemed that the Heisenberg principle of physics,
that the instruments of measurement affect what is
being measured, applied in social research, perhaps
even more markedly.

We concluded that it would be highly desirable to
develop, for the situations of concern, what Webb had
termed "unobtrusive measures."[1] We wished to see
whether, instead of having the researcher interact directly with the social system under study, it would be
possible to discern attitudes and responses to events,

government officialdom, and government programs from
behavior that could be observed indirectly or at a distance.  Such an approach is not new, but had not been
applied in a non-Western village culture that was in
the process of modernization and in the beginning
throes of revolutionary political change through guerrilla warfare.

The task would require successive steps of research,
beginning with the known interactive methods and gradually changing them, comparing the results from each
step with those from the previous one, until analysis
based on such data as routinely gathered village statistics or provincial archives could be tested for interpretation of attitudinal and cultural trends in the
village society.  We wished to test whether it would
be possible, for example, to find from such data whether
young men were leaving the village, and where they
were reappearing, since this would say something about
the drift of traditional family patterns; it might be
possible to do this from routine census data.  Or, the
record of interaction with officialdom for routine
business purposes might be correlated with particular
economic changes, described in other statistics.  Would
any of these economic and demographic changes corre-
late with other social change, such as variations in
religious practice?  And if so, what could all of it
tell about the day-to-day life of a society in transition?  In particular, would it be possible to show
that routinely gathered statistics, and other "neutral"

observations, were correlated with particular attitudes
toward local government, institutions, and behavior
that bespoke instabilities of a fundamental character
in the society?

It was conceded that this would be an extremely difficult task. But the methodological problem converged
with a practical one--the budding insurgency in Northeast Thailand. This was replete with the usual factors of injustice within the society and stressful
interactions among the rich and the poor, the young
and the old, in a situation of rapid social change.
And there was apparent political stimulation, training,
and material support for the insurgents from Laos and
North Vietnam, across Thailand's northeastern borders.
There were the usual village propaganda meetings, raids
on police posts, and assassinations of government officials. The Royal Thai Government, with diverse political, economic, and social advice, with American
financial help, and with American military assistance,
had undertaken a large number of programs to provide
physical security in the villages, local economic development, community development, modification of the
political system, and paramilitary training for local
defense forces. The approach was a combination of
trying to improve economic conditions, trying to provide the villages with some means of defending themselves against guerrilla raids, changing police and
military procedures to make them at once more effective
against the insurgents and less irritating to the gen-

eral populace, and amnesty for guerrillas who returned
voluntarily to the fold--all in an attempt to convince
both the general population and the insurgents to give
their loyalty to king and country.

But the problem was, precisely, that no one knew
whether the multiplicity of programs undertaken by the
Thai government was satisfying the population or not,
whether it was meeting their aspirations or frustrating
them, whether it was gaining their loyalty or driving
them deeper into revolution. As is usually the case,
these activities were measured by physical inputs and
outputs--how many roads were built, how many wells were
dug, how much the crop harvest increased, how many
village police were trained, and so on. The crucial
questions of attitude and aspiration, which would determine the outcome in the long run, were anybody's
guess.

In one Northeast Thai province, for example, the
governor became famous for a vigorous program of development associated with amnesty for terrorists, and
it appeared that the number of insurgent incidents was
declining markedly. He was the hero of the American
community. But a native Thai political scientist who
undertook a study of village attitudes, with ARPA support, said he found evidence that the villagers were
unhappy, because they felt that in order to get any
attention from the governor one had to become a Communist Terrorist first. Was this "normal" grousing, or
did it bespeak a volcano rumbling under the surface?

There were as many judgments on this as there were
people who considered it. This was just one of many
indicators that better means were needed for such assessments.

We decided to combine the practical and methodological problems to see whether it would be possible to
learn more about which programs were successful and
which were not, so that the government could plan its
future moves based on more accurate feedback from past
efforts than it had been able to obtain thus far. At
the same time, the attempt would be made to develop
newer, unobtrusive, easily applied techniques for
making such assessments. This was to be a major undertaking, planned as part of the Rural Security Systems
Program (see page 301), to last five years, which we
called Program Impact Assessment. It was planned that,
while Americans would initiate the task, when the techniques were developed the entire responsibility for
assessment of government programs would become that of
the Thai government, and would be supported by a
trained staff of Thai researchers who would be distributed as appropriate among the government agencies involved. This meant that the staff would have to be
educated and trained in the methods of social research.
It was planned that a cadre of American- and European-
trained Thai social scientists would be involved from
the beginning. They would, hopefully, be responsible
for all the planning and the work by the end of the
third year, and the Americans associated with the pro-

ject would become advisory and supportive.*

This ambitious effort faced three major hurdles beyond those of undertaking and developing the technical
aspects of the project.  First, Ambassador Unger was
very cautious.  While he appreciated the methodological

---

*This project was one of the prime targets of the
agitation and adverse publicity regarding participation of university social scientists that was described earlier.  Its morality was questioned; the
project staff were accused of working with American
imperialism and a reactionary local government to find
ways to suppress the population.  The accusation was
made that the sophisticated approach would help the
government repress an already underdeveloped and
underprivileged peasantry.  There is, of course, always the question of how the results of research will
be used.  In this case, the members of the research
community who were involved were well aware that providing data on popular attitudes and responses to
programs could have a negative result.  However, detailed knowledge of Thai society indicated that in
many respects the government, while it was an oligar-
chy, was rather more flexible than most such governments in responding to the demands of external events
as they were expressed through popular behavior.  The
hope was that in examining very closely how the population was responding to particular programs, and in
trying to devise programs which would cause responses
of satisfaction and popular support for what the government was trying to do, the government itself would
become more closely involved with its population,
starting a cycle from which there would be no return,
and in which the relationship between government and
governed might evolve in mutually beneficial directions.  Obviously, there was no certainty that this
would happen.  It is clearly a matter of individual
judgment and decision as to whether one believes it
is worth making the attempt, or that the attempt,
once made, will have the desired outcome.

problem, this was of relatively minor concern to him.
What concerned him most was the difficulty and risk of
having American researchers who were outside the official American community be in a position to probe into
the details of local government programs which, un-
avoidably, would have to involve some analysis of local
politics and the American Mission's interaction with
those politics.

Second, it was not at all certain that local Thai
politicians would be in a position or have the desire,
against their vested interests, to change programs if
they found them to be ineffective or counterproductive.
This would also be true of the leaders of the American
Mission agencies, such as AID's U.S. Operating Mission
(USOM) in Bangkok, which was responsible for supporting
most of the Thai security-related development programs,
since as often as not they had some stake in any local
program, having urged its implementation, having
helped to plan and fund it, and in some cases having
conceived it and then negotiated long and hard to have
it accepted.  It was quite possible that in these circumstances both local and American officials would
have preferred not to know of the faults and failures
of the programs if these were identified by the research studies, and would ignore them or find ways to
attack the validity of the research if results of this
character emerged.  On the other side, we saw evidence
that the local Thai social scientists were likely to
be young and idealistic, so that they might prove fer-

tile ground for revolutionary ideas and actions if indeed the above outcome should come to pass.

The third major problem occurred within the DOD it- self. In keeping with the character of insurgency and counterinsurgency, which represented a type of warfare departing far from, and encompassing much more than, purely military affairs, most of the specific research in the Program Impact Assessment effort was to deal with the economic and social development aspects of government actions rather than with the military as- pects. This raised the question of whether the work was appropriate for the DOD to undertake, and whether it could be defended before Congress, since we were making every effort to assure direct and obvious rele- vance to DOD's mission and responsibility.

To resolve the last problem, all the written materi- al on the program was given a military conflict- oriented cast, which distorted it from the beginning. We tried to minimize these distortions, but did not feel able to describe freely what was intended in all its subtle ramifications; and this had adverse conse- quences later. It was the language of defense-oriented counterinsurgency, stressing internal security problems and inhibition or modification of armed rebellion, which the university community, attacking this program, picked up and perhaps justifiably gave the negative interpretation that they did.

The first two problems were closely interlinked. From the research point of view, the question about

the potential response to negative results could only
be answered in the doing--by obtaining specific results
and seeing what effect they had.  But this approach did
not suit the ambassador all at once.  He would, I am
sure, have preferred that the proposal not be made at
all.  He agreed to have one American social scientist,
Dr. Paul Schwartz of the nonprofit American Institutes
for Research, who was to be the leader of the research
group, come to the country and work in the embassy,
more completely defining the program and working through
the official American community to probe delicately
toward the local government agencies and obtain their
reaction, based on specifics rather than on generalities they were not likely to understand.  If successful,
then more American personnel could appear, and the program could be advanced slowly.

It is a tribute to this principal investigator's
ability to grapple successfully with real-world problems  that after three months the ambassador was urged
by key members of his staff, and agreed, to give the
go-ahead for a broader and more intensive effort.  The
program moved, within six to eight months, from dealing
with innocuous subjects far removed from the substance
of the counterinsurgency problem, to evaluating some
of the action programs that were at the heart of the
local government's social development and counterinsurgency effort, such as community development, police
training, and road building, using indigenous Thai
researchers and with the full support of the Thai gov-

ernment agencies responsible for those programs.

This sounds like, and it was, one of the few success stories in this rather gloomy narrative. However, its path was not easy. Despite the great attention to "doing it right," the program suffered from the problems outlined above, and from others as well. One of the first and most difficult tasks was to help the Thai government officials understand the nature and potential value of the work. The first year of effort devoted much attention to this, with the consequence that methodological soundness, with its attending time and complexity, was sacrificed in favor of early results that would demonstrate the principle of evaluative research. Essentially, then, the first year and a half was devoted to the opening phase. It would be another two years (from 1969 to 1971) before it would be possible to tell whether the work could be undertaken with the necessary sophistication and would have the desired impact.

In the meantime, the usual turnover of official personnel continued (including my own final departure from the Pentagon in September of 1969). That was the time, also, when Senator Mansfield persuaded Congress to write into law the concept of "relevance" for DOD research that had been one of the principles of operation for ARPA's social research program. And, of course, the principle then took on the rigidity of enforcement that distinguishes legal requirements from the flexibility of voluntary action. As a result of

this pressure, and with no strong advocate for social
research remaining, the ARPA program succumbed, consciously or not, to the general trends affecting all
research having to do with counterinsurgency and
social systems. Thus, the planned five-year program,
after two years, and just at the point where payoff
was imminent--or at least at the point when one might
determine whether any payoff was in the offing and
how it might be brought about--appeared as though it,
too, would die. A successful effort was made to have
the AID mission in Thailand assume support of the project. Since the programs that were being evaluated
under the Program Impact Assessment effort were largely
under AID cognizance, this appeared appropriate. Shortly after this was agreed--over a year after it was
decided that ARPA could no longer support the work--
Congress reduced the AID program. In addition, the
report of a presidential commission recommended the
disbanding of AID and distribution of its functions to
other agencies.[2] The research continued into 1973,
however, gradually moving along the path initially
charted for it. At any stage of its existence, it was
not certain that it would enter the next stage. The
methodological developments were advanced, and the
Thai government has gradually been assuming responsibility for the evaluative activities, so that the project itself succeeded. However, the ultimate question
--whether the work has had the desired impact--still
cannot be answered.[3]

Thus, again, an attempt to undertake research work requiring long-term program development and stability was distorted and interrupted by short-term and extraneous considerations having nothing to do with the merits or requirements of the work. The pace of events in the real world and the time required for exacting and careful scientific work appear incompatible, to say the least.

All of the issues dealt with thus far have had to do
with defining the problems on which research studies
would be performed, and with obtaining the agreement
of the entire "system" that these problems should be
studied.  The next important step was to gather data
in the field based on sound research designs, and to
extract useful and reliable results from those data by
means of sound scientific analysis.  The research designs and the analyses had to be planned together, of
course, because no amount of analysis could yield valid
and reliable results if the research design did not
provide for the necessary and appropriate data to be
taken.  The constraints of field operations profoundly
influenced the research community's ability to fulfill
this, its raison d'etre and supposed stock-in-trade.

A number of adaptations of American social science
methodology had to be made to work across cultures.
To obtain the information on attitudes toward events
and on aspirations that was desired from local subjects of research, it was, first, necessary to determine whether the "instruments" of measurement were
valid in other cultures.  A number of techniques for
cross-cultural research--for example, Hadley Cantril's
self-rating scales[1] and Bavelas' Echo technique, already described--existed that would have to be rede-
veloped for, and tested in, the specific cultures
where they were to be used.

These were used occasionally; and Philip Worchel of
the University of Texas was also able to adapt such
methods as the thematic apperception tests for use in
Vietnamese culture.  Primarily, however, straightforward interviews were used, and the value of having social scientists undertake the interviews appeared to
lie mainly in the fact that some of them--those with
appropriate training in psychology--could structure
the interviews in a neutral way so that more information could be obtained than would be obtained by a
layman, and it would be obtained in a form that could
be checked for internal consistency.  But even this
was often not done well, especially when the researchers were of disciplines, such as traditional political
science, that had not especially trained them in the
necessary approaches.

One innovation, a matter of necessity, made most of
the studies possible in the first place.  However knowledgeable the research professionals might be about
the countries, their histories, their people, and
contemporary events, most of those who were anxious
to undertake this work (the anthropologists were the
primary exceptions) had not been there and could not
speak the language; nor did they have the deep and intuitive feeling for the culture that would accompany
real fluency in the language.  Some attempted to learn
the language, but in the few months or year available
to them for language training prior to undertaking research they could only learn enough language for normal

pleasantries and to request necessities of life, at
best.[2] Almost all the researchers, therefore, turned
as a matter of necessity to the most ready expedient,
the use of intermediaries who were bilingual local
nationals, for administering questionnaires and assistance in reduction of the raw data represented by the
responses.

This approach had two main advantages in addition
to expediting the performance of the studies. American
researchers who were new to the local scene had much
to learn "on the job" about the local culture and background, and their interaction with their indigenous research assistants helped to accelerate the process
markedly. In general, the assistants were university
students, or even graduates, often in the social sciences, and they were quick to understand what was wanted and needed. Further, when the questionnaires were
taken to the field to be administered, the foreign
presence of an American researcher, which could be expected to influence the respondents' attitudes and
answers, could be minimized or eliminated.

There was, however, another side to this. First,
the bilingual capability of the research assistants
was highly varied, so that it was not clear what effects
their translation and retranslation of questions and
responses between two languages would have, or what
variability would be introduced into the results
thereby. These biases were almost never themselves
the subject of investigation (e.g., by having other

individuals translate back to English a question that had been rendered from English to Vietnamese, for comparison with the original). The expedient was essential if any work were to be done at all in the time available, and other pressures on the research designs inhibited attention to what appeared at the time to be a fine detail.

Then, it would nevertheless be known to the respondent that his questioner was somehow connected with the government (because only the government in most places would undertake such studies),* and the indirect connection with the Americans could be inferred. In one case, a local social scientist having excellent credentials criticized an entire area of research because, he said, the respondents were slanting their answers to questions according to what they felt the government wanted to hear. He offered to undertake a replication of some of the research, since he was not connected with the government, to illustrate what the differences in the responses would be. Some further confirmation that he might be right was offered by comments of an American anthropologist in the area, who lived among the people and spoke the language fluently and understood the culture intimately.

The experiment appeared worthwhile. But it was never undertaken for reasons that were largely politi-

_____

*In some cases where local university scholars undertook social studies on their own, the local press accused the government of having inspired them clandestinely.

cal, and that illustrated well the further problems of
working even with the most highly qualified indigenous
social scientists.  For it was found with experience
that while the idea of separating politics from scientific objectivity is deeply ingrained in Western philosophy, it was much less firmly held in the non-Western
cultures with which our program interacted.*  In almost
every case, it was found that the local social scientists wanted to use their research either to provide
data that could be used for political purposes (which
therefore made their "objective" analysis of the data
suspect), or to use the fact of their working on a
subject related to affairs of state as a stepping
stone to political power.  Thus, the desirable trend,
which appeared a priori "good," toward involving qualified local nationals in social research that was intended to be objective had its own built-in limitations.

The combination of the press of time, sensitivity
of research subjects, and wartime constraints and dis-
locations, all interfered with the planning and implementation of scientifically sound research designs.
In a detailed analysis of most of the research studies
performed in Vietnam, Webb[3] showed that in all but one
or two studies there was little or no attention to the

---

*As we have seen, the attempt at politicization of
social research in the United States was one of the
consequences of Camelot and the Vietnam war, and
was (and still is) a radical idea in the American
scientific context.

basic qualities of research design that would have giv-
en scientific validity to the studies. For one thing,
the studies were begun at one point in time in a dynamic
situation, after the forces driving the changes had
had a profound impact, since few had thought before
the conflict started that it might be of interest and
importance to explore the initial conditions. Thus
there were virtually no baseline data comparable with
that now being taken, against which to compare and to
assess the effects of change. There had been academic
peacetime research in Vietnam by university scholars
and by the French, and these results served as broad
and unstructured guides for those who wanted to search
them out; but it was obviously difficult to compare
the situations of refugees or Viet Cong defectors before and after they became refugees or defectors. In
the first case, it was not known who would become a
refugee, and villages varied enough so that study in
one did not necessarily apply in another, although
broad and generalized (and therefore not very informa-
tive) inferences might be risked; and in the case of
the VC there was obviously no opportunity for conscious
and structured access to the people before they became
defectors. In addition, the society had been in rapid
flux and turmoil since the Japanese invasion in 1942,
so that a "baseline" in, say, 1958 would be of uncertain value for comparison with 1964 and beyond.

There were, however, opportunities to compare
"before and after" on a local scale and in particular

subject areas, but these were not often seized. Even
when such a plan could be made deliberately, events
were more likely than not to interfere. One study in
Vietnam, for example, planned to determine the effects
of a new government-sponsored "village TV" program.
With advanced knowledge of the program, surveys of
attitudes on particular subjects were undertaken in
villages where the government planned to place tele-
vision sets, before the villagers were aware of the
plans. There were then to be periodic surveys after
TV entered these villages; and it was even planned to
have control villages that would not have TV, to pin-
point any effects of TV more exactly in terms of attitude change over time. The trouble was, when the TVs
were distributed the researchers had no influence on
the operational plans, and the sets didn't go to the
originally planned places, so that the careful research
design was destroyed.

Since most studies were performed by means of
straightforward interviews, they included all of the
weaknesses and biases that this implied. Only a few
studies used more than one method to gather attitudinal
and historical data, so that results based on data
from different methods could not be compared; the variability due to the methodology itself could not be
ascertained. Before-and-after comparisons and control
groups could rarely be built into the designs. Therefore the studies represented, primarily, the taking of
a single data point in time relative to any events, and

such observations could be made by almost any intelligent observer, not necessarily a social scientist trained in sophisticated methodology.

Even these crude observations often lacked statistical validity within their limited scope. In those cases where it was possible to compile data from a large sample of respondents, it would be found that more often than not it had been impossible to randomize the choice of subject with respect to the uncontrolled variables and still obtain a large enough sample of each population to achieve statistical validity. A sample of prisoners, for example, would cover a span of several years in the times when they joined the National Liberation Front, how long they had been members, and when they became prisoners. Similarly, the experiences of individuals in the VC of the sample, and where these occurred, varied widely (even a hundred-mile distance in Vietnam could mean vastly different conditions of combat and interactions with the population). And access to prisoners anywhere was determined far more by the political desires and whims of the Vietnamese government officials who provided that access than by the desires of researchers for the requirements of their research designs.

By the time a sample of as many as 150 prisoners was sorted into classes where even a few of these variables could be considered fairly constant for a study of why they joined and why they defected, there might be only one or a few individuals in any group described

by particular values of the variables; and there were
rarely enough individuals in a single group (e.g.,
people in one age group who came from one village at
about the same time) to allow statistically valid comparison of the effects of one variable (e.g., the difference between relatively well off and very poor villagers). The next sample of 150 prisoners was likely
not to have individuals from the same population as
the previous group at all. Therefore, even though in
time a very large group including well over 2,000
prisoners was interviewed, scientifically significant
results could not be derived from the interviews.

Similarly, although attitudinal research was performed in villages, this was usually done on a one-
village-at-a-time, one-time-each basis, so that comparisons between villages in different circumstances, with
statistically significant numbers of villages, to explore in detail the effects of specific events was
rarely possible. Even worse, studies on related subjects were never started with similar hypotheses to be
tested (if, indeed, they started with any). And even
when the samples might be similar the parameters describing them were not standardized--for example, one
study might divide the male population into groups of
"zero to 15, 16 to 25, 25 to 40, and over 40," while
another would consider groups of "under 15, 16 to 45,
over 45." How, then, draw conclusions about a particular age group based on all the available data? Thus,
although some numbers of studies might be undertaken on

particular questions, the data usually couldn't be combined or the results compared very precisely.

This is a very sketchy outline of some very complex problems in research design. A detailed review would bring to light many more subtle problems. But the problems mentioned above are not subtle, nor were the researchers, by and large, poorly prepared for the technical aspects of their tasks, inept, or intellectually incapable of understanding research design problems. Why did such crudities creep into the work? The answer lies in the exigencies of field research in a country at war, and also in the misconceptions many of those who supported the idea of such research held about what was involved in actually doing it.

The most critical problem was that of "sensitivity." As we have noted in several contexts, the readiness of high-level, operational directors or commanders to permit entry of researchers into particular geographical areas, or to talk with particular people, varied inversely with the interest and importance they attached to the subject under examination. There were many reasons for this--fear that a delicate situation would be disturbed, fear that unfavorable information might be made public, a desire, perhaps, not to obtain critical results that would lead "Washington" to want to meddle. But it became almost axiomatic that the more substantive and important the problem requiring the research, the less access would be permitted to the sources of necessary data.

These inhibitions were unevenly distributed and took
many forms, for there were subjects of importance on
which those in control genuinely desired information.
But even then they kept a firm and stultifying hand on
the reins.  Permission might be given to enter one village in a "hot" area, while a sound research design
might require interviews in eight.  Access might be
given to one group of defectors who had not held very
important positions in the Party apparatus, while permission would be denied to see the few "high level"
defectors whose motivations for joining the Party, if
understood, might be indicative of the requirement for
a whole new outlook on the nature of the opposition.
The variation of the methodology might be restricted by
constraints on time and access, and by explicit direction, so that certain techniques could not be used; or
the number of researchers who could go into the field
was limited, so all the data could not be gathered in
the requisite form in the available time.  Of course,
all studies on important subjects did not suffer from
such constraints, but enough of them did to establish
a tendency on the part of the researchers--who were
vitally interested in and captivated by their work--to
gather whatever meager data could be obtained under the
constraints that were imposed, and to try to make the
best of whatever data they could gather in later analyses.  This invariably made for single or small samples
of observations across broad ranges of variables, without careful sampling or control of important parameters,

and consistently worked against good research design.

The time pressure was one of the most important factors. We have already seen, in another context, that
results on most subjects were needed "yesterday," often
for understandable reasons. Since carrying out the
full effort on a complex research design could take a
great deal of time, the temptation, when the researcher
felt himself in a position to influence policy, was to
cut corners. The time pressure, and the need to "produce," worked in more subtle ways, even on those projects where the overt need to hurry did not exist. In
the Program Impact Assessment project, for example,
while one of the main objectives was development of
methodology, this had to be disguised by promising
early assessment of real programs (this, despite the
reluctance on the part of officialdom to hurry into
such assessments). The methodological problem was two-
fold, however: development of indirect measurement
techniques to observe and interpret social attitudes
and behavior; and development of approaches whereby
the responsible local government officials would desire,
permit, and participate in the application of those
techniques. While the first could be disguised in the
act of obtaining substantive results on program evaluation, the second could not be evaded--it was necessary
if any research were to be done at all. Therefore, the
first program assessment efforts had to be highly simp-
lified, in keeping with the level of sophistication of
the officials involved, and they amounted to little

more than demonstration of what evaluative research was
like.  By the time this succeeded, and interest was
shown in proceeding to more elaborate and firmly based
methods, the existence of the project was in doubt because of its DOD sponsorship, so that it appeared the
real substance would never be reached.  This pressure
was later alleviated with the transfer of responsibility
to AID; but the budgetary vicissitudes of that agency
in the years around 1970 could offer no assurances of
orderly process and completion, either.  This sort of
problem, which in one form or another was endemic in
almost all the work, made it difficult to keep science
in the forefront.

It was also found, to the surprise of many, including the social scientists themselves, that properly
designed social research would be expensive; this interacted with the generally somewhat negative external
view of social research to constrain the limits to
which rigorous design could be pushed.  For example, in
Thailand, during 1968, the government was toying with
the idea of extending its capital-based TV network into
the farther, least accessible reaches of the country,
as a means of enhancing social cohesion and reducing
existing separatist tendencies. 'It requested help for
a pilot test to assess whether the impact would be
worth the effort and expense.  Here was a chance to
undertake a study at a relatively leisurely pace, obtain
baseline data, establish controls, and give attention
to all the details that would make for a scientifically

sound effort. We therefore worked with the government
to determine a group of villages where TV would go,
then identified villages where it wouldn't, initially,
but where the people were likely to know about it, and
identified others where there would be no TV and it
would probably be some time before people would know
about it--eight villages in all, in a complex design
with multiple controls and baseline data established
for all. Before and after surveys would be made, using
a number of different kinds of measurement "instruments,"
and a fairly large crew of Thai field assistants had
to be trained and dispersed to the villages periodically. The villages were in isolated locations and had
to be reached by helicopter if months were not to be
spent on each data-gathering sortie. The project
would have continued for two years, with periodic surveys to ascertain the impact of TV (if any) over time.

When the projected cost of the study was determined
we were shocked to learn that what was in effect a relatively small project to determine the reaction of the
population of a few villages to government TV would
entail a cost approaching a half-million dollars. It
didn't appear that, if Congress asked the questions,
this could be justified--intuition said that it might
"buy" $50,000, but not $500,000. So the project was
scaled down, with the carefully worked out research
design, and therefore statistically valid, internally
consistent, reliable results, being the primary casualties. The Program Impact Assessment effort was also

expensive; the upshot was that while it was underway
we put all our effort and energies for political defense into it, so that all other such work suffered as
we tried to keep the total of social research within a
tolerable budget figure.

It was easier to spend more money per project in
Vietnam under the pressure of wartime needs and MACV's
insistent requests for projects. But whereas elsewhere
there might be reasonable time to undertake carefully
designed research, even if we had wanted to in Vietnam
we couldn't. The combination of pressure for instant
results and rapidly changing people, situations, and
conditions meant that nothing would hold still for
carefully planned research, no matter how hard we
tried. We have already seen what happened when we
tried to undertake "before and after" surveys of village
TV in Vietnam. In the case of the prisoner and defector interviews, the combination of access problems and
movement of the war conspired to prevent any thorough
searching out of groups with even moderately uniform
backgrounds. Similarly, the attempts to study the
problems of refugees in a province could be interrupted
by major military operations of either side that would
change the situation, mix, and outlook of the population being studied. The problem of measuring specific
population parameters under such circumstances was
much like that of trying to measure the length of a
car from the side of the road while it moves past the
measurer at 60 mph. In the case of the car, instru-

ments could be devised for such measurements. In the
case of the social system, this was much more difficult
because we had to observe the system "on the fly" even
to determine what to measure.

Most of the research community was well aware of
the risks of biased effort in their work, for all the
reasons given. This had to be balanced against the
continuous pressure to undertake studies of this or
that subject. In addition, the opportunity to study,
learn about, and try to influence the management and
course of an event as important as the Vietnam war in
contemporary U.S. history was one that no one in the
research community, workers and management alike, was
willing to pass up lightly. Therefore, the perisha-
bility of the situation and the data were always balanced against purity and rigor of scientific research
requirements. The urge to push on at all costs inevitably relegated careful science to the back seat.

The impact of these imperfections varied with the
task at hand. In the case of motivational and attitudinal research, they could be profound, although the
researchers always managed to convince themselves that
there were some deep insights and common threads that
pointed toward "truth." In the case of studies performed to elucidate the patterns of more objective
events, such as a study that was undertaken to observe
the interaction between Viet Cong and government operations in a village over a period of time, or another,
in a Mekong Delta province, to piece together the inter-

locking patterns of VC political and military activity
in an area straddling one of their main supply routes,
the effects of the biases were easier to fathom and
rectify. For in these cases there were other data in
the records of the war and the military operational
system, and the memories of some of that system's members, against which to check.

A different pattern of biases appeared in the tasks
which might be called technical assistance--those in
which the research community was asked to help set up
a data system (e.g., the Hamlet Evaluation System) and
analyze the results. Although all the researchers involved felt intuitively that the kind of data that
could be obtained and the circumstances under which
they were obtained by the operational commands in the
field would inevitably bias the results, the operational community's "headquarters," driven by ever more insistent demands from Washington for better "indicators"
of how the war was going, insisted on using the latest
approach to analyzing numerous statistics, no matter
how imperfect the data or how biased the consequent
results might be. There was an interesting evolution
here, from a relatively fruitless search for "indicators" of success, through attempts to solve analytical
problems which dragged on and on without useful results
because the basic data were simply not good enough, to
simply setting up a computerized data system for the
operators to use and then working with that system to
modify and improve it to remove biases which everyone

sensed intuitively were there but which no one could
define rigorously.

At the same time, there gradually emerged two more
aspects of research in the field situation that hadn't
been reckoned on when we started.  The first was what
appeared to be the impossibility of integrating the
quantitative and nonquantitative disciplines in social
research in the field.  Much of this went back to the
data problems that always existed.  The social scientists strove mightily to add quantitative statistical
aspects to their work.  Some succeeded in some circumstances; but most of the time it was clear that, although they peppered their reports with tabulations
and statistics, the chief value of their work derived
from the insights they reached intuitively as the work
progressed.  These insights were usually fascinating
and instructive, although it might be hard to prove
by rigorous analysis of the data that they were generally valid or "true."  For example, while virtually
all Viet Cong prisoners claimed to have joined for
ideological reasons--driving out the American imperial-
ists and their lackeys, and variations thereof--their
actual reasons for joining seemed to be mostly very
personal.  These could vary from inability, for bureaucratic reasons, to attend a desired secondary school,
to love of adventure, to fear of the press-gang, to
the fact that the prisoner had lived all his life in
a VC area and could conceive of no other way to go.
Many were motivated by real injustice that they had

experienced or witnessed.  But with the poor statistical samples that characterized these interviews, it
would be difficult to know just how the different reasons for joining were distributed across the prisoner
population and, by inference, the population of communist troops.  Any program to entice defectors for amnesty, or to induce surrender of VC units, or to inhibit
communist recruiting would, ideally, be based on knowledge of why most of those troops were there.  Ultimately, therefore, the insights about why men joined
the VC were interesting, but not of much practical
value, nor could the "truth" be "proved," even though
it might be sensed intuitively.

At the opposite pole were the operations research
people, who manipulated any data they could get--because
the military statistical system was never, however much
we tried to influence it, set up to permit detailed
analysis of events and their causes--attempting to find
patterns of enemy activity that would show the directions for counteroperations best to succeed.  Most of
the time these results were dry and told nothing the
military couldn't sense intuitively.  For example,
one lengthy report analyzing dozens of operations
proved only that the VC operated most of the time at
night and in a certain relationship to the waxing and
waning of the moon.  Strangely enough, no one had previously demonstrated these facts with assembled and
integrated data; but once demonstrated it was so obvious that the analysis did not appear significant.

These differences between the disciplines seemed to
result more from profound differences in the mental
"sets" of the quantitative and nonquantitative groups
--subcultures within Snow's two cultures,[4] if one will
--than from simple matters such as training.  This was
indelibly impressed on my mind by a conversation between Murray Gell-Mann and Michael Moerman that took
place at the Jason summer study on Thailand mentioned
earlier.  The conversation opened on the question of
how many people might be listed as authors of a seminal
paper in Gell-Mann's and Moerman's respective fields.
In physics, the number could be many, each of whom
contributed importantly to the theory or experimental
verification of the discovery.  In anthropology, the
author had "pride of ownership" over "his" village,
where his research would make his reputation, and he
must do this alone.  He could not, and in his professional circles was expected not to, share the credit
with anybody.  Further, while the anthropologist would
certainly try to adhere to rigorous practices of observation and analysis, he would much rather be famous
for a well-turned, insightful phrase than for the extent and precision of his observations.

We never succeeded in bringing the two outlooks together by joining the different disciplines in a single
successful study.  Occasionally, a social scientist--
almost invariably a psychologist--was employed who
understood some of the mathematical approaches of
statistics and operations research, or an operations

analyst was found who had an understanding of the patterns of motivation of behavior.  The results were then
impressive.  (But that did not mean that they were
used, as we shall see.)  Moreover, the appearance of
the combination couldn't be predicted in advance, because the man who did the work not only had to be of
the right discipline and background, he had to be willing and able to go overseas to do it, sometimes without
his family.  The selection process, though it was intended to be purposeful, was, in effect, almost random.

The second aspect of the field research that gradually emerged was that the field situation posed unanticipated but poignant ethical problems of a kind different from the relatively broad questions of purpose
and morality that were appearing in the criticisms of
the social scientists who worked for the government.
But the net effect on the researcher's ability to
serve his conscience, his science, and his government
simultaneously was the same.

The most obvious problem came about when the researcher, who spent a great deal of time with the local
population, gained their confidence and started to
learn about the inner events and motivations of the
community he had joined.  He might, for example, learn
that certain unsuspected members of the community were
insurgents, or even that they planned some action inimical to the local government or the remainder of the
community.  He was at the spot to gain data of assistance to the local government, and supported by U.S.

government funds allocated to help the local government.
Thus far, his problem was more or less standard, and in
our experience most researchers who faced it would
favor their local informants and their information
sources, and keep quiet.  But his problem usually went
deeper.  The researcher had many acquaintances among
the local population, and his personal sympathies might
go to people in both of the rival groups.  It was thus
not a question of having sold one's soul to the devil,
but rather of keenly-felt personal sympathies that
might go both ways--more akin to the doctor-patient
problem in a divided family.  In all the years of this
research program, the problem arose only a few times.
Gerald Hickey, in Vietnam, had managed to gain the
respect of both sides, and to maintain his detachment
nevertheless, to the point where he could remain aloof
at appropriate times and yet not jeopardize their lik-
ing and respect for him.  Many of the other researchers
were troubled by anticipation of the question, and
some of us in ARPA even considered the advisability of
devising a policy to guide the researchers we supported.
But in the end it remained a matter of individual judgment, and must have been painful for many.

Such intelligence-related aspects of the work affected the program in other ways, simply because of
the uncertain boundary between field studies to gain
information for  research and those by other agencies
to gain intelligence.  The confusion the question engendered on the part of some of the congressmen who

participated in the Camelot hearings has already been
noted.  In another, more complex case, a study was undertaken to explore the impact of various psychological
warfare gambits initiated by the government on changing
attitudes in the villages of a Mekong Delta province
where the VC were very active in 1967 and 1968.  The
research leader was a Vietnamese social scientist,
familiar with and widely acquainted in the geographical
area.  The research technique to be used was that of
arranging a number of "participant observers" in several villages to report what was happening on the spot
as the "psywar" schemes were implemented.  The latter
might be as simple as passing out some small but valuable tool having a pro-government slogan on it, or as
complex as starting a series of conflicting but adverse
rumors about the VC.  It became apparent as the initial
phase of the study was coming to a close that the participant observer arrangements had led to the establishment of what could easily be interpreted as, and
in fact could easily become, a private intelligence
net.  Our Vietnamese scientist, we suspected, might
not be above using it for political purposes in the
ever-present Saigon intrigues, in which he had displayed
some extensive interest during several conversations.
This approached too close to the boundary for comfort,
and it was decided not to continue the effort.  We
were aided in this decision by the fact that the research scheme was found to be simply not very useful;
the data obtained by this technique were of an uncer-

tain quality, not easily subject to checking by other means.

Other problems of an ethical character have been mentioned earlier, in connection with the differing views of the university and military groups regarding project management, accounting for expenditures, and employment of families, and in the general antipathy between the two groups with respect to bureaucratic constraints and, in some cases, about how widely the results of research could be published. The trend toward conservative interpretation of the issues by the government officials involved, including myself, was continually reinforced by apprehension about the potential impact of adverse, critical, or satirical press reports, and by the presence of the General Accounting Office, which for a substantial part of the period under discussion was investigating the operations of Project Agile at congressional request. One was not inclined to take risks with the GAO looking over one's shoulder--or at least, risks were taken primarily when the stakes and the solidity of the work appeared high enough to warrant and permit a strong defense. Many projects that might otherwise have appeared "worth a try" were ruled out for this reason.

The net effect of these problems--the difficulty of merging disciplines and the ethical problems attending extensive field work--was that methodological innovation and careful research design that would run costs up tended to be avoided in favor of getting the job

done with least risk and in minimum possible time.  In
retrospect, it seems that the appreciation of what
<u>scientific</u> research had to contribute, in contradis-
tinction to simply gathering information about interesting subjects, was largely lost.  Studies were undertaken for the sake of doing the studies, and in all but
a very few, considerations of careful and scientific
research design to be certain of the validity of the
results drifted invariably to last place in the order
of priorities.

Despite all the problems, the overseas social research
produced new knowledge and understanding, fresh and
sometimes startling insights, wherever it probed.  If
the research designs did not ordinarily lend scientific
validity and confidence to what emerged from most individual studies, the subjects overlapped enough with
each other, with the knowledge of the few anthropologists who had spent years in the areas being studied,
and with the efforts of the operating people to make
sense of related events, that it seemed possible intuitively to separate that which "rang true" from that
which should be viewed with suspicion and distrust.
Whether we had scientific proof or not, we felt we
were learning much that was new and valuable.

In particular, a picture of the diverse revolutionary
movements of Southeast Asia began to emerge, with details of what motivated their members, explication of
the points of conflict within the existing societies,
and with understanding of how these movements made
their way through the peasant populations, gaining or
forcing adherents, and destroying the writ of the existing order and governments.  The behavioral patterns of
those governments became clear also.  There emerged a
detailed view of the traditional, cultural, and institutional constraints that put the governments at odds
with increasingly large segments of their populations.
One began to perceive and understand the emergence and

expression, in modern idiom, of age-old conflicts between diverse groups and subcultures, and to trace the
twin impacts of change from a colonial to a nationalis-
tic world, and from a traditional to an increasingly
modern society.

The actions of governments could be put in perspective. It became possible to predict which actions
might be effective, and which would simply exacerbate,
or put a new twist on, existing conflict. One could
usually foretell when a course leading to the latter
result would be taken, because to do otherwise would
run against deeply ingrained behavior patterns and
might threaten the continued existence of governing
elites. It became obvious, for example, that the Thai
government would use military force to try to put down
a rebellion among the Meo tribes in their northern
provinces that they half feared and half viewed as sub-
human, rather than try to rectify the effects of long-
standing attitudes and injustices inflicted on the
tribes by the dominant Thai population. Such a course
seemed inevitable, just as did the resistance of the
white population of Mississippi to school integration
in 1954. As another example, we found how and why, in
some areas such as the Mekong Delta region of South
Vietnam, accommodations could be made, and were made,
among local population, government, and insurgents
when this suited the best interests of all, with the
result that conflict was contained at a certain level
and never got worse—although by mutual agreement it

never got better, either.  These were but two examples
among a constant stream of them that emerged from the
deepening insights the research results stimulated.

But, just as in Mississippi in 1954 and following
years there were some members of the governing elite
who recognized the inevitable and were willing to accept change and seek reconciliation, there were significant parts of the governments of these countries who
were willing to try a departure from the past.  In
Thailand, for example, there was one general in the
Communist Suppression Operations Command who tried to
take an approach that combined efforts to lure adherents away from the terrorists, and attacks on their
bases, at the same time that Thai army commanders were
undertaking harsh measures against villages suspected
of harboring terrorists.  And the point was, the United
States was dealing with all such groups, and exerting
the influence deriving from its presence, the distribution of its military and economic aid, and the advice
that went with them.  Thus the knowledge gained from
the social research could have been used, with perhaps
some significant effect, to guide the advice and the
disbursements.  This may have worked if the American
community had approached the problem with some coherence
of viewpoint.  But the American government, and its
representatives overseas, brought their own sets of
complexes and contradictions to the situation.

The United States was always ambivalent about
whether it was simply giving aid to be used freely by

the recipients according to their own conceptions of
need and utility, or whether it would use its aid to
exert "leverage"--to induce the recipients to do certain things and act in certain ways.  It was obvious
that aid couldn't long be given for activities that
defied the directions which a majority of Congress
would approve; there was also the problem that the
various members of the American community in a country
had their own ideas about how economic or military aid
(for whose oversight they were responsible) should be
used, and there was no unanimity on that score.  There
was a diversity of ideas and beliefs as great as, or
greater than, that within the host country, and various
American officials aligned themselves with various sets
of ideas or factions within the host government's
councils.

There was also tension between the idea of assistance willingly and freely given, with the desire not
to earn the constant accusation that the recipients
were "puppets," on the one hand; and the need to look
out for Uncle Sam's interests and dollars, according
to one's best understanding of the situation, the conditions behind the appropriation of those dollars, and
the needs of the local government and population, on
the other.  And some solutions, such as the idea of
accommodation in the Delta provinces, were simply outside the range of acceptance of the collective value
system, which urged the use of American as well as Vietnamese troops to try to suppress the Viet Cong there.

Thus, research might indicate the real possibility of
reducing conflict through accommodation among government officials, populace, and insurgents, and some U.S.
officials might want to use our aid to encourage that
view. But to most of them, it would defy the idea of
"winning," which was the reason we were there; and it
would look much like a form of corruption; and our resources would, some could say, be used to support "the
enemy"; and such a solution was simply beyond the pale.

There is nothing new here; the description fits the
pattern of real-world political milieux everywhere.
The point was that it was precisely to help all groups
involved to guide themselves by something better than
"seat-of-the-pants navigation" that the social research
had been undertaken. Other products of the research
had indicated how the American presence and aid fitted
into and affected the local picture, and the small a-
mount of research on the advisory function had shown
ways in which advice at various levels might be effectively given and sometimes willingly received. Thus,
imperfect as it was for all the reasons given, and
more, the research had developed results that could be
useful and that would meet the needs originally perceived. All of the trouble and the problems would
have been well worth wrestling with if the research
had fulfilled these ultimate ends. But the crazy-
quilt pattern of power politics and value conflicts
made the use of the results an "iffy" proposition,
sometimes apparent and beneficial, sometimes hard to

trace, and many times patently nonexistent.  On the
whole, for all that it taught to some of those involved,
the impact of the research on the most important affairs
of state was, with few exceptions, nil.

A key problem of implementation arose from the difference between the "language" of the research community
and that of the operating community.  Often, the social
scientists wrote beautiful reports of their work.  They
presented the background to the study they were describing in all its intricacy and subtlety.  The conditions of the study would be described, and the methodology, and the data sources, and how the results were
analyzed.  More often than not, conclusions were presented, each in a paragraph or a page, with qualifying
conditions and subsidiary speculations.  Recommendations
were direct, but not necessarily any more brief.
Buried somewhere, usually toward the end of the background discussion, would be a statement of the problem
being studied.  This was the language of social research.

And the busy executive would not wade through it.
He knew the background (he thought) and was indifferent
to methodology.  He wanted a concise statement of the
problem studied and the results, and would leave the
remainder to the appendices, for others to judge.  If
the study could be reduced to a one-page "fact sheet,"
so much the better; but he would not read a hundred or
more pages of eloquent and often irrelevant verbiage
to get the answers to questions he felt he already un-

derstood pretty well (chances were, he didn't understand them that well, but he was not about to take the
trouble to find that out). If the results challenged
his intuition, he was more likely to dismiss the report
as poorly done than to inquire searchingly into the
basis for his own beliefs, or ask for a critical review
of the report to see whether it might possibly be correct.

Now, there is an element of parody in these descriptions. There were social scientists who wrote concise
and lucid reports, and there were officials who would
read lengthy reports and learn from them. But the
trend was the other way, for valid "cultural" reasons.
Much as he wished to convey his results to the "user,"
the researcher wrote also to satisfy his own need for
thorough presentation of that which had occupied his
mind for months or years, and to meet what he felt
would be the judgments of his colleagues about his
scientific ability and integrity and the soundness of
his work. The "user" was usually on a 20-hour day,
and days or weeks behind in all his work. Although he
wanted to be enlightened and educated, he was willing
to take scientific rigor on faith, and wanted the answers to his questions swiftly and without the need to
work too hard to get them. Along with his "fact sheet,"
he might have some brief judgments by his staff as to
the validity of the work and how seriously the results
should be taken. Needless to say, the staff might
have their own fish to fry, and their comments might

not always do justice to the research results. Thus,
the study report and the official whose personalities
matched, as it were, were a rare combination; but the
combination was essential for the work to be taken
seriously.

There were other impediments to acceptance of research results. We have already seen the reasons for
frequent lack of coincidence between the appearance of
a study report and its reaching the official who originally asked the question. In these circumstances, a
report was not often able to find its way into the
hands and mind of someone who really wanted the results
and was prepared to act on them. Or, as an alternative,
a report on some critical subject could reach the desk
of the one who could act, but the arrival was in a
sense random; it could come at the wrong time and be
ignored, or at the right time and influence events profoundly. In either case, there was a large element of
chance involved. Two examples are illustrative.

At about the time the United States entered into
the Paris peace negotiations in 1968, some of us, including Chester Cooper, who was then working with
Governor Harriman on the search for a settlement of
the Vietnam war, became concerned that, whereas the
North Vietnamese negotiating team and positions had
both the venerability and rigidity of twenty years of
Viet Minh doctrine, it was not at all clear that the
United States had either a unified position or an understanding of the implications of some of the proposals

that were being made.  Since Cooper was in a position
to influence the negotiating positions on our side, or
at least to obtain a hearing for new ideas and insights,
it was agreed that State should ask DOD to undertake
some appropriate studies to illuminate some of the issues better.  In due course, the request arrived
through appropriate upper-level channels (from William
Bundy to Dr. Foster), and the studies were initiated.
In some months the first results began to appear.  They
included, among other things, a perceptive analysis,
from available prisoner interview and Hanoi radio data,
of how the VC might view the advantages and disadvan-
tages to them and to the Vietnamese government of a
ceasefire, which was being discussed at the time; and
an historical analysis of how the Viet Minh had used
the issue of French prisoners of war to further their
cause in negotiations with France at Geneva, in 1954.
But by the time the reports appeared, the personnel
composition at State had changed.  Cooper had left,
and there was no one we could identify as really desiring to have these reports.  They were distributed, but
there was no feedback.

At about that time, however, I learned that a general with whom I had worked closely during the Camelot
crisis had become the military member of the U.S. negotiating team in Paris, and I sent copies of the reports
to him.  While the course of the negotiations might be
too slow to see whether they had an impact, at least
we got some feedback, and the U.S. negotiating team

seemed to have enough time for some reading.  As soon
as this general was replaced by another, the feedback
stopped, although we still sent reports when they were
completed.  Ironically, by the time the prisoner issue
came to the fore, some three years later, and the report on the related subject of the French prisoners
could have warned of some of the booby traps, that report must have been buried deep in the previous Administration's files.  At least, it seems that it must have
happened that way, from the way the clear lessons about
North Vietnamese use of the prisoner issue appeared to
have been ignored.

In the second case, two reports, separated by about
three years in time on the same subject, met vastly
different fates.  The subject was the effectiveness of
the Regional and Popular Forces in Vietnam--those semi-
civilian quasi-soldiers who had borne  the brunt of the
war in the villages for all the years it had continued.
It was obvious, in 1964 and 1965, that their ability
as soldiers, their training, and their morale, left
something to be desired.  When the opportunity offered,
I had asked Jeanne Mintz, a SORO social scientist who
was interested in the problem, to write a report using
the results of a small research project then underway.
Based on some seventy or eighty interviews with American soldiers and civilians who had returned from Vietnam, and who had served there at all levels and in all
kinds of jobs, the report--anecdotal rather than scien-
tific--brought to light the various problems the RF/PF

faced: low pay; lack of training and leadership; neg-
lect by the Vietnamese government; failure of survivors'
benefits--all the things that would make for a poorly
organized and motivated fighting force.

The report was delivered and duly sent to all the
places where it could be of interest. But from the
response, or rather the lack of it, and the lack of
action afterwards, it seemed to have dropped into noth-
ingness. Three years later, another report on the subject was written. This was the result of one of the
few studies in Vietnam, performed under the aegis of
the Simulmatics Corporation by the psychologist Philip
Worchel of the University of Texas after a request
from the military command, that was able to follow a
somewhat rigorous research design and careful scientific methodology. Interestingly, the results--the
reasons making for good or poor RF/PF units--were much
the same as those that had emerged from the earlier,
cruder effort, which had been based on the intuition
and experience of American participants rather than on
study of psychological motivations of the RF/PF themselves. The second report was prepared, as well, in
a style designed to catch the official eye. But from
all the response, it seemed that it, too, would be
consigned to limbo. Then, on a visit to Vietnam in
October of 1967, I chanced to have a conversation about
the RF/PF with General Westmoreland. When I asked, it
turned out that he had not seen the report but was interested; I had a copy in his hands the next day.

In the ensuing months, it was clear that this time
a research product had struck home. Reforms of the
entire RF/PF system were being instituted, and combat
reports indicated that they were beginning to give a
much better account of themselves, often defeating
North Vietnamese army units. Of course, the time was
right for such a change; it was the height of the war,
and much increased emphasis was then being given to the
pacification program in general. So the report on the
subject finally entered the system at the right time
and at the right level, and, one likes to think, it
helped rectify a problem when the awareness was there.
On such chancy stuff was the impact of the entire research effort based.

Part of this "impact" problem, of course, was the
exact manner in which often unexpected results struck
the preconceptions of the recipient who was responsible
for the action. We have already seen how this interaction helped shape the research program through selection of subjects for research. With respect to the
research product as well, if the subject were neutral,
or if the results fell in with the preconceived needs
and desires of the officials who would have to act on
them, the research reports were well received and well
used. For example, the continuing work to establish a
reasonably sound statistical basis for interpreting the
hundred or more detailed "rating" questions that contributed to the Hamlet Evaluation System "scores" for
thousands of hamlets and villages was always viewed as

necessary and helpful, and helped shape that system into as reasonably rigorous an accounting of intangibles as the data would allow. Similarly, an effort by an expert in psychological testing techniques to prepare culture-free tests, independent of literacy, for assessing military aptitudes and guiding the military assignments of conscripts, led to the institution of an entire new system for drafting and training the armed forces of a country (the country was not in Southeast Asia). This happened because the country's leaders knew there was a problem and wanted to remedy it; they asked for, and were receptive to, suggestions for change.

But on matters that challenged the old ways of doing things, or that indicated failure in a government program to which there was strong commitment by important officials, there was never such easy acceptance. One of the major questions raised at the initiation of the Program Impact Assessment effort, described earlier, was whether anything would happen if programs were assessed as nonproductive or counterproductive, and ways emerged to change them that ran against the cultural grain of interested officialdom. Was it worthwhile to spend considerable sums of money, displace people overseas, and undertake an arduous effort, if the final outcome would be to have the results of all this ignored? Obviously, it was decided to take this risk. But in part, the awareness of the risk led to the very cautious approach, starting with relatively inconsequential programs, that both the research and the official communities adopted.

Worchel, who after his Vietnam research became the
Director of ARPA's large research unit in Thailand
(1968-1970), suggested an indirect approach to the
acceptance problem.  He postulated that the problem
potentially facing officialdom was that of recognizing
publicly that programs and actions for which they were
responsible were having deleterious or counterproductive effects.  When faced with stated conclusions and
recommendations to do something differently, the admission of failure must be explicit if the recommendations were accepted.  The natural reaction was defensive
and resistive.  The proposal, then, was that the research community should not draw firm conclusions or
make explicit recommendations.  It should simply design
its research to elicit the facts, making causes, effects,
and consequences very clear.  These would be presented
to the officials, who could draw their own conclusions
and devise their own solutions.

In theory, this seemed a reasonable approach and
entirely consistent with the role of a social research
investigator.  The problem that could be immediately
anticipated, however, was that "none are so blind as
those who will not see"; confronting an official with
incontrovertible evidence of the consequences of his
actions would not assure that he would act differently.
And, of course, it would be an unhappy lot for the
social scientist to have to ferret out data and interpret events based on them, and then to have to refrain

from drawing the inescapable conclusions and making the
burning recommendations, while watching the one who
needed the assistance refrain deliberately from drawing
those conclusions, or acting inappropriately (in the
scientist's view) on them.  But one form of being ignored is in many senses much like another, and it was
decided to test this approach as part of the Program
Impact Assessment effort.  Unfortunately, in the event
the delays attending the interagency transfer of the
program were lengthy, and the DOD overseas social research program began to wind down rapidly shortly after
this decision was taken.  Thus, we in DOD had no opportunity to test the viability of the approach.  Even in
1973, after the program per se had been well accepted
by the Thai government, it was not clear that it would
have the desired effect on their social programs.

In another case there was, at long last, the
appearance of success in this area, without any certainty of the existence of its substance.  We had given
a relatively modest amount of support to a Thai social
scientist to enable him to carry out some studies of
social developments in farming villages.  The objective
was to ascertain whether some of the stresses of modernization were creating restiveness among the younger inhabitants and causing them to join the insurgents.
While some of the American social scientists criticized
the technical quality of his work, he managed to keep
its political implications submerged, and to make a
reasonably complete report on the attitudes toward the

government and its works of key social groups in the
villages.  These results were sufficiently impressive
to Thai officialdom that, some years after the work
was initiated, the social scientist and his Thai co-
workers were given an official position as a supporting
research arm of one of the agencies concerned with con-
trolling insurgency in the country.  This result alone
was highly gratifying, since it represented the hoped-
for outcome of the financial support given to the individual, under circumstances when the entire idea of
supporting indigenous researchers overseas was being
challenged in Congress.  However, the agency to which
this research group was attached was not the one exer-
cising the ultimate power of decision in governance of
the countryside.  At the time of writing, therefore,
it is not yet clear whether the data developed and
presented by this group will be taken seriously enough
at the high levels of Thai government to affect the
established patterns of official behavior.

In matters where research results might have had a
profound impact on large-scale events, where they
dealt with the fundamental premises, understandings,
and approaches to matters of war, peace, and interactions with foreign populations and governments, it
proved impossible in the long run for those results to
have any effect at all.  Secretary McNamara, for example, had established a standing rule that all "software"
reports--operations research and social research--
emerging from DOD studies in Vietnam were to be sent to

him with a covering summary sheet, outlining the results and their value. We knew that he read many of
the reports that were sent--especially those dealing
with the impact and operation of the Viet Cong and the
Government of Vietnam (GVN) in the villages. A picture
of the events gradually emerged from those reports,
showing how during that period (1964-1967) the VC were
gradually extending their writ among the population;
how the GVN through sheer ineptitude played into their
hands; and how, often, American policy or local advice
would exacerbate the situation or simply fail to have
the desired effect. This is not the place to dwell on
the history of the Vietnam war. But it can be observed
that the knowledge transmitted by the reports could
have had no effect because, by then, the inexorable
course of the war, with its attendant policies and behavioral patterns, had been set. The changes that
might have been required would have run counter to the
direction in which "the system" was already fixed, and
it is clear in retrospect that far greater forces than
the observations of a small number of researchers were
not able to change it until the VC themselves did so
in a far harsher way, with their 1968 Tet offensive.

But even when the system was more fluid and more
open to suggestion, those with responsibility for the
grand sweep of events did not seek answers from those
with research expertise. In one case, early in 1964,
the late George Carroll, a thoughtful official who was
responsible for coordinating Vietnam affairs in ISA and

who had "connections" into the White House, asked me
whether our research had turned up any traditional Vietnamese institutions on which a democratic government
credible to Vietnamese could be built.  It didn't take
long to have prepared for him (through the agency of
SORO's CINFAC) a report on the Vietnamese village councils.  These comprised a venerable form of local government, predating the French in Vietnam, to which respected village elders were "elected" by approbation.  Although the village-council system had been corrupted
and emasculated by the French and by Ngo Dinh Diem,
who appointed his loyal followers to the councils, it
was still more or less respected by the village populace, and was familiar to them as the local government
that took over when "the Emperor's authority stops at
the bamboo fence."  A system of representation in which
village councils were elected, and they in turn elected
representatives to higher bodies through district and
province until representatives were sent to the national
government, would have been congenial to Vietnamese
from ancient times.  But on the day the memorandum
containing this proposal and the descriptive report on
the councils reached Carroll, we were both astonished
to hear the White House call for national elections in
the American style in Vietnam.  To our knowledge, no
one familiar with Vietnamese history had been consulted
before that proposal was made.  Village elections were
held many years later, but were never related to national representation; and the sorry history of South

Vietnamese national elections in the American pattern,
and their outcomes, from that first suggestion until
the Fall of 1971, is well known.

Many experts on Vietnam pointed out to American officials from the earliest days that the very choice of
"hamlet" rather than "village" for significant attention
bespoke American ignorance and was unfamiliar to Vietnamese. The hamlet was the smallest group of dwellings,
in the heavily populated rice-growing parts of South
Vietnam, clustered where convenient to the rice fields
and to the roads or canals to market. But several
hamlets made a village, and the village was the smallest
administrative unit. Thus the creation of a system of
"strategic hamlets" served to confirm the isolation of
the population included in them, away from their familiar informal groupings and displaced from their land,
their access to markets, and the graves of their ances-
tors. This added to the burden, already difficult
enough, of trying to make that alien system succeed;
and of course, it did not. Similarly, the later use
of a Hamlet Evaluation System in relation to pacification could show half the hamlets in the country free of
VC guerrillas, but would mask the fact that guerrillas
might command all or parts of adjacent hamlets, so that
few villages might be truly "pacified." It was not
until 1970 that this distortion of view in the American
influence on the administration of Vietnamese society
was rectified in the official record-keeping on the
war.

None of this is to say, of course, that these considerations, if reflected earlier in official policy,
would necessarily have changed the course of the war
very much.  But it would seem that a necessary, if not
a sufficient, condition for rendering assistance to one
side in a society undergoing revolutionary conflict
would be to understand thoroughly the forms and traditions of that society.  Then, at least, reforms could
have a starting point rooted in the culture rather
than imposed, unfamiliar, from the outside.  In this
the research community could have helped; but it was
rarely if ever asked, nor was much heed paid if it
spoke.  (This leaves begging the question of why the
official Vietnamese did not point these things out.
It is sad to have to note that the urban elite that
ruled a peasant multitude in turmoil, an elite influenced by their French-oriented upbringing, were separated from that multitude almost as much as were the
Americans, and could have benefited equally well from
the advice.)

Even on a more mundane level, policy and long-
standing patterns of operation transmitted from one
soldier to the next couldn't be modified easily.  Some
of the same reports that were sent to the Secretary of
Defense, including an excellent analysis of the American advisor and the reasons for his ability or inability
to relate to his Vietnamese counterpart, were made required reading for the MACV staff by General Westmoreland.  They may have proven useful to some individuals,

but as a general matter, the beneficial changes that could have been made in the selection, training, and assignment patterns of advisors, or in some specific operations that affected and interacted with the village population, were rarely discernible. And we have already seen that some vital subjects, such as the impact of the war on the population, were not even open for study, even though the researchers had already observed enough to suggest that then-current directions for waging the war might be counterproductive. Much of the knowledge and understanding of the motivations, organization, and operations of the VC had their roots in the thousands of interviews the social scientists conducted with prisoners, defectors, and villagers. The results may not have affected policy, but they did eventually permit the assembly of a "VC Manual," in English and Vietnamese, that set forth what was known about the VC and the NLF organization and methods. This became a reference book and training aid, and doubtless served in the education of thousands of officers and men concerned with trying to fathom the working of that organization. This was a clear demonstration, again, that where research results could fit into the pattern desired by "the system" they could be accepted. Even so, there was no way to ascertain whether the availability of this book made much difference in the struggle against the VC in the villages, after all.

    This pattern of acceptance was not limited to Vietnam, which might be said to be a special, although all-

pervading, case.  In another instance, in 1969, we had
decided that several years of research in Thailand, a
country faced by lesser, but nonetheless threatening,
guerrilla warfare, had amassed a wealth of information
that would be of vital interest and importance to the
officials responsible for determining American policy
with respect to that country.  A volume was prepared
that integrated the results of three years and several
million dollars worth of work into a fairly coherent
picture of the conflict within Thailand and its culture.
The volume had the requisite "executive summary."  It
was distributed to all those in the Administration who
it was believed had an interest in and responsibility
for policy toward the country in question.  A number
of kind and complimentary letters were received in
return.

But it was discouraging to learn that the staff of
Henry Kissinger, whose understanding of the country
and its problem would at that time be the most critical
for policy about Thailand, had been instructed to prepare a "fact sheet" on the report for his use.  He
hadn't time to read it; all his time was being taken up
by the President.  Of course, any fact sheet simply
represented a brief, one-sentence-each summary of the
volume's main points.  These could not help but be
assembled selectively, and so constitute a very subtle
form of recommendation for action.  True, such recommendations would, as sifted by the staff, be influenced
by the knowledge developed in the research.  But the

problem of educating a key official to the subtleties
of the policy choices on which he would be likely to
have the final say would not be met. Perhaps at that
time Thailand wasn't important enough in the larger
scheme of things to warrant more attention, since peace
in Vietnam was obviously first on the list. One never
knew whether to be grateful that the results of millions
of dollars' and many years' worth of effort could, by
whatever indirect means, be given any hearing at all,
or to decry the missed opportunities when they weren't
given the hearing for which they were designed.

Thus far we have been exploring whether and how the
research results could have any influence on events at
all. To place the whole exercise in somewhat better
perspective, it must be noted that there were times
when we were fearful of that influence and wished fer-
vently that it did not exist. One such case occurred
at about the time the prisoner of war interviews from
Vietnam were becoming available. Some of the DOD
officials who had initiated that work felt it most important that Secretary McNamara be kept up to date on
the results as they became known, and arranged to have
him briefed periodically by the project director--a
dangerous procedure with unevaluated research results.
The project director played it straight, and pointed
out that the results he was briefing were preliminary,
simply "impressions." But it seemed to some of us that
the nature of those impressions might possibly be
highly misleading. In the particular matter of the im-

pact of the war on the population, the "impressions"
were that the villagers were blaming the VC, not the
Americans, for the death and destruction--because the
VC were there, that's why the bombs fell.

Some of us felt that even if this knowledge emerged
from talks with a number of villagers, it paid to be
suspicious when the results of research were so close
to what one might want to hear. We didn't know how
seriously Secretary McNamara was taking these results,
or whether he, too, might share this suspicion. We
felt that such stuff shouldn't even be taken to him
until the "preliminary" data could be much better wrung
out by detailed analysis. And so we undertook to get
the periodic briefings turned off--itself a delicate
procedure. About the time we succeeded, more extensive,
detailed, and fully analyzed results began to be available, and they showed that indeed the "preliminary
impressions" had been warped, and the attitudes described were not generally descriptive at all. The
analysis, and later research studies of refugees and
why they had left their homes, showed that the Vietnamese peasants blamed the war for their problems:  the
VC, the government, the bombing and fighting--they
simply wanted to be left in peace. If someone on the
outside wanted to blame the VC for the population's
problems, or blame the Americans, he could find support
for either view in the interviews.

All of which illustrates that, much as we wanted
the results of this social research program to influence

events and policies, we were always treading a fine
line between trying to get the work used and trying to
inhibit excessive and premature enthusiasm. The controls that were exerted had to be based largely on the
judgments of the research managers and a host of other
officials above, below, and to the side of them.    In
the long run, the performance in terms of the main purposes of the research was spotty, to say the least.
Some few studies had a profound effect; some were helpful to executive officialdom; most did not and were
not.  The chances of any one study having major influence were small.  The closer a study came to dealing
with problems in which important policy issues were at
stake, the less likely that it would matter.  Many factors influenced the reception or impact of a particular
report, the greatest number of them accidental and un-
predictable.

One conclusion that can be drawn is that to achieve
a few relevant, high-quality outputs that might have a
predictably great effect, very many studies in related
and overlapping areas would be needed.  But the constraints on social research in this context, internal
and external, were such that the necessary large volume
of work could not be undertaken.  When all was said and
done, therefore, an enormous amount of effort and
adrenalin were expended to accomplish the relatively
small amount of work that was completed, with little
certainty that any of it would be useful, and great
certainty a posteriori that most of it would not be.

Now, this is nothing to cry over because such is the
fate of much research  including that performed in the
life sciences and that which leads to hardware.  But
there are some important differences.  Everyone knows,
for example, that hundreds of approaches have been or
will be necessary to find a vaccine for polio, or to
find cures for various forms of cancer, and that hundreds of millions can be spent following false leads
before the few correct (because they succeed) directions
are found.  It is recognized and accepted, also, that
in this work many individual research efforts will produce nothing useful; many will produce interesting and
useful knowledge or methodology, even if they did not
succeed in their original objectives.  Similar occurrences are routine in attempts to develop new electronic
circuitry or new machines to perform old jobs more ef-
ficiently, or to perform new jobs.  Sometimes the projects that did not succeed could have been predicted
in advance by specialists, but the projects go ahead
anyway.

There are many cases, in fact many cases never
recognized, where Congress and the public have accepted
with relative equanimity the expenditure of $5 million
and sometimes $50 million or more worth of bad physics
or bad engineering.  The MOHOLE project, to drill
through the outer crust of the earth for geological
research, caused hardly a stir outside the scientific
circles directly involved when it was cancelled.  No

one outside ARPA noticed when I cancelled a clearly unworkable radar map-matching project I found when I entered there, even though the single project had already
spent more money than a year's entire social research
budget. But the threshold of forgiveness is low with
respect to social research, and the expenditure of
even $5,000 of public funds on something that appears
unproductive can, as we have seen, call down the wrath
of the gods on the spender and place an entire departmental research budget in jeopardy. There are many
reasons for this. Two important ones are the sensitivity of the subject matter, which is almost always higher
in significant social research than in the life and
physical sciences and engineering; and the need, which
is generally not recognized with regard to social research as it is relative to the other subject areas,
for specialized expertise to judge the technical quality, feasibility, and value of the work. At least, in
social research the willingness on the part of the lay
public to recognize when and why some expertise may be
needed to make a judgment is not very great.

The point is that the recognition of the speculative nature of all research is not readily granted to
social research, so that in the latter, where it is
paid for by the public, every project must count, and
precisely because it doesn't, and can't, there will
never be enough projects for the few high payoff, high
impact efforts to have much probability of being under-

taken.  (Note that the few highly successful projects
described earlier accounted for about 10 percent of
the total expended on this program.)

While at one level of awareness we were learning about and trying to grapple with the diverse problems that may be called internal to the research and its application, at another level we continued to feel the pressures of the outside world.  The interest of the press and Congress in DOD's social research, especially that undertaken in Vietnam, did not abate.  Although our redefinition of the program made it less visible for a time, this couldn't, and didn't, last very long.  If we were performing problem-oriented studies, some of which were worked on by social scientists, then we began after a year or so to be questioned about the projects, whatever they were, that were performed "mostly by social scientists."

By describing them in "plain English," assuring in the descriptions their relevance to the DOD's mission and their heavy orientation to the war in Southeast Asia, we managed to stave off disaster.  Not one Agile social science project was noted by Congress or cancelled by congressional instruction during the 1966-1969 period.  But by adhering to the self-imposed rules outlined previously, we had essentially put the handwriting on the wall ourselves.  It was obvious that any social research program tied to both the military mission and the war would not long survive the growing public disaffection with both.  In effect, then, we were simply buying time until the inevitable happened.

Other than the congressional committees' continuing
questions about diverse projects, the one positive action they took, ironically, was on the question of
"coordination." However much we felt we took pains to
assure that all interested branches of the administration were informed of and were able to comment on our
work and help shape our program, the congressional
committees still believed we were going ahead with insufficient intragovernmental coordination. In its report on the FY 1968 budget, the House Defense Appropriations Subcommittee said of Project Agile:[1]

...this year brought out the fact that the program is
being extended to other geographical regions [than
Southeast Asia]. The Committee believes that much
better coordination among the various departments and
agencies of the government is required before a useful
and meaningful program in many of these areas can be
undertaken.

This was to be a recurring theme. The Senate Foreign
Relations Committee had continued to express its un-
happiness with Defense "foreign policy research." The
General Accounting Office (we supposed, at the committee's behest, but we never learned for certain) continued its probes and made its report. The House Defense Appropriations Subcommittee's report in 1969
(FY 1970 budget) contained these words:[2]

Some studies in foreign countries raise the question
as to whether or not they should be funded under the
foreign assistance program rather than in the Defense
budget. Additionally, ARPA has made no attempt to

have participating countries share in the cost of such
projects.

Of course, the program was planned that way, since the
rationale was that these programs were in American self-
interest, to improve the effectiveness of our planning
and implementation of military assistance programs.    In
retrospect, it is clear that the constant calls for
more coordination, as they shifted ground, were really
reflections of a deeper dissatisfaction.    The above
words showed that we were being hoisted on one of our
many self-made petards, and that Senator Fulbright was
finally making his point.

In the summer of 1967, the Defense Science Board
held another brief study session, chaired by Rains
Wallace, in which he and a number of the social scientists who had participated in, or managed, the DOD's
behavioral and social research programs tried to chart
a new course in the afterlight of the Camelot events
and the effect they had had on the outside world's
interest in DOD social research.    Among other things,
in a report that ranged over the DOD's entire social
science program, the report selected "for increased
effort and funding," the area of "increasing understanding of operational problems in foreign areas."
It said specifically:

Despite the difficulties attendant upon research in
foreign areas, it must be explicitly recognized that
the missions of the DOD cannot be successfully performed in the absence of information on (a) socio-

cultural patterns in various areas including beliefs,
values, motivations, etc.; (b) the social organization
of troops including political, religious and economic;
(c) the effect of change and innovation upon socio-
cultural patterns and socio-cultural organization of
groups; (d) study and evaluation of action programs
initiated by U.S. or foreign agencies in underdeveloped
countries. Solid, precise, comparative and current
empirical data developed in a programmatic rather than
diffuse and opportunistic fashion are urgently needed
for many areas of the world. This goal should be pursued by: (a) multidisciplinary research teams;
(b) series of field studies in relevant countries;
(c) strong representation of quantitative and analytic
skills; (d) a broad empirical data base.

And it was also observed, with regard to the problem

of involving first-rate professionals, that:

More high quality scientists could probably be interested in DOD problems if DOD would more frequently
state its research needs in terms which are meaningful
to the investigator rather than to the military....

While the full dimensions of the DOD's problems were

only slowly becoming apparent at the time, it is easy

to see now that the report was bucking the long-term

trend, and some in the DOD noted at the time that such

recommendations had passed beyond the realm of politi-

cal feasibility.

The report reached the news,[3] and its recommenda-

tions were quoted extensively. Senator Fulbright im-

mediately questioned whether the DOD really meant to

implement such recommendations. He was reassured that

the DOD would view them with caution and, in fact, they

quietly died (at least those recommendations having to
do with research on and in foreign areas).

Meantime, the National Academy of Sciences/National
Research Council committee that had been established
after Camelot had kept at its work.  Its base and interests were broadened, as illustrated by the title of
the report it issued in 1968:  "The Behavioral Sciences
and the Federal Government."[4]  After cautioning that
"There is no assumption....that knowledge is a substi-
tute for wisdom or common sense for decision-making,"
it went on to say that "The behavioral sciences [anthro-
pology, economics, history, political science, psychology, and sociology] are, nonetheless, an important
source of information, analysis, and explanation about
group and individual behavior, and thus an essential
and increasingly relevant instrument of modern government....There is need to be concerned as much with the
development of the behavioral sciences as with their
use...."

A number of recommendations were made:  to strengthen
the behavioral sciences and their role in federal
policy planning; to use the National Science Foundation
as a source of support for basic research to build the
necessary "technical" base and underlying subject knowledge; and to achieve better social science representation in the councils of science--the Office of Science
and Technology and the President's Science Advisory
Committee--closest to the head of government.  These
will be of interest in a later context (Chapter 22).

With respect to the kind of work we were trying to
have done through ARPA, the committee report recommended:

That each major department and agency, with the assistance of an advisory panel of behavioral scientists,
develop a strategy for the use and support of the behavioral sciences and maintain under continual review
a long-range research program that includes:

    a. A broad spectrum of research activities from
       applied research to investigations of fundamental
       behavioral and social processes relevant to de-
       partment or agency missions;

    b. Opportunities through internal staffs and contract
       and grant arrangements to utilize research re-
       sources both inside and outside the government;

    c. Continuing programs for the systematic mainte-
       nance of historical and operating records as
       essential sources of research data; and

    d. Application of behavioral science knowledge and
       methods to program evaluation and analysis with
       provision for experimental projects designed to
       provide relevant information for future planning.

This was almost identical with the Smithsonian report's
recommendations, and represented advice that the DOD
had diligently been trying to follow since 1963. The
report also stated that:

3. The major mechanism for relating research programs
   in international affairs on an interagency basis is
   the Foreign Area Research Coordination Group (FAR).
   FAR, however, is a voluntary group of some 20 participating agencies with no binding authority over
   its members and no firm lines to the policy planning process. The Foreign Affairs Research Council
   in the Department of State serves as another

clearing-house through its function of reviewing
research projects for their sensitivity to foreign
policy issues.  Neither mechanism provides a basis
for defining government-wide objectives for research in international affairs.  There are no organized means of assuring that areas of research
essential to policy planning are supported and that
cumulative bodies of knowledge on international
problems are developed.

...the Committee recommends:

4. That, in the field of foreign affairs, long-range
   behavioral science research objectives be drawn up
   by an interagency planning group headed by the
   Department of State, with the support of the Office
   of Science and Technology, and that the research
   programs of all departments and agencies that operate overseas, including the United States Information Agency, Agency for International Development,
   Department of Defense, and the Peace Corps, be continually related to these long-term objectives
   through the Foreign Area Research Coordination Group
   and foreign affairs planning mechanisms like the
   Senior Interdepartmental Group.

Thus, a number of continuing threads, positive and

negative, were entangled.  The idea of an interagency

coordinating group once again reared its head with (it

turned out) about as much chance of being adopted this

time as any of the other times.  And it appeared (to

one not familiar with the internal deliberations of

the group), that State had finally found a friendly ear

for its contention that FAR should be in the driver's

seat for research having to do with foreign areas.  In

the last analysis, a recommendation to this effect by

the NAS/NRC committee was mischievous, because the

committee could ignore the key problem that had plagued

the idea of FAR control from the start:  giving one
department of government authority over programs in
another department.  But, worse still, FAR was, by the
report's own findings, not organized for or adequate to
do the job.  While the NAS/NRC committee hoped they
could rise to it, or be made to do so, the negative advantages of the management practice of giving responsibility and authority for a job to a manager one knows
in advance is inadequate, in the hope that the capability will grow, should by this time have been obvious,
at least in this context.  This was the trap we fell
into before Camelot, in assigning work to the Army and
its instruments, and there was no reason to believe in
this case that the outcome would be different.

At any rate, it turned out to be irrelevant, for
Senators Fulbright and Mansfield were preparing moves
that would continue the trends against social research
regarding foreign areas, regardless of what the scientific community desired or recommended; and that were
to have much more profound implications for basic
science in general.  In 1969, the dissatisfaction in
Congress with the DOD, its wars, and its works, was increasing.  There was a new Administration making a
point of trying to bring the war to a conclusion, and
at least somewhat agreeing that "priorities" had to be
"reordered."  In August of that year Senator Fulbright
introduced an amendment to the FY 1970 Defense authorization bill to reduce the DOD research budget by $9.5
million--$3.5 million to be taken from Federal Contract

Research Centers, $1 million to be taken from "foreign research" and "social and behavioral sciences," and $5 million from Project Agile.[5] The amendment was incorporated in the bill, which passed in the Senate and was ultimately sustained in the House and in Conference.

Shortly afterward, Senator Mansfield introduced another amendment, which became Section 203 of the bill, and which said:[6]

None of the funds authorized to be appropriated by this Act may be used to carry out any research project or study unless such a project or study has a direct or apparent relationship to a specific military function or operation.

In approving its version of the bill in September, the House Armed Services Committee included Section 203, saying also:[7]

We interpret 'military function or operation' in its narrowest sense.

The final Act included Section 203, of course.    In introducing his  amendment, Senator Mansfield stressed basic university research sponsored by the DOD as the culprit, saying later[8] that the DOD was supporting $400 million of "non-mission oriented research and development projects," with basic research "of the kind traditionally carried out in the universities at a level of $311 million in comparison with $277 million for the National Science Foundation."  Congress, he said, "by writing Section 203 is giving clear notice (among other things):

5. That primary responsibility for government support for behavioral science research and training conducted in foreign countries by universities in the United States be placed in agencies and programs committed to basic research and research training, particularly the National Science Foundation, the National Institutes of Health, and the proposed Center for Educational Cooperation under the International Education Act.

But though he stressed basic and university research, he devoted the details of his reasoning to DOD research in the social sciences, giving a long list of DOD-supported social science projects (ironically, not including any from Agile's program) that he said were not relevant to the DOD mission.

The impact of Section 203 was not limited to social science projects, however, nor was it intended to be, for Senator Mansfield indicated his intent to attain the "reasonable goal" of reducing the $311 million of DOD funding of academic research to no more than 25 percent of that funded by NSF by the end of FY 1971. Yet it was only by FY 1973 that the NSF budget was increased by more than $100 million above its previous level, so that if this had been followed faithfully universities would have lost over $200 million per year in support for scientific research.[9] Senator Mansfield thought that the President "as a matter of national policy, might decide to reduce the overall level of support for academic research. That latter, I would add, would not be a national calamity."

Only time will tell whether it was.  But since DOD
support for basic science was one of the pillars up-
holding it, the Mansfield amendment, Section 203, can
be said to have marked a turning point in national support for scientific research, and the beginning of a
leveling off and downturn in federal budgeting for such
research, from which the universities and the scientific
community in general have not yet recovered.[10]  The immediate impact of Section 203 was to eliminate about
$10 million worth of DOD research projects.  However,
there were now more stringent limitations on the work
DOD could support, and it appears that most other federal agencies are taking heed, and are wary of supporting research that cannot be shown to meet the same
criteria of mission specificity in their own areas.
As we have seen in connection with the constraints on
DOD work overseas, one of the best ways to stultify
free inquiry into important questions, "applied" or
not, is to subject them to the test of being necessary
to support an immediate operational mission.  And as
Nichols has pointed out[11] the Mansfield amendment threw
into focus the problem of science policy, and became a
rallying point for those who did not believe the "tired
rhetoric" supporting R&D, and felt there were better
things to do with the public's money.  If Section 203
was not the entire moving force behind the changed
national attitude to and support for science, it added
a strong force to the downward trend, and thus it

seemed that the waves made by Camelot were now, four
and five years later, eroding much wider and farther
shores than just "DOD social science research."

Senators Fulbright and Mansfield worked closely together to assure that the provisions of Section 203
were carried out.  The occasion for a sharp exchange
with the DOD arose in October, 1969, when Senator Fulbright sent Dr. Foster, the Director of Defense Research
and Engineering, a clipping about a Themis contract
that had been awarded to the University of Mississippi,
and asked whether the project in question didn't stretch
the constraints of Section 203.[12]  Ironically, this
wasn't a social science project in the usual sense of
those the Senator objected to; it had to do with birds,
and illustrated well the problem of what I have described as the "lunatic fringe" among research scientists.  For while this project may not have done as
much violence to scientific, ethical, and humanitarian
considerations as the others from the periphery that
had been seeking my own support, it was "far out"
enough to tickle a newshawk's curiosity.  The contract
--a serious one--was to investigate the possibility of
training birds to perform various military tasks.
There had been some recent experience in this area.
It had been shown, for example, that pigeons could be
trained to recognize certain kinds of routine military
targets in an aerial photograph more reliably than
human photo-interpreters could, and that they could be
trained to recognize people in ambush in real life,

stop in front of them, and peck a radio transmitter to give an alert. The contract apparently (I have no first-hand knowledge of it, but am surmising from what I have seen written) intended to see whether such skills, and related ones, could be extended in scope and to other species of birds. It may well have been trying to stretch an originally interesting idea too far.

A group working with birds for such purposes had tried to obtain Project Agile support for their work for some years. I had declined, on the basis of my past view of some of the early results. These demonstrated that even if an important range of skills could be trained into birds, the military system as a whole was unlikely to take the accomplishment seriously, and therefore the effort would be a waste of money. But the birds' trainers in that case persisted, and eventually found a source of support in the DOD. Perhaps this same group had turned up at the University of Mississippi--I don't know--and perhaps the University of Mississippi group found support elsewhere when their Themis contract with the Army was eventually terminated. We had found that a determined and persistent group could easily keep itself alive by following the money and adapting to the current "buzz-words." The news report described it thus:[13]

Flying Off to Combat?--Birds Alerted for War--Would you believe that war is for the birds?

At any rate, the response to Senator Fulbright's
letter, on November 3, after explaining the bird contract, said that:[14]

The research programs of the military departments and
Defense agencies are under continual review by elements
of DOD and receive, in addition, the critical scrutiny
of my office. It has long been DOD policy to support
only research which is relevant to military functions
and operations. Most of our projects in the research
and exploratory development budget categories (from
which comes most of our university funding) are, in
fact, relevant to many military operations. From time
to time, however, we eliminate support for research
fields which are no longer relevant to DOD needs;
high energy physics is a recent example. I do not
expect, therefore, that implementation of these sections
will entail any new type of review or selection.
Nevertheless, Secretary Laird, Secretary Packard, and
I have been instituting a number of new management
approaches which will provide a basis for more coherent
and explicit presentations to the Congress about the
basis for our budget requests.

This triggered a storm. Senator Mansfield said, on the
Senate floor,[15] that "Congress, when it enacts its
laws, does not attempt to waste time on futile gestures
....It is very upsetting to see any executive agency
disabusing the clear expression of congressional intent
....," and Senator Proxmire added that "There is no
question that Federal research has been overwhelmingly
sponsored by the Department of Defense in the last few
years....If we provide funds for the Department of
Defense, this is one area where we do not adequately
scrutinize them..." (This depended, of course, on how

much of the DOD's $7-8 billion of RDT&E money is con-
sidered "research." Nichols has pointed out[16] that
the DOD share of federal support for university research
went from 47% in 1955 to 14% in 1971, while HEW's share
grew from 19% to 45%, and NSF's from 5% to 18%.

So violent was the reaction that Deputy Secretary of
Defense Packard had to repudiate his DDR&E, writing to
Senator Mansfield:[17]

There is absolutely no question that the Department
will comply fully with the law. I have directed all
components to review critically all current and proposed research and development projects and studies
to ensure that they have a direct, apparent, and
clearly documented relationship to one or more specifically identified military functions or operations.
Any project or study which does not fulfill the cri-
terion of Section 203 will be terminated.

Congressman Daddario, head of a House Subcommittee on
Space and Astronautics, in his last term prior to re-
signing to run for Governor of Connecticut, pointed
out the dangers of this course of action:[18]

I fear that there exists today a very real danger that
research in the universities and elsewhere, now funded
for defense appropriations and which should be continued
in the national interest, will be fatally disrupted by
a mechanistic and legalistic application of the stric-
tures of section 203....

Congress must give urgent and immediate thought to
arrangements that will identify and provide for the
orderly, uninterrupted transfer and continuation of
any research adversely affected by section 203, which
should still be carried on in the national interest.

But the problem was not treated with urgency.

Senator Fulbright returned to the attack the following year.[19] Noting that he had been refused a copy of
a study he said was prepared for the DOD by the Institute for Defense Analyses on the Tonkin Gulf incident,
as well as his continued irritation that the DOD was
still letting contracts on such subjects as "Soviet
military policy," or "European security issues," he
introduced a two-part amendment that, in his words,
would:

First.  Limit the Defense Department's spending for research by outside organizations on foreign affairs
matters to not more than the amount appropriated, or
transferred by other agencies, to the Department of
State in the preceding fiscal year for such research;
and

Second.  Insure that congressional committees are
given access to Government-financed research studies
carried out by private individuals or organizations
unless "executive privilege" is invoked.

Senator Fulbright pointed out that despite substantial
budget cuts, "The military is spending nearly 20 times
as much on foreign affairs research as the agency assigned the primary responsibility for conduct of the
Nation's foreign policy."

However, now that the primary objectives of all the
years of pressure on DOD's "foreign affairs research"
had been achieved, this represented but the winding up
of a campaign, as indicated by the following exchange
between Senator McIntyre of New Hampshire, who had

chaired a subcommittee on R&D of the Armed Services
Committee, and Senator Fulbright:[20]

Mr. McIntyre
   ...The Defense Department's foreign area research program has always represented only a small
part of its work on the behavioral and social sciences.  The great bulk of its effort has been expended
in the areas of:  first, human performance--studies
of the performance of men under stress; second,
manpower selection and training--studies of the
best methods for training men for various positions
in the Armed Forces; and third, human factors engi-
neering--studies to insure that military hardware
is designed for safe, efficient, and effective use
under battlefield conditions.  The foreign area
research budget of the Department is itself divided
into two components--foreign military security environments and policy planning studies.
   ...The fiscal 1971 Defense Department budget included a request of $9.9 million for foreign area
research.  In light of the Department's reluctance
to approve outright transfers of funds to the State
Department and in light of the policy expressed in
section 203 of last year's bill, the committee
subjected this request to a thorough, almost pains-
taking examination.  As a result of this examination,
it recommended a reduction of $3.1 million--over 30
percent--from the Department's proposed budget,
bringing it to a level of $6.8 million.  This reduc-
tion was directed primarily to work in counterinsurgency operations and work proposed by the military
services but deemed more appropriate either to the
State Department or the International Security
Affairs Office of the Department of Defense.  The
remaining funds are earmarked for projects which,
while of interest to the State Department, bear a
clear relationship to the Defense Department's own
mission.
   ...As for the Defense Department itself, its
foreign area research budget has now declined from
$16.1 million in fiscal 1968 to a committee-

recommended fiscal 1971 budget of $6.8 million, an overall reduction of 58 percent.

I would like to ask my colleague, as chairman of the Foreign Relations Committee, what actions he has taken to increase State's own foreign area research budget in recent years, and just what he feels has to be done by the Congress to get State moving in this area?

## Mr. Fulbright

...I do not know how to inspire the State Department to assert its responsibility in this area. The State Department has not in recent years had very much influence in the budget process. Matters that are clearly within the State Department, such as the exchange program, have been restrained very severely through the budget and by action of the Appropriations Committee.

As a matter of fact, the Senator knows that all agencies other than the Department of Defense have great difficulty when it comes to getting money.... The State Department has had other pressing budget problems and they have not tried very hard, apparently, to get more money for research. I have counseled that they do so but there have been no effective results.

## Mr. McIntyre

...The Senator just supported the amendment I offered, which is an outgrowth of section 203, which is the application of the relevancy test, which has given us quite a few problems in connection with the defense budget. This amendment is an attempt to bring the National Science Foundation into this picture more clearly as an institution solely devoted to research. When there is budget stringency and a need to cut, the cut is too often at the research end. This amendment points one direction in which we have to go. But there have to be increases, too, in the research budgets of other mission agencies. The State Department is one of these.

It is said the Department of Defense is doing too much in research. The Department of Defense will meet that argument by saying, 'Those areas where we

are carrying on research may well go to the National
Science Foundation and to the State Department, but
we think these areas of research are important and
should be done, and no one else is now doing them.'
So we will need the Senator's cooperation, as
chairman of the Committee on Foreign Relations, to
bring about this reordering of research within the
Government today.

Senator Fulbright then withdrew the first part of
his amendment.

This appears as good a place as any to bring to a
close this chronicle of the DOD's efforts to enlist
social research in support of its overseas operational
assignments. It is now time to look back and see what
the broader meaning of these events might be. But the
stage might well be set by a somewhat wry epilogue.

This is provided by still another report of the NAS/
NRC committee which, having published the report about
social science research for the federal government in
general, and having experienced some turnover of its
membership, turned its attention back to the problem
that originally led to its creation: the DOD's social
science research program. After two more years of de-
liberation, and some drafting, it published another
report, "Behavioral and Social Science Research in the
Department of Defense: A Framework for Management,"
in February, 1971. It is not necessary to dwell in
detail on its findings and its reasoning; suffice it
to say that the nature of the subtleties and sensitivities in social research overseas was recognized. One

area was that of the clash of values between the researcher and the supporting agency, about which the
report had this to say:

The most significant distinction among the categories
of research is that foreign military security--
environments and policy--planning research is inherently
politically sensitive, while manpower research is not,
although it, too, has had its controversial projects.
Indeed, research on man-machine relationships and
"human engineering" has an Orwellian tone, but by and
large a psychologist could work on problems of improving selection and training choices through psychological
testing without having to confront possible conflicts
between his own value system and the value system implicit in the area of research.  This is less true for
categories of security-environments and policy-planning
studies.  Regardless of questions of political sensitivity, much policy-planning research has to be done
by and for the Department of Defense because it deals
with issues of strategy, force structure, and budgets.
The Department of Defense should not be foreclosed
from undertaking such research.  (emphasis added)

Another problem area was that of having applied research
done in such a way that basic knowledge could be applied
to and influence real problems.  The report's words
have a familiar ring:

In the national security area, the methodology of social
science research now permits and warrants substantial
funding for such efforts as simulations of the operational environments that policy-makers may posit as
constituting the range of possibilities for which the
nation must be prepared.  Computer-based simulation
studies on a large scale are likely to be expensive.
They may be used either for fundamental research or
for engineering development, and it is particularly
difficult in the social sciences to draw a dividing

line between different stages of research and development. But, under whatever label, they constitute a qualitatively different mode of behavioral research than is encompassed by the traditional expectations of many foreign-affairs practitioners, who believe that the social sciences can provide little or nothing beyond humanistic, individual, historical research. The limits of utility on "engineering development studies" in the behavioral and social science areas of Department of Defense research are not yet known with any precision. However, it is clear that those limits have not been approached and that an adequate effort to develop the engineering side of behavioral and social science research has not yet been undertaken. The potential for such work is perhaps especially great in the area of manpower research (psychological testing mechanisms, for example), but it also exists in the policy-planning and foreign-area spheres.

Among the recommendations were the following:

  ...The Department of Defense should actively seek the transfer of responsibility for the support and management of foreign area research, and it should strongly endorse the creation of a government-wide institutional structure--to which it would have access and in which it would have a chance to voice its informational needs--in which this responsibility should be lodged.

  ...The national security agencies jointly establish a task force on social and behavioral science research priorities in the area of national security policy.

  ...The Department of Defense, in order to bring about a more effective managerial relationship between the producers and consumers of research:

  ...provide funds for retrospective studies in the social and behavioral sciences designed to establish the relationship, if any, between basic research and programmatically useful results.

...allocate funds for evaluative studies of on-going
programs that allow for the questioning of policy
assumptions and the proposal of programs alternative to those under analysis, in order to suggest how programs might be modified in the
future.

And so, despite the subtle differences in context and
appreciation of the problems, it would seem that <u>plus
ca change, plus c'est la même chose</u>. The lessons
gained through eight years of trying to do what was
being recommended anew had, apparently, not yet sunk
in.

# V  REFLECTIONS

During the Camelot hearings of the Fascell subcommittee, Congressman Frelinghuysen asked:[1] "What have you learned as a result of your experience which has resulted in the termination of the project?" The only answer I could give him at the time was the immediately obvious and superficial one: we had confirmed our suspicion that the Army's approach to social research on the problem of revolutionary change would not work, and, since the DOD still felt it needed the knowledge and data that the research sought, we would have to find another, more subtle way to get the job done. This was, of course, not a satisfactory answer for Congress, as they conveyed by their subsequent action in cutting the budget for this kind of work.

The Camelot experience represented but the beginning of learning. It led to experimentation with various approaches to the research, and with diverse institutional arrangements for its support. With all that under our belts, it is possible to answer the congressman's question with more insight. To state the conclusion first, it is roughly as follows: in our culture, government support of social research to help government's own ends must be approached with circumspection, great selectivity, limited purposes, and careful attention to the potential effects of the very performance of the research, as well as the results, on the researchers, the objects of the research, and the general public.

It can be argued that Congress had known this all
along, and that the proposition was stated, in different words, at the time of Camelot.  But the expression
then was essentially a reaction to particular events.
It referred explicitly to the DOD, and it was stated
in terms of propriety.  It is my contention at this
juncture that the lesson has wider application.  If
the reasons for the problems and ultimate failure of
the DOD program can be explained by factors more universal than those particular to the setting of an un-
popular war in unfamiliar lands then those factors
should be identifiable in other situations.  If they
are, then social research in those situations may fare
about as well (or as poorly) as did the DOD's social
research efforts in its particular problem area.

It appears to me now that the key question is not
the propriety of work undertaken by a particular agency,
but rather the feasibility of this kind of work in the
social and cultural setting of government trying to
get its job done in the public eye.  It is a matter of
how the parties to the research contract interact,
and of the effect of their interaction on the subjects
of research and on outside observers.  Let's explore
their motivations from the vantage point of all that
has passed.

To perform effective research, the social scientist
would like to keep the situation he is studying fluid
but under careful control.  He wants, ideally, to be

able to examine all the important variables of the
problem, keeping most of them fairly constant while
others are varied systematically, and data on their
effects and interactions are carefully recorded. That
is, he would like to change some variables (here, conditions of a social group) while others remain about
the same, so that the effects of such changes can be
observed and analyzed in a systematic way. All this
means, from the scientist's viewpoint, that a social
program should not "gel" very early. In fact, the
initial purpose of his research is to ascertain the
direction in which a social program should be molded
and guided before it is allowed to assume immutable
characteristics.

The bureaucrat, on the other hand, has a job to do,
with operational objectives that, however defined, are
normally viewed by him as clear and straightforward.
The task may be educating people, or raising them from
poverty, or helping them form economic institutions to
create jobs, or helping them form quasi-political institutions to deal with the more formal elements of
government. The achievements are likely to be measured
as concrete outputs:  so many children in school; so
many curriculum changes; so many jobs; so many neighborhood associations. Whether the children become
educated or the jobs are "satisfying" takes too long
to determine, and is left for the next generation to
judge.

While the program director wants to keep his "op-

tions" open at the beginning, this is not so much for
the purpose of understanding the subjects' responses
thoroughly and adapting the program to them, as it is
to help ascertain the overt signs of potential success
--public acceptance, and the accommodation of all of
the various political, economic, and bureaucratic
interests involved.  Once the bureaucrat sees his path
through this essentially political jungle, he wants to
fix the program and change it as little as possible.
Each undertaking within the program represents a commitment of prestige and money on the part of the bureaucracy, in a visible arena.  Changing the program can
easily be read by the bureaucrat's political superiors
and by the public as a sign that the bureaucrat does
not know what he is doing.  In many cases, there will
have been, and may continue to be, vocal opposition to
the program, the effect of which is to cause the
bureaucrat responsible for its implementation to fix
its dimensions and parameters even more rigidly than
he might otherwise have been moved to do.

Thus, the ultimate desiderata of the researcher and
the bureaucrat diverge from the beginning.  The researcher wants to be able to design and mold a social
experiment so that its results can help design a better
social action program.  The bureaucrat wants to get a
job done, where that job is likely to have been defined rather vaguely by the instruments of society at
large, and more precisely by himself and his colleagues.
These divergent motivations lead to clashes over matters

revolving around timing and publicity. The bureaucrat has only so much time before he must undergo the usual tests of bureaucratic success. The researcher, on the other hand, wants his research and data gathering to be paced by the changes in behavior and attitudes of the subject population. Thus, each of the participants has his critical milestones. Events in the bureaucrat's life are tied to budget cycles and electoral cycles, whereas events in the researcher's life are tied to the evolutionary periods of attitudes and social institutions. The lengths of the respective periods can differ by years or decades.

Among the main personal satisfactions for the researcher, other than that in a job well done, are the fame and fortune that arise from making his work known and having it recognized by his colleagues. It is important for knowledge and for future programs that the current program's vicissitudes, the false starts and their effects, and the fortunate or unfortunate chance variables be made a part of this published record. Since he is dealing with a society and all its interacting segments, some of these variables involve the people guiding the program as well as those affected by it. To the bureaucrat, publication of such information is anathema. His budget and his success lie not with his mistakes, or with his learning processes, but with his ultimate achievements. Exposure of his intermediate operations, especially before his results are made apparent, exposes him to scandal in the press,

questioning by Congress, the displeasure of his superiors, and the machinations of his rivals. He is
therefore motivated to suppress the material that is
the scientist's nourishment.

The disparate motivations interact strongly with
the events under study. While the researcher's ultimate objective is to affect them, the best usages of
science require him to observe them first. The operator, on the other hand, wants to affect events immediately, and once he has found the means to do so he wants
to sustain their momentum. In some situations, such
as those which have been the subject of this book, the
events, once initiated, may be beyond anyone's control,
and they may move too fast for careful observation.
Moreover, as they become more important and sensitive,
observation becomes more difficult because access to
the population and the key players is reduced. This
happens partly for lack of time, but primarily because
the stress of the events themselves makes both population and bureaucracy less willing to subject themselves
to examination, and less able to perceive what is happening and to articulate their reactions clearly. The
bureaucracy's need for secrecy intensifies while it
evaluates the effects of the events, both on its own
position and efforts and on the population it simultaneously serves and tries to lead.

If the bureaucracy controls access to the so-called
target population by virtue of its sponsorship of the
research, it is able to enforce its need for privacy

or secrecy easily, by denial of that access.  In such
circumstances systematic collection of data becomes
difficult, if not impossible, and the research is
forced into an increasingly unscientific mode.  The
less rigorous and carefully controlled the research
becomes, and the less coherent and definitive the data,
the more the researcher is forced to make intuitive
judgments to fill the gaps, if he is not to give up
altogether (and the impulse to keep going, when the
affairs under study are of vital concern, is difficult
to resist).  But when the researcher, who is really an
observer on the outside looking in, makes intuitive
judgments instead of reaching conclusions based on
data, these judgments place him in conflict with the
bureaucrat, who is really in control of the relationship,
and whose own judgments are the ones that lead to action and (he believes) control his future.  The researcher thus finds himself increasingly less able to
influence events and to achieve his own professional
objectives.  If he becomes sufficiently frustrated he
will turn on the bureaucrat in a mood of disaffection
and criticism.  And, of course, the bureaucrat will
fight back, using the ultimate sanction, withdrawal of
sponsorship and money.

All these problems are, however, merely reflections
of something more basic--they are rooted in fundamental
clashes of values among the participants in the drama
of social research.  Myrdal has pointed out that social
research is not value-free.[2]  In the case of government

supporting social research to help achieve its ends,
each of the participants has his own value system.
The researchers adhere to a set of premises about the
world.  (These were illustrated for the beginning of
the events described here, in Chapter 3.)  The government must share these premises if it wants to employ
the researchers, and if the latter are to be willing
to work for that government.  In finer detail, the members of the government bureaucracy must share values
with its leaders--the President and his appointees--
if the President expects the bureaucracy to carry out
his instructions effectively.  The frustration of President Kennedy with the State Department was an illustration of the consequences when such a coincidence
of values fails to exist within the executive branch.[3]

The population being studied must also share premises and values with the researchers (or at the very
least they must feel neutrally about any differences)
or they will not respond to the researchers as the
latter go about their business of gathering information about the population.  Suspicion on this point
led South Vietnamese officialdom to control carefully
the American researchers' access to particular prisoners; and there was, in turn, suspicion on the part
of at least some American researchers that respondents
were telling them only what the respondents thought
the researchers wanted to hear.  This suspicion was a
tacit recognition that ideas of "objective" inquiry
play a different role in Vietnamese and other Eastern

cultures than they do in our own.

A high Thai government official once asked me why American anthropologists were so interested in the hill tribes on the fringes of his country. If they came to Thailand for research, why didn't they study the Thai (i.e., the dominant ethnic group)? No amount of explanation of the inherent interest these anthropologists had in learning about primitive and disappearing cultures would quell his suspicion that the tribesmen were being examined to satisfy ulterior purposes in the control of Thailand's border areas. It also emerged in this conversation, interestingly enough, that study of the Thai culture might lead to data proving the Thai ancestry of peoples in neighboring countries; those countries had been formed, I was told, in part by accretion of provinces stripped from Thailand by the French and the British. This proof of their Thai origins could support hopes of reconquest, just as study of the hill tribes could fuel suspicion of further colonialist adventures. The basic idea of performing research primarily to know, taken for granted by the Americans, was alien to local officialdom. Of course, that officialdom had occasions to learn of policy recommendations, made by the "objective" researchers, that were inimical to its own interests--for example, that rebellious hill tribes could be "pacified" by changing Thai law to accommodate the swidden agricultural and other customs of the hill tribes, instead of forcing the tribes to accommodate to laws not written with them in mind.  Even the people being studied assumed that the researchers were there with some ulterior purpose, and indeed the researchers often had to earn their welcome by demonstrating support for the people they worked with if they became involved, by their very presence, in issues affecting those people. The Americans' desire to be wanted and helpful against injustice fell right in with these local purposes.

These examples illustrate the need for consonance or reconciliation of values among the major participants in social research.  Of course, the government bureaucracy, the researchers, and the population being studied are the ones directly involved in the issues. But the majority of the public also has values, premises, and points of view.  Although this public is composed of many diverse elements, it is probably a safe generalization that it is tolerant of "long-hair" stuff such as social research if that research doesn't challenge its ideas of propriety, thrift, and suspicion of the obscure or dishonest in government and its activities.  Should such a challenge arise, the press is ever ready to expose it, and Congress to act by cutting off funds and otherwise prohibiting the activity.  There will be no outcry of opposition to reduction of research, especially social research, by the general public.

This is not to imply that any of these responses are "wrong" or unjustified.  Again, Myrdal[4] has made the point that values operate on two levels.  One is

a "higher" level which in our society specifies what
is "right" and "wrong" in the view of the vast majority
of the people--for example, in our society adherence to
the Ten Commandments can be considered "right," and
coercion is "wrong." Most people adhere to values at
this level more when acting or reacting as part of a
group than as individuals. Then there is a lower, or
"practical" level, where individuals reconcile their
sometimes unhappy daily interactions with their fellows,
for personal interest and gain, with the higher level
of social objectives that continues to hold the lure
of ultimate attainment. When events are important
enough to shake people out of their daily interests,
and to make them feel that some group is violating the
higher values, the response is natural to want to call
those violators to account; there is likely even to be
a certain unconscious assuagement of conscience in
this, relating to their earlier support or tolerance
of the undesirable behavior. As we have seen in connection with the Vietnam war, when members of the
press and the university community of social scientists
began to turn against the war, those performing social
research for the government in connection with the war
came, to them, to acquire the same sinister qualities
and motives that were ascribed to the government, and
especially to the U.S. military that was actively prose-
cuting the war.

Further, I have noted earlier that in social research on substantive questions a phenomenon akin to

the Heisenberg principle of physics appears to operate.
The fact and means of measurement and observation affect and change the phenomena being observed and all
the participants. Even if they begin by supporting
the government view, the researchers will elicit new
facts and insights, and will form new viewpoints that
lead them to understand the government approach and
programs differently, and, quite likely, to want to
change them. The government bureaucracy will, in the
fashion of all bureaucracies, recoil defensively. The
population affected by the government programs, the
subjects of the research, will become sensitized to
the issues by the very fact of the research. That
population's outlook and its responses will change;
and these changes will become more widely known, and
will affect the more general public, whose views and
tolerance will change as well. The more fundamental
the issues, the more likely that these changes will
take place. The closer to problems of human survival
and dignity the issues of concern, the more profound
and emotionally charged the changes are likely to be.
The longer the research takes, the more likely that
these changes will occur before it is completed. For
reasons such as these, even if government initiates
the alliance with science, that alliance is unlikely
to continue amicably until the task is done.

Seen in this light, the events, conflicts, and outcome of the Defense Department's attempt to use social
research to help it grapple with the problems of revo-

lutionary warfare on a world-wide scale are easy to
understand.   Viewed in retrospect, Camelot and the subsequent storms were simply the shocks of adjustment as
stresses were relieved and the entire, intricate, delicate structure of relationships took on a new form.

All of this is, of course, speculative theorizing
that cannot be "proved" with the evidence I have available.  But it seems to me to meet the test of reason-
ableness, and it appears to be supported by extensive
and detailed observations made in the course of the
program we have been examining here.  If there is more
general value to those observations, the conclusions
derived from them should apply to other social research
programs that have been of interest to and supported
by the government.  While social research is not my
field and I claim no special expertise in its history
or applications, my meager readings suggest that this
wider relevance does indeed exist.  It seems not inappropriate to close with a few observations as to why
I believe this is so.  Others may find that it is a
worthy subject of research to test more rigorously the
hypothesis I have tried to convey.

It is readily observed, first, that the kinds of
phenomena encountered during the DOD's overseas research efforts in Southeast Asia were not unique to
that program or situation.  Sommer[5] has written of
the difficulties of performing field research in such
areas as the black ghetto.  They include the inability
of the researcher, especially if he is white, to over-

come his obvious "separateness" from the group being
studied; the aversion of both observer and observed to
the "prying and spying" that attends the gathering of
social data; fear of observing illicit behavior; lack
of patience; and personal danger and discomfort--in
short, all the problems encountered by the DOD's researchers in Vietnam and elsewhere, even apart from
the added difficulties imposed by interactions with
officialdom.  As to the latter, Campbell[6] has observed,
in connection with such events as the Connecticut
clampdown on speeding in 1955 to reduce highway deaths,
that:

....given the discrepancy between promise and possibility, most administrators wisely prefer to limit
evaluations to those the outcomes of which they can
control, particularly insofar as published outcomes
or press releases are concerned.

Moynihan confesses that "I have been guilty of optimism
about the use of knowledge gained through social science in the management of public affairs."[7]  He points
out that, in the first half of the twentieth century:

Social science was asked....to attest to the equality
of the races; to legitimize the demand of wage workers
under capitalism to organize and bargain collectively;
to provide measures of intellectual worth so that applications for college admission and such might be
judged by objective criteria; to prescribe measures
for a high-level functioning of the economy.  All
these it did.

But, he asserts, the "old symbiotic relations" between

social scientists and social activists are breaking
down over the problems of implementation. He also
notes that:

The methodology (of social science) is now quite beyond the comprehension of non-social scientists. In
particular, it is beyond the ken of the lawyer class
that tends to wield the levers of power in American
Government.

This all sounds familiar. It is reinforced by all the
signs of malaise in the partnership between social
science and government on the domestic scene brought
out in a lengthy 1967 staff study, "The Use Of Social
Research in Federal Domestic Programs," of the House
Committee on Government Operations.[8]

The more recent signs of disaster or indifference
emerging from value clashes in government-supported
social research and experimentation are legion. The
affair of the Blackstone Rangers in Chicago,[9] the
failure of the Clark Plan[10] for restructuring the District of Columbia school system, and the repudiation
by the President of the recommendations of his commis-
sions on pornography[11] and population[12] provide examples
of the heat that can be generated when the social
scientist espouses a view, in his work, that is not
shared by the public or the government which supported
that work. The failure of powerful research results
to influence institutions when the findings challenge
established values is illustrated by two court decisions (in California and the District of Columbia) re-

quiring equal taxation for and distribution of educational funds among jurisdictions,[13,14] in the face of
the Coleman findings[15] that educational success and
funding are not correlated; and by the failure of the
results of the New Jersey income tax experiment[16] to
change national and state policies opposed to financial
support for the working poor.

These are all questions that go to the very heart of
the deep social ills that plague modern American society. If they cannot be studied with government support,
or if, when they are studied, the results are ignored
or rejected, how can the social scientists who have
tried to rationalize the issues be more effective in
helping the government and the public to recognize the
true nature of the phenomena and seek solutions that
appear to be more in keeping with the facts that might
emerge from study? Or, stated otherwise, are there
ways in which social scientists and government can undertake investigations to shed light on these complex
questions, so that society can gain from the resulting
knowledge, even though the findings may challenge the
prevailing values? Experience has shown that there
may be some ways.

First, the results of the DOD's efforts, and the
burgeoning of evaluational research in connection with
government programs that are avowedly experiments,
show that where clash of values is not a severe problem social scientists can be employed to design experiments and evaluate the results. A measure of social

experimentation is coming to be accepted.  Such things
as the New Jersey income tax experiment, experiments
with educational contractors who are willing to accept
the "payment for performance" principle for teaching
children to read, health insurance experiments, all
show that in areas where society is willing to countenance some slight departure from the norms--where no-
one's ox is particularly gored--social scientists can
help design the experiments and evaluate the results.

But even here, caution is necessary.  We know that
members of the public cannot be manipulated just to
collect objective scientific information even if the
results are obviously important to the public at large.
It is now recognized as an ethical principle that some
type of informed consent is necessary before people
should be involved in an experimental manipulation.
Moreover, the results may, or may not, be used, depending on the circumstances and motivations of those
involved, as we in the DOD learned during the Program
Impact Assessment effort.  A 1970 report on evaluation
in federal domestic programs[17] points out that "The
recent literature is unanimous in announcing the general failure of evaluation to affect decision making
in a significant way."

Submerged value clashes can rise to the surface, or
early results can stimulate them.  A good recent example came to light when a group of Stanford Research
Institute contracts to evaluate preschool education
programs were suspended by HEW, because SRI was accused

by two young lawyers of wasting the $12 million in-
volved.[18]   One defense that was given against this
charge, to the effect that since "The government was
consciously investing in building up a capability in
this field....there might well have been some waste...
as there was in the early days of defense contracting,"
can be viewed in juxtaposition with the remark made by
the lawyers that the $12 million "could have financed
a whole class of students through Stanford."  Large
expenditure for research, with a substantial fraction
"wasted" in learning a new area, is still more likely
to be overlooked in the physical than in the social
science arenas.

Second, the social scientist can contribute as a
consultant; he can give of his knowledge to government
administrators and planners, directly or through advisory committees.  Many have been effective in such
roles.  But they must recognize that situations may
arise in which their greatest contribution to society
may be the publicity attending their resignation from
such positions.  The conflicts of values and objectives
can obviously work in the person-to-person consulting
relationship as well, and the one who would continue
to be heard (and paid) must have a high frustration
tolerance insofar as the following of his advice is
concerned.

The social scientist can, as an alternative, join
the government as an administrator, at least for a
time.  He can then use his knowledge, gained from his

past research, to try to "move the system" and have
some of his ideas implemented.  This has the great advantage that he needn't depend on a government-to-
scientist relationship, or on the vicissitudes of
sponsored research, to make the attempt.  But he will
have to recognize at the outset that, even as a member
of the bureaucracy--indeed, particularly as a member
of the bureaucracy--he will face the same constraints
that he would have faced as a researcher trying to work
under the sponsorship of that bureaucracy, or the constraints faced by any other government official trying
to get a job done.  He will, again, have to have a
very high tolerance to frustration (or, if one will,
patience), and temper his commitment to the ideal with
satisfaction about what he finds possible, which is
likely to be very much less than he had initially
hoped for.  He will have to give up being a scientist
and behave like an administrator.[19]  Eventually, the
constraints and the environment will impose on him the
values and outlook of the bureaucracy.  In addition,
the intellectual capital he brought with him to the
government will become stale, outdated, and obsoles-
cent; he will find himself routinely administering
the few good program ideas he was able to have accepted
without disasters imposed by internal bureaucratic
conflicts or the curiosity and sensation-seeking of
the press.  And then it will be time for him to leave
the government.

If the social scientist explicitly wants to under-

take extensive research on the key social issues of
the day, he had best do so with private sponsorship.
This is not to say that he would always be successful,
even then. But the constraints and conflicts of
sponsorship will be smaller; he will not have to face
accountability for using public funds for purposes the
public does not approve. He will run less risk (but,
nevertheless, some risk) of being accused, by the subjects of his research, of being the representative of
their oppressors. And he will be in a better position
to be responsive to and concerned only about the demands of his interests, his profession, and his peers.
Of course, his impact on society may still be small,
distant, or irrelevant. But to the extent that the
flow and evolution of the ideas of the age can have an
impact on what people believe and on what government
does, he will, by having eschewed government sponsorship, be in a position to press the logic of his findings at least as effectively as he could from a base
of government sponsorship, and probably more effectively.

And so, I am led to the final thought deriving from
the experiences described in this book. As they did
in the context of those experiences, the community of
social science is likely to urge, and has urged, increased government support of research on the great
social problems of the day. With due recognition for
the government's need to collect data to help it plan
and evaluate the social programs it is expected to

undertake, I have reached the conclusion, nevertheless, that the opposite of the social scientists' recommendation is in order.

The research itself is needed, without question. Some of it, especially in the evaluation area, is necessary and feasible for government to sponsor. Beyond this, its support should be subject to the economic and political laws of the intellectual market place. And the government should do less, not more, to influence the workings of that market place. It should support less, not more, research into the workings of society. It should select that which it does support carefully, attending only to those ideas and objectives finding ready acceptance elsewhere. It will find soon enough that it is, itself, subject to the effects and influences of research on social problems performed outside its purview. In the area of learning about societies, their values, and their behavior, I now believe that government can be most effective if it follows, rather than leads.

REFERENCES

Chapter 1

1  "Two Communist Manifestos," texts of statement is-
sued in the name of World Communist Leaders Meeting in
November of 1960 and of an Address by Premier Khrush-
chev on January 6, 1961, The Washington Center of
Foreign Policy Research Affiliated with The Johns
Hopkins University, 1961, pp. 51-52.

2  Schlesinger, Arthur M., Jr.:  A Thousand Days:
John F. Kennedy in the White House, Cambridge.  The
Riverside Press, 1965, pp. 358-378.

3  "The Differences Between Comrade Togliatti and Us,"
editorial in the Peking People's Daily, December 31,
1962.  Reprinted in English in The Washington Post,
January 3, 1963.

4  Remarks of Secretary of Defense Robert S. McNamara
at the Annual George C. Marshall Memorial Dinner,
Association of the United States Army, October 10,
1962.

5  Public Papers of the Presidents, John F. Kennedy,
1962, U.S. Government Printing Office, Washington,
D.C.

6  Rostow, W., Address to the Graduating Class, United
States Army Special Warfare Center, June 28, 1961,
printed in the Congressional Record, Vol. 108, August
6, 1962, p. A-6013.

7  Department of Defense Appropriations for 1963,
Hearing before the Subcommittee of the Committee on
Appropriations, House of Representatives, 87th Congress,
2nd Session, Part 2, pp. 49-50.

8  Ibid.

9  Gillert, Lt. Col. G.J., Jr., "Counterinsurgency,"
Military Review, April 1965.

10  See, for example, U.S. Congress. Senate, Committee
on Foreign Relations. Laos: April 1971. A staff
report prepared for the use of the Subcommittee on U.S.
Security and Commitments Abroad. U.S. Government
Printing Office, Washington, D.C., 1971.

11  Gillert, p. 27.

12  New York Times, May 6, 1962, p. 28; May 13, 1962,
p. 1.

13  Composite Report of the President's Committee to
Study the Military Assistance Program, W.H. Draper,
Chairman, August 17, 1959.

14  Orlansky, Jesse, "The State of Research on Internal War," Institute for Defense Analyses Research
Paper P-565, August 1970.

Chapter 2

1  "Behavioral Sciences and the National Security,"
Report No. 4 together with Part IX of the Hearings on
Winning the Cold War:  The U.S. Ideological Offensive,
by the Subcommittee on International Organizations
and Movements of the Committee on Foreign Affairs,
House of Representatives, December 6, 1965, pp. 68-72.

2  Bray, Charles W., "Toward a Technology of Human
Behavior for Defense Use," American Psychologist,
Vol. 17, 1962, pp. 527-541.

3  "Social Science Research and National Security,"
by Ithiel de Sola Pool, A.J. Coale, W.P. Davison, H.
Eckstein, K. Knorr, V.V. McRae, L.W. Pye, T.C. Schel-
ling, W. Schramm. A report prepared by the Research
Group in Psychology and the Social Sciences, Smith-
sonian Institution, Washington, D.C., under Office of
Naval Research, Contract Nonr 1354(18), Task Number
NR 170-379, March 5, 1963.

## Chapter 3

1 "A Threat to the Peace--North Vietnam's Effort to Conquer South Vietnam," 2 Parts, Department of State Publication 7308, December 1961.

2 Carver, George A., Jr., "The Faceless Viet Cong," Foreign Affairs, Vol. 44, No. 3, April 1966, p. 347.

3 See, for example, Morganthau, Hans, "A Political Theory of Foreign Aid," American Political Science Review, Vol. 56, June 1962, pp. 301-309.

4 "Ethical Standards of Psychologists," The American Psychologist, January 1963, amended by the APA Council of Representatives, September 1965 and December 1972.

## Chapter 4

1 Lyons, Gene M.: The Uneasy Partnership. Russell Sage Foundation, 1969, p. 151.

## Chapter 5

1 Milton, Helen S., "Cost-of-Research Index, 1920-1970," Operations Research, Vol. 20, No. 1, January-February 1972, pp. 1-18.

2 Departments of State, Justice, and Commerce, the Judiciary, and Related Agencies Appropriations for 1965. Hearings before a Subcommittee of the Committee on Appropriations, House of Representatives, 88th Congress, 2nd Session, U.S. Government Printing Office, 1964.

3 U.S. Statistical Abstract, U.S. Government Printing Office, 1970, p. 526.

4 Department of Defense Appropriations, Hearing, Armed Services Committee, U.S. Senate, S201-18.13, April 5, 1972, U.S. Government Printing Office, pp. 3219-3349.

5  Much of the material about Project Agile gathered
by the Students for a Democratic Society is also contained in Klare, Michael T., War Without End: American
Planning for the Next Vietnams, Vintage Books, New
York, 1972.


## Chapter 6

1  Lyons, p. 188.

2  Cooper, Chester L., The Lost Crusade: America in
Vietnam, Dodd, Mead & Company, New York, 1970, p. 255.


## Chapter 7

1  Subcommittee on International Organizations and
Movements, p. 190, contains Department of Defense
Directive Number 5129.22, April 10, 1961, promulgating
the Defense Science Board Charter.

2  Reingold, N., ed., Science in the Nineteenth
Century--A Documentary History, Hill and Wang, New
York, 1964, p. 200.


## Chapter 8

1  Forrester, Jay W., Urban Dynamics, MIT Press, Cambridge, Mass., 1969.


## Chapter 9

1  Subcommittee on International Organizations and
Movements, p. 20.


## Chapter 10

1  New York Times, April 14, 1966, p. 1.

Chapter 11

1 "Science and the Citizen," Scientific American,
Vol. 225, No. 5, May 1971, p. 45.

2 Subcommittee on International Organizations and
Movements, pp. 51-54.

3 Ibid., pp. 9R-10R.

4 Walsh, John, "Social Sciences Cancellation of
Project Camelot...brings Research Under Scrutiny,"
Science, Vol. 150, September 10, 1965, p. 1211; also,
December 10, 1965, pp. 1429-1431.

5 "Internal War Potential (Estimate)," Punch, July 7,
1965, p. 8.

6 The Washington Star, July 8, 1965.

7 For a discussion of the TAT see, e.g., Buros, O.K.,
ed., The Fifth Mental Measurements Yearbook, The
Gryphon Press, Highland Park, N.J., 1959, pp. 301-313.


Chapter 12

1 Department of Defense Appropriations for Fiscal
Year 1966, Report of the Subcommittee of the Committee
on Appropriations, House of Representatives, 89th
Congress, 1st Session. U.S. Government Printing
Office, Washington, D.C., p. 50.

2 "The Behavioral Sciences and the Federal Government,"
Advisory Committee on Government Programs in the Be-
havioral Sciences, National Research Council, National
Academy of Sciences, Publication No. 1680, Washington,
D.C., 1968.

3 "Behavioral and Social Science Research in the De-
partment of Defense--A Framework for Management,"
Advisory Committee on the Management of Behavioral
Science Research in the Department of Defense, National

Research Council, National Academy of Sciences.  Washington, D.C., 1971.

4  Lyons.


Chapter 13

1  Subcommittee on International Organizations and Movements, p. 107.

2  Ibid.


Chapter 14

1  Subcommittee on International Organizations and Movements, p. 1R.

2  Ibid., p. 5R.

3  Ibid., p. 17.

4  Ibid., p. 8R.

5  Ibid., pp. 79-80.

6  Ibid., pp. 92-94.

7  Defense Department Appropriations for Fiscal Year 1966, p. 50.

8  Congressional Record, Senate, October 22, 1965, p. 27466ff.

9  Thouless, Robert H., How to Think Straight, Simon and Schuster, New York, 1947, p. 4.

10  See, e.g., Congressional Record, Senate, August 22, 1967, pp. 23524-25; April 18, 1968, pp. 9980-85; April 22, 1968, pp. 10174-76; July 9, 1969, p. 18899.

11  Subcommittee on International Organizations and Movements, p. 97.

12 "Federal Support of International Social Science and Behavioral Research," Hearings before the Subcommittee on Government Research of the Committee on Government Operations, United States Senate, 89th Congress, 2nd Session, June 27, 28; July 19, 20, 1966. U.S. Government Printing Office, Washington, D.C., 1967, p. 1.

13 Ibid., p. 14.

14 Ibid., p. 16.

15 See n. 2, Ch. 6.

16 New York Times, May 14, 1968, p. 1.

17 New York Times, July 11, 1967, p. 1; July 12, 1967, p. 42; July 23, 1967, Section IV, p. 9; August 3, 1967, p. 2; August 4, 1967, p. 3.

18 See, for example, Shapley, Deborah, "Defense Research: The Names Are Changed to Protect the Innocent," Science, Vol. 175, February 25, 1972, p. 866.

19 Pike, Douglas, Viet Cong: The Organization and Techniques of the National Liberation Front of South Vietnam, MIT Press, Cambridge, Mass., 1966.

20 Congressional Record, Senate, April 18, 1968, p. 9985.

21 Ibid.

22 Congressional Record, Senate, July 9, 1969, p. 18903.

Chapter 15

1 Horowitz, Irving Louis, "The Life and Death of Project Camelot," Trans-action, Vol. 3, No. 1, November-December, 1965, pp. 3-7, 44-47.

2   Subcommittee on Government Research, p. 239ff.

3   Horowitz, Irving Louis, ed., The Rise and Fall of
Project Camelot:   Studies in the Relationship between
Social Science and Practical Politics, MIT Press,
Cambridge, Mass., 1967.   (The revised edition, 1974,
also contains the passages discussed in this book.)

4   Silvert, Kalman H., "American Academic Ethics and
Social Research Abroad," American Universities Field
Staff, Reports Service, West Coast/South America Ser-
ies, Vol. XII, No. 3 (KHS-1-65), July 1965.

5   Subcommittee on Government Research, p. 225ff.

6   Ibid., p. 201.

7   Subcommittee on International Organizations and
Movements, p. 9R.

8   Horowitz, Trans-action, p. 44.

9   Ibid., p. 47.

10   Nisbet, Robert A., "Project Camelot:   an Autopsy,"
The Public Interest, Fall, 1966, p. 52.

11   Washington Star, September 12, 1965.

12   Klare, Michael T., "Counterinsurgency's Proving
Ground," The Nation, April 26, 1971, pp. 527-28.

13   Beals, Ralph L., Politics of Social Research--An
Inquiry into the Ethics and Responsibilities of Social
Scientists, Aldine Publishing Company, Chicago, 1969,
pp. 187-188, 197-198.

14   Ibid., pp. 193-194.

15   Washington Post, April 21, 1967, p. A-6.

16   See, for example, "The Politicization of the Pro-
fessions," The Humanist, September-October, 1971,

pp. 26-31; Science, Vol. 176, May 5, 1972, p. 496;
Haberer, Joseph, "Politicization in Science," Science,
Vol. 178, November 17, 1972, pp. 713-723.

17  Thackray, Arnold, "Reflections on the Decline of
Science in America and on Some of Its Causes,"
Science, Vol. 173, July 2, 1971, pp. 27-31.

18  DeGrazia, Al, "Government and Science--An Editorial," The American Behavioral Scientist, Vol. IX, No. I,
September, 1965, p. 40.

19  Congressional Record, Senate, January 22, 1969,
pp. 1442-1447.

## Chapter 17

1  Department of Defense Appropriations for 1968,
Hearings before Subcommittee of the Committee on
Appropriations, House of Representatives, 90th Congress,
1st Session, Part 3.  U.S. Government Printing Office,
Washington, D.C., p. 176.

2  Wolf, Eric R., and Jorgensen, Joseph G., "Anthropology on the Warpath in Thailand," New York Review
of Books, Vol. XV, No. 9, November 19, 1970, pp. 26-
35, Part III.

3  See, for example, Newsletter of the American Anthropological Association, Vol. 11, No. 7, September, 1970,
p. 2; Vol. 11, No. 8, October, 1970, p. 1; Vol. 12,
No. 1, January, 1971, p. 2, p. 9; Vol. 12, No. 3,
March, 1971, p. 1, p. 11; Vol. 13, No. 1, January,
1972, pp. 1-4; Vol. 13, No. 2, February, 1972, p. 1.

4  Wolf and Jorgensen, Part II.

5  Ibid., Part III.

6  Wall Street Journal, November 18, 1971, p. 1;
New York Times, November 21, 1971, p. 79.

7  Congressional Record, Senate, April 18, 1968,
p. 9984.


Chapter 18

1  Webb, Eugene J., Campbell, Donald T., Schwartz,
Richard D., Sechrest, Lee, Unobtrusive Measures: Non-
reactive Research in the Social Sciences, Rand McNally
& Company, Chicago, 1966.

2  President's Task Force on International Development.  "U.S. Foreign Assistance in the 1970s:  A New
Approach," March 4, 1970.  Quoted in U.S. Department
of State Bulletin, April 6, 1970, pp. 447-467.

3  Informal communication from Eugene Webb, member of
Program Impact Assessment Scientific Advisory Panel,
July, 1973.


Chapter 19

1  Cantril, Hadley, "A Study of Aspirations,"
Scientific American, Vol. 208, No. 2, February, 1963,
pp. 41-45.

2  Sinaiko, H. Wallace, "Foreign Language Training:
An Investigation of Research and Development for Viet-
nam," Institute for Defense Analyses Study S-232,
March 1966.

3  Webb, Eugene J., "A Review of Social Science Research in Vietnam...," Institute for Defense Analyses
Research Paper P-450, December, 1968.

4  Snow, Charles Percy, The Two Cultures and the
Scientific Revolution, Cambridge University Press,
1959.

## Chapter 21

1 Department of Defense Appropriations for 1968, Report of the Subcommittee of the Committee on Appropriations, 90th Congress, 1st Session. U.S. Government Printing Office, Washington, D.C., p. 57.

2 Department of Defense Appropriations for 1970, Report of the Subcommittee of the Committee on Appropriations, 91st Congress, 1st Session. U.S. Government Printing Office, Washington, D.C., p. 81.

3 Horowitz, Irving Louis, "Social Science Yogis and Military Commissars," Trans-action, May 1968, pp. 29-35.

4 "The Behavioral Sciences and the Federal Government," U.S. Government Printing Office, 1968.

5 Department of Defense Appropriations for 1970, Senate Appropriations Committee Report No. 91-607; 91st Congress, 1st Session. U.S. Government Printing Office, Washington, D.C., p. 134.

6 Public Law 91-121, 91st Congress, S. 2546, November 19, 1969, p. 2.

7 Department of Defense Appropriations for 1970, Report of the Subcommittee of the Committee on Appropriations, House of Representatives, Report 91-522, September, 1969. U.S. Government Printing Office, Washington, D.C., p. 46.

8 Congressional Record, Senate, November 6, 1969, p. 13899.

9 U.S. National Science Foundation Data Book, NSF 73-3, January 1973.

10 Nichols, Rodney W., "Mission-Oriented R&D," Science, Vol. 172, April 2, 1971, pp. 29-37.

11 Ibid., p. 29.

12  *Congressional Record*, Senate, November 25, 1969, p. 14971.

13  Quoted in the *Congressional Record*, Senate, December 1, 1969, p. 15207.

14  *Congressional Record*, November 25, 1969, p. 14971.

15  Ibid., p. 14969.

16  Nichols, p. 32.

17  *Congressional Record*, December 6, 1969, p. S-15929.

18  *Congressional Record*, House, December 18, 1969, p. H.12740.

19  *Congressional Record*, Senate, August 28, 1970, p. S-14568.

20  Ibid., pp. S-14569-70.


Chapter 22

1  Subcommittee on Organizations and Movements, p. 85.

2  Myrdal, Gunnar, *Objectivity in Social Research*, Pantheon Books, New York, 1969.

3  Schlesinger, Arthur M., Jr., *A Thousand Days*, Houghton Mifflin Company, Boston, 1965, pp. 406-407.

4  Myrdal, pp. 16-17.

5  Sommer, Robert, "Some Costs and Pitfalls in Field Research," *Social Problems*, Vol. 19, 1971, pp. 162-166.

6  Campbell, Donald T., "Reforms as Experiments," *American Psychologist*, Vol. 24, No. 4, April 1969, p. 409.

7  Moynihan, Daniel P., "Eliteland," Psychology Today,
September 1970, pp. 35-37, 66-70.

8  "The Use of Social Research in Federal Domestic
Programs," A Staff Study for the Research and Technical
Programs Subcommittee of the Committee on Government
Operations, House of Representatives, 90th Congress,
1st Session, April 1967. In four parts. U.S. Govern-
ment Printing Office, Washington, D.C.

9  For summary, see Facts on File, December 12 and 18,
1968, p. 536.

10  Clark, Kenneth B., with the assistance of the
staff of the MARC Corporation, A Possible Reality,
Emerson Hall, New York, 1972. See, especially, p. 34,
re differential compensation.

11  United States Commission on Obscenity and Pornography Report, September, 1970, U.S. Government Printing Office, Washington, D.C.

12  Commission on Population Growth and the American
Future Report, 1972, U.S. Government Printing Office,
Washington, D.C.

13  Serrano vs. Priest, 96 California Reporter 601
(August 30, 1971 as modified on denial of rehearing
October 21, 1971).

14  Hobson vs. Hansen, 327 F. Supp. 844 (1971).

15  Coleman, James S., Equality of Educational Oppor-
tunity, U.S. Department of Health, Education, and
Welfare,  Office of Education, 1966.  U.S. Government
Printing Office, Washington, D.C.

16  Kershaw, David N., "A Negative Income Tax Experiment," Scientific American, Vol. 227, No. 4, October
1972, pp. 19-25.

17  Wholey, Joseph S., Scanlon, John W., Duffy, Hugh
G., Fukumoto, James S., and Vogt, Leona M., "Federal

Evaluation Policy," The Urban Institute, Washington,
D.C., June 1970, p. 46.

18  Science, Vol. 177, September 15, 1972, p. 973.

19  See, for example, Klein, Stanley D., "Psychologist
at City Hall--A Problem of Identity," Proceedings,
77th Annual Convention, American Psychological Association, 1969, pp. 853-854.